engineering
a compiler

engineering
a compiler
VAX-11 CODE GENERATION
AND OPTIMIZATION

Patricia Anklam
David Cutler
Roger Heinen, Jr.
M. Donald MacLaren

digital

Printed in U.S.A.
10 9 8 7 6 5 4 3 2
Documentation number EY-00001-DP

The manuscript of this book was created using generic coding and, via a translation program, was automatically typeset on DIGITAL's DECset Integrated Publishing System.

VAX-11, VAX/VMS, PDP-11 are trademarks of Digital Equipment Corporation; MULTICS is a product of Honeywell Inc.

Aho/Ullman, *Principles of Compiler Design,* © 1977. Addison-Wesley, Reading Massachusetts. Figures 12.12 and 13.8. Reprinted by permission.

Library of Congress Cataloging in Publication Data
Main entry under title:

Engineering a compiler.

Includes index.
    1. VAX-11 (Computer)—Programming.
2. Compiling (Electronic computers)
3. Code generators. 4. PL/I (Computer program
language) I. Anklam, Patricia, 1949–
QA76.8.V37E53 1982   001.64'25   82-9633
ISBN 0-932376-19-3

Preface

This book is for students, for computer scientists, and for practicing software engineers who have a special interest in compiler design and implementation. It describes practical experiences in the development of a production-quality compiler with a code generator capable of generating highly optimized object code for multiple source languages. In examples and discussions of source language issues, we generally refer to a specific compiler implementation—a PL/I General Purpose Subset compiler for Digital Equipment Corporation's VAX-11 machines. However, the methods used in the compiler are applicable to most languages; thus this book should prove useful to anyone interested in the field.

Chapter 1 describes how the project got started and how we acquired the excellent compiler we started with: the PL/I compiler developed by Robert A. Freiburghouse and originally marketed by him through his former company, Translation Systems, Inc. This chapter also discusses the overall structure of the compiler as it existed when we acquired it.

Chapter 2 discusses our experiences in bootstrapping the original compiler onto our VAX-11 machine. It provides some insights about bootstrapping in general and describes the decisions we had to make and the tools we had to create in order to debug the compiler early in its development. The chapter concludes with a description of the overall structure of the compiler in its current state.

One of the tools introduced in Chapter 2 is TBL, a table-building language that is used to describe local code generation in a procedural fashion. TBL is actually very flexible and we use it in several places in the compiler, not just in the local code generator. TBL and its compiler are discussed in Chapter 3.

The backbone of our compiler's design is the Intermediate Language, which serves as the boundary between the language-specific "front end" and the machine-specific common code generator (the "back end"). Chapter 4 describes the steps the front end must perform to transform a program's source statements into semantically correct trees and to accumulate symbol table information required by the back end. Chapter 5 presents the Intermediate Language itself. It is worth noting that the symbol table structure and the intermediate language have a long history, going back at least to 1970, when Freiburghouse designed version 2 of the MULTICS PL/I compiler ("The In-

v

ternal Representation of PL/1 Programs," Internal Memorandum, October 1970). Although the design has evolved over the years, the operators and symbol table nodes of the VAX-11 PL/I compiler are still very similar to those of the MULTICS compiler, with one major difference. The PL/I compilers developed at Translation Systems, Inc., keep the internal program representation in a linear file of operators representing a sequence of trees, rather than as a complete tree in memory. We discuss the advantages of this approach in Chapter 5.

Chapters 6 through 10 provide detailed technical discussions of VAX-11 specific phases of the compiler, including tree writing and reduction, global optimization, code generation and the allocation of temporaries, register allocation and assignment, and peephole optimization. Although these chapters are ordered according to the sequence in which the phases execute during a compilation, they may also be read individually.

In these chapters, we discuss some topics in greater detail than others, and some topics generally found in books on compiler design are not discussed at all. For example, we tend to emphasize optimization and code generation techniques but make little mention of parsing. Our aim is to present information on aspects of the design that we feel are especially interesting or that we feel we executed particularly well. The technical content of these chapters is occasionally somewhat dense, and we assume that readers have some prior acquaintance with compiler design topics or some experience in software engineering, or both. The glossary provides some explanations of PL/I terms used in the text and should help fill any gaps.

Chapter 11 summarizes our experiences in taking the common back end and writing a second front end—for a C compiler—for it and compares these different front ends. Chapter 12 offers some brief conclusions about the process of compiler design in general. In the appendix we present some examples of code optimization.

Although this book is neither a textbook nor a scholarly survey of compiler design techniques, students should find much material of practical value in it. We have discussed engineering issues that are not covered in the academic literature, and we have tried to do so with a minimum of technical jargon and abstraction.

We would like to acknowledge the participation and contributions in the development work of the PL/I compiler and documentation of William Brown, Charles Spitz, Catherine Pacy, Peter Baum, and Thomas Diaz.

Successive drafts of this manuscript were edited, reviewed, and aided by Ann Staffeld, Jonathan Ostrowsky, Jay Palmer, Rodger Blair, Andrew Bodge, Larry Jones, and Myles Connors. For help in preparation of early drafts, we owe thanks to the Graphic Services group at Digital's Spit Brook facility, in particular Deborah Malone and Paul King, and the library staff, Charlie Matthews and Dottie Mamos.

Special thanks for help and assistance go to the Digital Press staff for superb editorial support. This manuscript was produced by Digital's Educational Services Development and Publishing in Bedford, who accepted generically encoded, machine-readable text from the authors and translated it on a DECset typesetting system. We are thankful to Rudolf Riess and Mary Ann Cotter for undertaking the translations, to Jane Blake for the careful final editing of the manuscript, and to Gillian Cowdery and Frances Giannopoulos for the book and cover design.

We appreciate the support and encouragement of C. Gordon Bell, William Heffner, Bill Johnson, and Armen Varteressian, who gave us time to work on this project.

Finally, we acknowledge once again the engineering achievements of Robert Freiburghouse, whose early compilers and compiler-writing techniques provide the groundwork for the compiler we describe here, and whose encouragement of our project and thoughtful readings of early drafts are greatly appreciated.

Patricia Anklam
David Cutler
Roger Heinen, Jr.
M. Donald MacLaren

Contents

Figures

Selected project notes, taken by David Cutler, appear on pages 91, 93, 120, 123, 133, and 154.

Cartoons by Stanley Roberts, Digital Equipment Corporation, appear on pages 37, 39, 72, 77, and 96.

1

Where We Began, and Why

When we began the compiler development project, as a team, we had few pre-conceived notions of how certain tasks within a compiler ought to be done. Two of us had participated in the design of operating systems for Digital Equipment Corporation's PDP-11 and VAX-11 computers. One, a technical writer, had previously documented operating systems. The fourth member of our team had experience in compiler design and language theory but had never worked on code optimization.

Background

The VAX-11, a computer architecture developed by Digital Equipment Corporation in the mid- to late seventies, is a 32-bit machine with memory management capabilities to support multiprogramming. One of the fundamental design goals of the VAX-11 architects was to implement an instruction set that would enhance the performance of code produced by high-level language compilers. Therefore, constructs such as case, call, and array accessing by register incrementation are built into the instruction set and map conveniently into single instructions or addressing modes on the VAX-11 processors. In mid-1977, before the first release of the machine and its virtual memory operating system (VAX/VMS), plans for VAX-11 language products emphasized the development of languages that were already available on the company's PDP-11 processors: initially (and especially) FORTRAN but eventually COBOL and BASIC. There was also some interest in PL/I, particularly because at this time two ANSI subcommittees were working on it. One was defining a subset of the full PL/I language, and many of Digital's competitors either had or were readying implementations of this subset. Another subcommittee was defining real-time extensions to the language to support process control environments.

Consequently, a task force appointed to study the market for a PL/I compiler recommended that Digital try to make a PL/I subset available within three to five years. To minimize the risk of designing and implementing a compiler from scratch, the task force recommended purchasing an existing compiler and modifying it to produce code for VAX-11 machines. The marketing report was reinforced by another Digital study evaluating the VAX-11 de-

1

sign and its suitability for compiler implementation. The latter report concluded that many features of both the architecture and the operating system seemed especially well designed for the PL/I real-time extensions. This finding was not surprising given that the VAX-11 architecture was designed with high-level languages like PL/I in mind.

There was never much discussion about which PL/I compiler to buy: the obvious choice was the one designed by Robert Freiburghouse and marketed through the company he founded, Translation Systems, Inc. His compiler was designed so that a PL/I front end, written in PL/I, transformed the source program into a common intermediate representation that could subsequently be read by different code generators that would produce instructions for various machine architectures. This compiler has also been successfully adapted by Wang, Data General, Prime, Control Data Corporation, Honeywell-Bull CII, and Stratus Computer, Inc.

Building the PL/I Team

In January 1978, the contract had been signed to purchase the compiler and to obtain its sources and documentation. Later that same year two of us (Dave and Roger), who had recently completed work on the first release of the VAX/VMS operating system software, expressed interest in doing the PL/I compiler project. Our motivation was twofold: first, we were tired of operating system development and wanted to take on a different, challenging project; second, we knew nothing about compilers (nor even of PL/I) and wanted to learn about them. We were confident that, given our intimate knowledge of the VAX-11 instruction set, we could write a compiler that would produce very efficient code.

We were soon joined by the PL/I language expert of the team (Don), whose concern throughout the project was the semantic and language-specific phases of the compiler. His extensive experience with PL/I and with compiler design in general ensured the conformity of the compiler (and its implementors) to the PL/I standard, both in fact and in spirit.

Documentation support was provided throughout the project by Patti, who joined the project to document the PL/I language and stayed to document the compiler and common code generator.

The Original Compiler

The compiler was "delivered" to us by way of an account on a MULTICS machine at the Massachusetts Institute of Technology. The account contained the compiler's sources and an executable version that ran on MULTICS. The compiler executed in five phases:

1. In a first pass over the source file, the compiler parsed the PL/I statements, created a symbol table from information in the source file declarations, and transformed the program into an intermediate form, a linear file of *operators*.

2. Next, a declaration validation phase read the symbol table and applied PL/I rules to declarations by filling in default attributes, checking for conflicting attributes, and so on.

3. In a second pass over the program, the compiler read the symbol table and the intermediate representation to apply PL/I-specific semantics, resolve references, calculate array extents, and so on.

4. In an optional pass over the operator file, the compiler performed global optimizations, including loop invariant removal, common subexpression elimination, and limited optimization of Boolean expressions.

5. Its storage allocation phase assigned static variables to memory locations, automatic variables to stack locations, output the storage map of the program, and wrote the initial object module records.

The compiler did not contain a code generator; we would provide that.

Each pass read a file created by a previous pass and output a new file. Because the compiler was developed initially for machines with limited address space, these intermediate files were true "files" in that they were written temporarily to disk space. Moreover, each pass executed independently of the others and, upon its own completion, transferred control to a utility routine that saved global variables in memory and loaded the next pass.

The compiler was almost machine independent. Machine dependencies (relative to source or target computer) were isolated in tables of constants specifying size and alignment requirements for data, a general-purpose data conversion routine, and some small routines in the storage allocator that emitted object records. The constant tables were built to be used on MULTICS to generate code for a computer with 16-bit integers and 32-bit addresses.

The great value of this compiler was that it correctly and efficiently handled the syntax and semantics of the PL/I General-Purpose Subset. In addition, it featured a very nice intermediate language and was programmed in such a way that it was easy to modify. We have extended and modified the compiler in many ways, but the treatment of PL/I syntax and semantics has changed very little.

Armed for the Dragon

When we approached our task we had, by way of technical information on the compiler itself, its sources and a set of design notes. We were able to compile examples on MULTICS and examine the intermediate language output. Consulting was available from Freiburghouse, but in the end we used only about two hours of telephone consultation.

Collectively, our team possessed PL/I expertise and a depth of experience in software engineering. And, of course, we had begun familiarizing ourselves with the literature on the subject. Our principal source was the classic by Alfred V. Aho and Jeffrey D. Ullman, *Principles of Compiler Design* (Reading, Massachusetts: Addison-Wesley, 1979). We used this source frequently, especially to understand the state-of-the-art theories on optimization.

Thus armed, we began our project.

2

Getting Started: Design Decisions

With the compiler sources available to us on the MULTICS machine at MIT, our first task was to get a version of the compiler running on our VAX-11 machine, which was at Digital's software engineering facility in Tewksbury, Massachusetts. This entailed, first, designing and developing a code generator for the VAX-11. The second task was to bootstrap the compiler.

A Code Generation Method

Although the original compiler did not contain a code generator, we had acquired with the compiler an intangible asset: the knowledge that Freiburghouse used a procedural form of table-driven code generation in his own PL/I compilers. In this method, one extends a simple procedural language, called TBL (Table Building Language), by adding primitive actions specifically related to code generation. The code generator is written in the extended TBL and compiled into a table by a TBL compiler. One must write an interpreter to interpret the TBL program contained in the table. The combination of TBL program and its interpreter is the code generator. We had no examples of TBL-style code generators to study, but Freiburghouse gave us a short lecture on the topic. We defer a detailed discussion of TBL to Chapter 3, but we will try here to explain the origin of the approach.

The concept of table-driven code generation is part of the folk knowledge of compiler writers. Most table-driven code generators work along the following lines. The table contains templates or patterns representing short sequences of machine instructions. To generate code for an instance of an operation, the code generator uses an algorithm to select the pattern that appears most suitable in the current context. A relatively simple routine then substitutes operands for parameters in the template and generates actual machine instructions. There are many possible variations on this theme; but the point of table-driven code generation is always to use templates to systematically represent a mass of code generation details. Another advantage is that the method is generally very space efficient.

The disadvantage of traditional table-driven code generation is that even with a complicated pattern selection algorithm the method is not very flexible. In particular, it is difficult to make use of information about language data types and sizes. The development of TBL may be regarded as a reaction to

5

this problem. Instead of having a table that contains code patterns, we have a table that contains procedures that generate code patterns. In the simplest case—an operation that always translates into the same single instruction—there is no practical differentiation between the two approaches. In the traditional method, a table contains just a template for that instruction. With TBL, the table contains just a single action that emits the instruction.

The advantage of the TBL approach is felt when, in order to generate good code, a decision must be based on many factors. Then the TBL method generates code one step at a time with all the flexibility of a procedural language available to control the generation. The TBL approach is still very systematic because the TBL dialect used is tailored specifically to code generation for the target machine.

The TBL approach described in this book was first tried experimentally by a student at MIT under the direction of Freiburghouse. MacLaren used it for a FORTRAN compiler on MULTICS in 1975, and Freiburghouse used it in all the PL/I compilers produced while he owned Translation Systems, Inc. We made our TBL a syntactic extension of Freiburghouse's TBL so that a single TBL compiler could be used for all the TBL programs in our PL/I compiler. The whole TBL approach seems so natural that we would not be surprised to hear that it has been used before, but we have not been able to find documentation of such use.

We did not decide at the outset to use TBL for our code generator (we were, for that matter, skeptical of any technique that depended on running an interpreter at compile time). However, we had no other approach in mind. We therefore decided to use TBL initially so we could get on with the bootstrap and to rewrite the code generator later, if necessary. The decision to use TBL proved a good one; we never modified the design. Our Local Code Generator (described in detail in Chapter 8) uses a TBL program to generate instructions on an operator-by-operator basis.

Using TBL requires a TBL compiler. We needed to write our own version of a TBL compiler mainly because the one on the MULTICS machine was written in PL/I and we did not have a PL/I compiler on our VAX-11 machine. And because we decided (for reasons explained below) not to perform the bootstrap on MULTICS, we could not use the TBL compiler there. So, one of our first tasks was to write a compiler so that we could write a compiler. The resulting TBL compiler is the first, the fastest, and most bug-free—albeit the simplest—of the three compilers we have written.

It was when we encountered problems in bootstrapping the compiler that we formally decided to use TBL.

Bootstrapping

The PL/I compiler we bought was written in PL/I. Writing a compiler in its own language is quite a common practice, and one nice thing about it is that the developers immediately benefit from improvements in the compiler. Another advantage is that the compiler provides a substantial test program for checking its own correctness and performance. The principal reason for writing a compiler in its own language, however, is that it makes transferring the compiler to a different computer architecture relatively easy. This transfer process is generally referred to as *bootstrapping the compiler.*

A typical bootstrap proceeds as follows:

1. Start with a complete compiler running on a host computer.

2. Replace its code generator with a code generator for the new, target machine. This code generator has to implement only the parts of the language used by the compiler, and it can cut corners in other ways that will be corrected later.

3. Build the new compiler by using the original compiler on the host machine. This produces a *cross-compiler* running on the host computer and generating code that will execute on the target machine.

4. Debug the cross-compiler by using it to compile test programs on the host computer. Take these compiled test programs to the target computer and execute them there.

5. Build the new compiler by using the cross-compiler. This produces a compiler that runs on the target computer.

6. On the target computer, debug the compiler by compiling and executing test programs there. Making changes and corrections requires recompilation using the cross-compiler on the host computer, and this may require backing up to step 3.

7. Finally, use the new compiler on the target machine to compile itself. Test it by checking that the two compilers produce exactly the same output on all test programs, including using the compiler itself as a test program.

This process sounds confusing, but the only step that is actually complicated is the development of the new code generator.

Our initial inclination was to bootstrap the compiler roughly as outlined above, using the MULTICS PL/I compiler as the host compiler. The code generator would produce output in VAX-11 MACRO, the VAX-11 assembly language, rather than in object code. This shortcut would save work initially and, we hoped, would avoid problems connected with differing data representations on MULTICS and VAX-11's.

A bit of experimentation with MULTICS caused us to change our plans. We found that the MULTICS system was heavily loaded. Compared with our local VAX-11 system, response time was slow, especially in compiling large programs. Because the MULTICS machine was located some distance away (in Cambridge, Massachusetts), we could use only slow-speed printing terminals, not the high-speed video display terminals we were used to. Moreover, there was no way to quickly obtain listings of any size. Even worse, we could see that the cycle of compiling a test program on MULTICS, getting it to VAX, running it on VAX, and modifying the Local Code Generator on MULTICS would be painfully slow. For these reasons, we adopted an approach that startled many people.

From the very start, we developed the Local Code Generator on the VAX-11. Our cross-compiler ran on two machines, the front end on the MULTICS in Cambridge and the back end on our VAX-11 in Tewksbury. Transfer of data between the two was accomplished via a magnetic tape containing the front end's output. A courier transported tapes between Cambridge and Tewksbury once a day. The result was a compiler with unusually quick turnaround on code generation modifications: to modify the compiler's code generator and retry it with all the test programs required only a few minutes because there was no need to run it through a front end again. However, the compiler's performance statistics were also unusual: complete compilation of a test program required from 12 to 24 hours.

To write the Local Code Generator on the VAX-11 we used TBL and assembly language. Our choice of assembly language caused some controversy, but it was the obvious choice. No really suitable high-level language was available on the VAX-11 at that time, and we were very familiar with VAX-11's MACRO language. MACRO also seemed the logical choice for the compiler's "kernel," the interpreter for the very large code generation TBL program, which has much code that manipulates data at the bit level.

On MULTICS, we changed the PL/I compiler to generate three output files:

- One file contained the symbol table contents (after execution of the storage allocation phase).
- The second file contained the operators (after global optimization).
- The third file contained storage allocation information for the VAX-11 Linker.

The files were written to tape using ANSI tape formats, despite the fact that the files contained only binary information.

At this point, we encountered the stumbling block we had hoped to avoid by doing a traditional bootstrap: we had to deal with the machine-specific binary representation of the data. MULTICS, a 36-bit machine, stores bit strings and character strings from left to right within bytes or words, depending on the size of the data structure being written; whereas the VAX-11 stores them from right to left. For example, on MULTICS the first addressed byte of a 36-bit integer is the byte containing the sign bit. On the VAX-11, the first addressed byte contains the integer's low-order bit. Therefore, the program we used to write the tape not only had to convert data from 36-bit words to 16-bit or 32-bit words (depending on the precise data structures) but also simultaneously had to swap bit strings.

For most of our debugging of the Local Code Generator, we used six small test programs, which we compiled each time we made changes to the code generator. In this case, compiling required merely reloading the three files from tape and running the new versions of the Local Code Generator to produce a machine code listing and a VAX-11 object module. We did not execute these programs. To verify the code, we looked at the machine code listing and ran the module through a VAX/VMS software utility program called the *object module analyzer.* This program reads object code and flags incorrect records. It was invaluable to us for debugging the compiler because we could easily tell whether the compiler was producing syntactically valid—though not necessarily semantically correct—object code.

At this early stage, we felt we needed to do only enough code generation to support the portions of the compiler that were written in PL/I (a common shortcut in bootstrapping). Because all compile-time data conversions were done by a separate machine-dependent conversion routine, we assumed that the compiler used only pointers, strings, and simple integer arithmetic. Thus, we wrote only enough of the code generator to handle these language functions. We were surprised to discover later that the compiler used fixed-point decimal arithmetic. This arose from an expression with integer constant operands. Unlike most such expressions, this one was not evaluated at compile time, and so it appeared in the compiler's object code.

Eventually, satisfied with our few artificial test programs, we tried a real program, HANOI. This entailed transliterating to PL/I a FORTRAN program that solves the Towers of Hanoi puzzle. It was the first PL/I program we compiled and executed successfully on VAX-11 and has remained one of our favorite benchmarks. The success of HANOI marked the approximate end of debugging our cross-compiler.

The next step was to get the front end running on the VAX-11. The organization of the cross-compiler permitted a novel approach. Instead of starting with the first phase (the parser), we started with the last one (the storage allocator). We compiled it with the cross-compiler and linked it with the code generator to produce an allocator plus a code generator on the VAX-11. We then changed the front end on MULTICS to dump the symbol table and operators to tape before the storage allocation phase. Thus, more of our new cross-compiler existed on the VAX-11, less of it on MULTICS. The arrangement is illustrated in Figure 1.

To test the compiler, we used our original six test programs and parts of the compiler. We compared the operator file and symbol table file produced on MULTICS by the original cross-compiler with the corresponding files produced on the VAX-11 by the new cross-compiler. We also compared object code from the two compilers. It took many iterations before the outputs matched.

We continued our backward bootstrap with the global optimization routine, then the second pass, and finally the remaining front end phases combined.

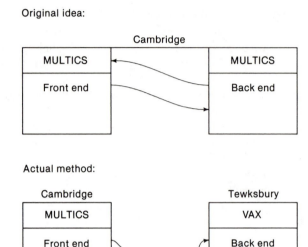

Original idea:

Figure 1. Bootstrapping backward.

Each stage of the bootstrap brought different problems to light. For example, while bringing over the large and complicated semantic analysis phase, we discovered that our register allocation scheme was inefficient and inadequate. In this initial design, we performed register allocation within the Local Code Generator in such a way that the Local Code Generator had to make special allowances each time it wrote an instruction that destroyed registers. It was messy. Our much more efficient, final version of the Register Allocator is described in Chapter 9. We also discovered that we had overlooked some of the symbol table that was required only by the compiler's first two passes.

The entire bootstrapping took about a month from the time the code generator we wrote seemed to produce valid code for the six test programs until all passes were running together on the VAX-11. Before that, we had spent about five months studying the compiler and writing the code generator and the TBL compiler. The completion of bootstrapping marked the end of the "risky" phase of our project; we had succeeded in getting a PL/I compiler to run on a VAX-11. Next, we had to define the kind of product we wanted to build.

A Project Plan

By the time we had finished the bootstrap, we had a much better idea of the complexity of the compiler. We therefore decided to begin by writing a PL/I product for the proposed subset standard (called the General-Purpose Subset) rather than for the real-time extensions. We also set a quality goal for our-selves: we wanted our PL/I compiler to be comparable in performance of gen-erated code to the VAX-11 FORTRAN compiler. Later, we decided that even this goal was not sufficiently ambitious. As development continued, we learned new ways to make the compiler produce faster, better code, and we added optimizations in almost every phase.

It took another year—and two additional programmers—to prepare the compiler for product field testing. During this time, we sharpened our diag-nostic and development tools; implemented a run-time system and a self-checking test system; designed, wrote, and reviewed a set of user manuals; and rewrote or modified more than half of the compiler. Among the major time-consuming tasks during this phase were changes to the compiler re-quired for conformance to the VAX-11 language standards (in particular, the calling standard) and enhancements to the I/O routines to take advantage of the VAX-11 Record Management Services (RMS) file system routines.

Tools We Needed

One of the things we needed right away were some good diagnostic tools. The original compiler had a routine called PRINTOPS that output the opera-tor file. We had already modified this routine so that it would dump the opera-tor and symbol table files from the MULTICS machine onto tape. We further modified it to get a routine that we could use to verify the intermediate repre-sentation of the program. When we had completed the external command in-terface to the compiler, we simply added the necessary option to the command data base so that we could selectively print different internal data structures during different phases of the compiler. Thus, to output the opera-tors in the parse trees after the compiler's first pass over the program, we would invoke the compiler using a command like:

```
PLI/DIAG=(OPERATORS,PASS1)
```

(Subsequent chapters present examples of the output from dumping the oper-ator file. Although it is not always easy to look at trees in linear form, this output helped us understand what the compiler was producing.)

In addition to PRINTOPS, we added a debugger (modifying the debugger used by the VAX/VMS operating system development team) and wrote routines to dump the Symbol Table (DUMPSYM) and the code blocks pro-duced by the Local Code Generator (DUMPCODE).

When the goal is a very high-quality compiler, continual verification of out-put is essential. We decided very early on that we wanted a thorough test system, and we hired a programmer to work full time developing one. The resulting test system, which is still in use, is totally self-checking; that is, it does not depend on hand checking of output, but instead keeps a data base of expected output and runs the same programs against each new version of the compiler. This approach ensured that we never introduced a bug that made a previously valid test program invalid without the bug being detected.

We also wanted a test system to which we could add test programs easily. Once our system was developed and under control, we added a test program each time we detected a bug, even if the bug and its fix seemed trivial. By the time we completed the project, the test system consisted of over 500 programs. Of these, 90 percent were test programs introduced to test features of the compiler; the balance were introduced as a result of reported bugs.

How We Changed the Compiler

During the year of compiler development following completion of the bootstrap, no phase of the compiler was left unmodified: some things were completely rewritten, some were modified gradually, and some new phases were invented. For example, we wrote a new lexical analysis routine, wrote the underpinnings of the Local Code Generator, pulled register allocation out of the Local Code Generator and introduced it as a unique phase of its own, and completely rewrote the Optimizer phase. We always, however, kept a version of our "bootstrap" compiler with which to test and compare new versions as we went along. It was our private benchmark.

A major change that we had not foreseen at the outset of development came about when we made the decision to structure the compiler so that the code generation phases (collectively, the "back end") could be used in common by compilers for different languages (individual "front ends"). In fact, before the first version of our PL/I compiler was shipped as a product, we had begun work on our second compiler, an implementation of the C programming language. Achieving the goal of a truly common back end required restructuring the front end to simplify tree management and introducing a routine (actually, a coroutine) called Write Tree to serve as the interface between the front and back ends. Eventually, this design resulted in a more comprehensive shell, or envelope, of common routines, including compiler initialization, source file input/output, and listing file output.

Introducing . . . The VAX-11 Compiler
and Common Code Generator

Before discussing specific aspects of the compiler design or individual executable phases in the next chapters, we present an overview of the structure and control flow of the VAX-11 Code Generator. (One of the phases of the VAX-11 Code Generator, in which the intermediate program representation is transformed into machine language code, is called the *Local Code Generator*. To avoid confusion, we consistently refer to the entire shell as the *VAX-11 Code Generator* and to the code generation phase as the *Local Code Generator*.)

Each numbered step, or phase, shown in the overview (Figure 2) is described below. Most phases are language and compiler independent; that is, the routines that execute them can be incorporated with little or no modification into a compiler for any programming language. The shaded blocks in Figure 2 show phases that are language and compiler specific. The designer of a front end for a specific language compiler must provide the routines to execute these phases.

The explanations of the numbered steps in the diagram follow:

1. Compiler invocation and initialization normally involves the specification of an input file or files, libraries, and compiler options. These are processed through an interface to the VAX/VMS command language.

2. The steps of parsing and semantic analysis represent the primary language-specific work to be provided by a front end.

3. As it parses and transforms a source program, the front end builds the Symbol Table and creates trees of what we call, simply, *operators*. To output the trees, the front end calls the VAX-11 Code Generator routine called Write Tree. Write Tree is a language-independent procedure that accepts the trees and writes them into a linear file of operators. The operator file is itself a representation of a sequence of trees. However, in the operator file the trees have a modified form. Write Tree changes some trees into a more restricted canonical form required by the Local Code Generator and the Optimizer and it reduces trees by performing optimizations—such as constant reduction—whenever possible. It also adds information about operand usage to the Symbol Table, contributing information needed by the Optimizer and Local Code Generator phases.

4. The Optimizer performs standard global optimizations such as removal of invariant expressions from loops, elimination of common subexpressions, and selection of local variables that are candidates for assignment to registers. To perform these optimizations, it does exhaustive program control and data flow analyses of the program on a block-by-block basis. It also performs a few optimizations that are targeted for the VAX-11 instruction set but that are in fact machine-independent. Execution of the Optimizer can be suppressed by a compile-time option.

5. The implementor of the front end must write a storage allocation routine. The storage allocation routine must, according to the requirements of the source language and information provided by the front end, select static or dynamic allocation for variables and generate object language to allocate and assign initial values to static and external variables.

6. The Local Code Generator reads the operator file created by Write Tree or the Optimizer. As it processes operators, it allocates data struc-

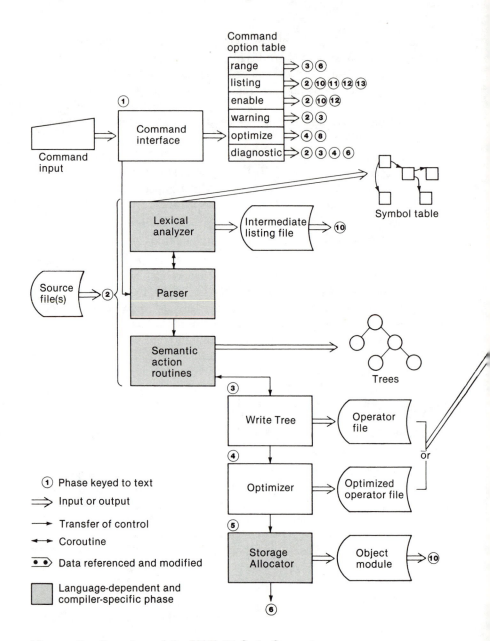

Figure 2. Overview of the VAX-11 Code Generator.

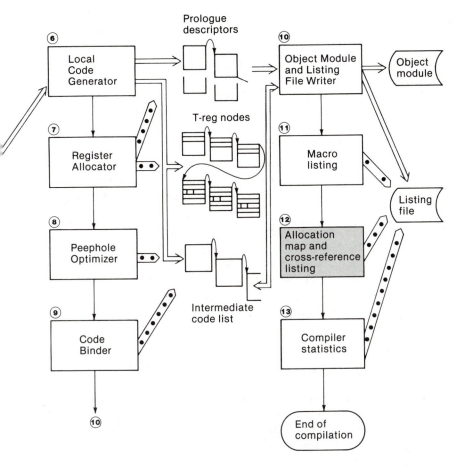

tures to represent temporaries and maintains information about these structures on a block-by-block basis. It also builds skeletal machine-language instructions, called *code blocks,* that reference the operators used as instruction operands.

7. The Register Allocator uses the data structures built by the Local Code Generator to assign temporaries referenced in instruction operands to specific hardware registers and updates the code blocks with the register numbers. Depending on the requirements of register usage for addressing, the Register Allocator adds code blocks as needed to the list of code blocks—the intermediate code list—to generate correct addressing sequences.

8. The Peephole Optimizer scans the code blocks in the intermediate code list and replaces selected code sequences with shorter or faster code sequences that produce equivalent results. The peephole optimizations can also be suppressed by a compile-time option.

9. Following peephole optimization, the branch/jump resolution phase (the Code Binder) resolves the virtual memory addresses of program labels and determines the appropriate machine instructions for transfers of control. It updates the code blocks with the correct information.

10. The Object Module and Listing File Writer reads the final code list and adds object module records to the object module file created by the Storage Allocator. It also reads the intermediate listing file created by the language front end and opens the listing file for output.

11. The MACRO listing is optionally written by a procedure that executes only if requested at compile time. It merges the machine language representation of the program into the source program listing during object module generation.

    Generation of a listing file is delayed until this time in the compilation so that the machine language code can be written in line—that is, the instructions generated for each source language statement are output in the listing immediately following the source language statement. (This output proved very useful during the development and debugging of the compiler.) This delay also permits incorporation of all diagnostic message text in the listing following the line number at which the condition occurred, even for conditions that are not detected until operator processing.

12. The writer of the front end must supply routines to be invoked during compilation that will write a storage map and cross-reference listing, if any, to the listing file.

13. Finally, the VAX-11 Code Generator shell gathers statistics during compilation if requested, including statistics on the performance of the back end, and prints these in the listing.

Figure 3 shows a more compact illustration of the possibilities for folding front ends into the shell, or envelope, of the VAX-11 Code Generator. It shows how we have used the back end in conjunction with both the VAX-11 PL/I and the VAX-11 C compilers.

This shell has proved to be quite flexible; in addition to our two compiler projects, the back end has been successfully adapted at Digital to two other compilers. One of these, an implementation of the PEARL language, was developed in Reading, England, with an early version of the back end (and with limited access to technical assistance and documentation).

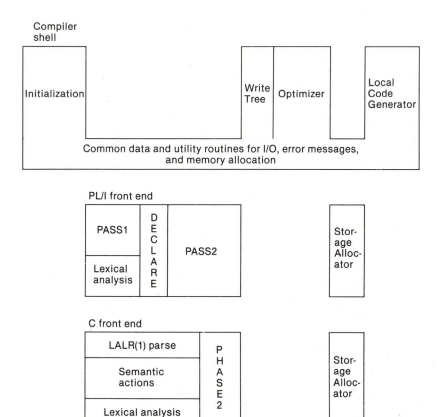

Figure 3. Using the VAX-11 Code Generator for different compilers.

3

The TBL
(Table-Building
Language)

The logic of four phases in our compiler—PASS1, PASS2, Write Tree, and the Local Code Generator—is encoded by means of the table-building programming technique we call TBL, or Table-Building Language. (We also use the acronym to refer to the TBL compiler, to source programs written in TBL, and to the TBL output file.)

TBL is not a programming language like FORTRAN, BASIC, or PASCAL. It is a general syntax shell into which a user can place an individualized repertoire of instructions. To avoid confusion with other language terminology, we call the user-defined instructions in a TBL program *actions*. The result is a very high-level language tailored to solve a particular programming problem—in the case of our compiler, four different problems: parsing, semantic analysis, semantic reduction, and code generation. Looked at another way, each user's set of TBL actions represents an abstract machine.

The purpose of this chapter is twofold: to introduce TBL in order to provide a better understanding of our implementation techniques in certain phases of the compiler and to demonstrate that a broad range of programming problems are candidates for TBL-style solutions. At the end of the chapter, we include a detailed, annotated TBL program and its interpreter.

How TBL Programs Are Constructed

A TBL compiler combines the action definitions of the user's abstract machine and a source program that references these actions, producing a table of numeric data. To execute the statements in the user's TBL program, an interpreter reads the numeric data treating specific numeric values as instruction opcodes. Figure 4 illustrates the steps and files required to build a TBL-driven program.

Each TBL-driven phase in our compiler has a small, unique interpreter. The interpreter can be viewed as the microcode in the user-defined machine; the TBL compiler's output is the assembly-language code.

The syntax of TBL provides for references to user actions with arguments and constant identifiers. Common programming constructions such as call, goto, case, if, and if_not are part of the user's repertoire only if they are defined in the TBL program along with the necessary underlying interpreta-

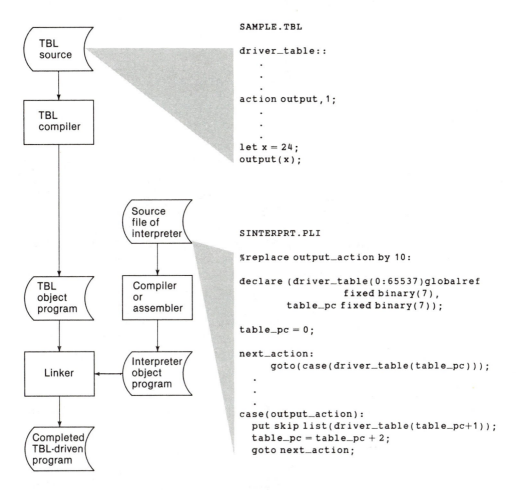

Figure 4. Files required to build a TBL-driven program.

tion. (For example, use of these constructions requires that the names *call, goto, case, if,* and *if_not* be defined as TBL actions and processed by the interpreter.) Before discussing in detail how TBL programs are constructed and encoded, we can illustrate the elegance of a high-level TBL program by showing a program fragment taken directly from the PL/I compiler's parser:

```
LET left_paren = 2;
LET right_paren = 3;
LET current_token = 128;
LET bad_syntax = base_error+22;
    .
    .
    .
```

```
if is_token_type(left_paren,current_token)
    THEN [
            call(expression_parse);
            match_token(right_paren);
            ]
    ELSE [
            emit_error(bad_syntax);
            ]
RETURN;
```

At first glance, this example looks very much like PL/I or PASCAL; in fact, the logical function of the fragment can be accomplished by a PL/I or PASCAL program combined with many subroutines. The important and less evident difference is in performance. The TBL scheme does not require a procedure invocation each time an action is referenced but simply a trip around a loop in the interpreter that determines which action to process. TBL is also a very space efficient method for representing the sort of complex decisions that must be made in code generation.

Since the user is free to define the actions of a TBL program, the languages may look somewhat bizarre. For example, they do not have anything resembling proper variables, and some do not even have assignment actions.

The "Language"

The requirements for constructing syntactically valid TBL source programs are quite simple. The language consists of:

- A set of rules defining language elements, including valid names, comments, and punctuation
- TBL compiler directives and constructs that permit definition of names, actions, and locations
- Statements using the directives and user-defined actions for which TBL writes an opcode and arguments to its output file.

All TBL statements have optional labels and are terminated by semicolons. Identifiers specify labels, constants, and actions. All identifiers used in a TBL source program that are not defined in the TBL source file are assumed to be names whose values will be resolved at link time.

Numeric values can be expressed as decimal integer constants or as constant identifiers defined with LET directives. Because all values are encoded into bytes, numbers must be in the range 0 through 255.

In our implementation, TBL programs begin with the specification of a name representing an external address. This allows the program's interpreter to reference the start of the TBL program by using this name. A comment begins with the /* character pair and terminates at the end of the line on which it appears.

Constant Identifiers

A LET directive defines a constant identifier and assigns it a value so that it can be used in future statements. For example, the LET directives:

```
LET true = 1;
LET false = 0;
```

define the names *true* and *false* with the constant values 1 and 0. Thereafter, references to these names cause the compiler to output the corresponding values.

Defining Actions

The ACTION directive declares an action, that is, an instruction for the TBL machine. For example, the actions illustrated in the parser fragment above are defined as:

```
ACTION is_token_type,2;
ACTION call,1;
ACTION match_token,1;
ACTION emit_error,1;
```

The numbers in these ACTION statements represent the number of arguments that must be specified for the action. Depending on the sophistication of the interpreter, arguments to actions are specified as any of the following:

- Decimal integer constants in the range 0 through 255, or constant identifiers (defined with LET directives) equated to integers with values in this range
- The names of user-specified labels in the TBL source file
- Names that are passed through by the TBL compiler and assumed to be resolved at link time.

Each interpreter is responsible for evaluating and processing argument values in a way consistent with the functions being performed by the actions. For example, if the TBL program defines an *add* action, the interpreter would probably treat its arguments as numeric data. Similarly, the interpreter would most likely treat the argument of a *goto* action as a location or a displacement from a location.

References to Actions

Once defined, an action is referenced by specifying its name and arguments, if any. The TBL compiler does not produce any output for an ACTION directive; instead, it assigns a number to each action according to the position of its corresponding ACTION directive in the source file. It then uses the action numbers as opcodes in the creation of the output file. For example:

```
ACTION set_token_type,2;
```

Assume that this ACTION directive assigns the opcode 23 to the action *set_token_type*. Then, if a statement such as

```
set_token_type(constant,current_token);
```

were encountered and the values of the constant identifiers *constant* and *current_token* were defined by LET directives as 10 and 130, the TBL output for this statement would consist of consecutive bytes containing the values 23, 10, and 130.

In our original design, all actions were expected to have a fixed number of arguments. However, we encountered instances in which actions needed to have variable numbers of arguments. We therefore modified the TBL compiler to interpret any argument count greater than 127 as meaning "a variable number of arguments," with the result that the first argument in a reference to the action specifies the number of arguments that follow. For example, a *call* action must be defined as

```
ACTION call,128;
```

so that it can be used to invoke subroutines with different numbers of arguments.

Recognized Actions

In addition to the user-defined actions, the TBL compiler recognizes several common programming actions and processes them in a predefined way. These actions represent the basic primitives of program control flow. Some users of TBL may not need them; thus, they are not processed by the TBL compiler unless specifically defined by the user. It is still the responsibility of the user-written interpreter to give the appropriate meaning to the underlying actions. For example, the syntax for a reference to a *goto* action is:

```
goto(target_label);
```

The TBL compiler has to recognize this construction and calculate the displacement from the reference to the *goto* action to the *target_label*. For our implementation of the TBL compiler and its interpreters, the targets of *goto* actions are signed 16-bit values. If the compiler did not calculate the displacement, the interpreters would be restricted to byte displacements since that is the size of arguments. This approach would have seriously restricted our TBL capabilities. (The displacement is calculated by the compiler, but the interpreter must still know what to do with it.) This implementation satisfies our requirements, but someone writing another TBL compiler might want to do it differently. In fact, we considered adding argument-size specifications to the ACTION directive to permit more general argument interpretation. Although this approach might have been more flexible, we decided it would be costly in terms of execution time; moreover, we have never had an absolute need for the capability.

The syntax for a reference to a *call* action is as follows:

```
call(target_label(arguments...));
```

For these actions, the TBL compiler generates a reference to the opcode for the *call* action, followed by the target address as if it were the target of a *goto* action, the number of arguments, if any, and the optional formal arguments themselves. Full implementation of the *call* action requires a *return* action, but there is no need for the TBL compiler to recognize it because there is no special processing required.

The syntax for the recognized *case* action is as follows:

```
case(selector, target-list . . . );
```

For this, the TBL compiler outputs the *case* action opcode, a byte containing the number of targets, the *selector* argument, and the specifications in the *target-list*. Each item in this list is treated as a *target_label* in a *goto* action.

The general syntax of *if* constructions recognized by our TBL compiler is as follows:

```
if test_action THEN [then_actions...]
                    ELSE [else_actions...]
```

(The *else* clause of this construct is optional and may be omitted. Brackets delimit the *then* and *else* clauses, serving as syntactic markers as in a begin/end construct in a block-structured language.) The *if* and *if_not* actions represent more structured forms of branch-true and branch-false constructions. These constructions are transformed to the following:

```
test_action;
if(label1);
then_actions;
goto(label2);
label1: else_actions;
label2:
```

The *test_action* is executed first; it stores status information in a Boolean variable in the interpreter. Then the *if* action executes and branches if the Boolean variable is false. Thus, the *if* and *if_not* actions depend on the user to implement them in the interpreter. The arguments of an *if* or *if_not* action are the same as target labels in a *goto* action.

In addition to these common forms, our TBL compiler uses *if* and *if_not* actions in constructing sequences of *and* and *or* clauses. For example:

```
IF action1 AND
   action2 OR
   action3 THEN [then_actions....] ELSE [else_actions...]
```

Sample TBL Program and Its Interpreter

The best illustration of TBL is a sample program complete with its interpreter. The sample program is shown in Figure 5. The output of compilation of *sample* is a sequence of bytes.

Figure 6 shows the interpreter, written in PL/I, for this output.

Figure 5. A sample TBL program.

NOTE The label *driver_table* marks the beginning of the TBL program; the compiler passes the name through to the output file. The interpreter uses this name to locate the beginning of the TBL program.

```
driver_table::
```

NOTE The program *sample* defines the recognized TBL actions *call, case, if, if_not, goto,* and *return* described in this chapter, as well as actions that permit simple arithmetic operations and comparisons— *add, sub, eql, neq,* and *assign.*

```
/* define actions...
  action call,1;
  action case,2;
  action if,0;
  action if_not,0;
  action goto,1;
  action return,0;
  action add,2;
  action sub,2;
  action eql,2;
  action neq,2;
  action assign,2;
  action output,1;
  action finish,0;
```

NOTE In this TBL program, constant identifiers with values greater than 127 represent variables; when the interpreter reads an argument whose absolute value is greater than 127, it uses the value as an index into an array of variables.

```
/* variables
  let x = 128;
  let y = 129;
```

Figure 5 *(concluded)*

NOTE These directives define the constants *alpha*, *beta*, and *gamma*, with values less than 127.

```
/* some numbers with names
 let alpha = 66;
 let beta = 33;
 let gamma = 99;
```

NOTE References to the *assign* action give constant values to the variables *x* and *y*. The *add* action adds the value of *y* to *x*.

```
/* assign values to x and y and add them
 assign(alpha,x);
 assign(beta,y);
 add(y,x);
```

NOTE In the *if* action, the reference to the *eql* action sets or clears an interpreter state bit. If these arguments have equal values, the bit is set, the *if* action is true, and its then clause is executed. Otherwise, the bit is cleared, the *if* action is false, and the actions in the else clause of the *if* action are executed.

```
/* check result
 if eql(x,gamma)
    then [
         output(x);
         ]
    else [
         output(x);
         output(gamma);
         ]
```

NOTE The *finish* action terminates the sample TBL program.

```
/* Terminate sample TBL program
 finish;
```

Figure 6. Interpreter for the sample TBL program.

```
1    /*
2      This program implements a simple TBL interpreter.
3    */
4    interpreter: PROCEDURE OPTIONS(MAIN);
5
```

NOTE   There is a one-to-one correspondence between the action numbers assigned by the TBL compiler to the actions and the label subscripts used to designate the action interpretation routines. Thus, the *add* action defined in position 7 of the **ACTION** directives in *sample* is equated in the interpreter with the constant identifier 6. This definition is then used as a subscript in the label array *case* such that *case(add_action)* (line 148) represents the interpretative routine for addition.

```
6    /*
7      define names for known actions
8    */
9
10     %REPLACE call__action BY 0;
11     %REPLACE case__action BY 1;
12     %REPLACE if__action BY 2;
13     %REPLACE if__not__action BY 3;
14     %REPLACE goto__action BY 4;
15     %REPLACE return__action BY 5;
16     %REPLACE add__action BY 6;
17     %REPLACE sub__action BY 7;
18     %REPLACE eql__action BY 8;
19     %REPLACE neq__action BY 9;
20     %REPLACE assign__action BY 10;
21     %REPLACE output__action BY 11;
22     %REPLACE finish__action BY 12;
23
24     /*
25       define error codes
26     */
27     %REPLACE stack__error BY 0;
28     %REPLACE inv__write__arg BY 1;
29     %REPLACE max__error__message BY 1;
30
```

Figure 6 *(continued)*

NOTE The TBL output file—or object program—is declared by a global reference to its starting address, *driver_table*. This is the global label defined at the beginning of the TBL source file. The table itself is declared as an array of bytes so that the interpreter can move through it referencing locations by subscripts.

```
31   /*
32   define the driver table starting address
33   */
34   DECLARE driver__table(0:65535) CHARACTER GLOBALREF;
35
```

NOTE The variables defined in the TBL source file are maintained in an array whose elements are subscripted from 128 to 255.

```
36   /*
37   define variable space for TBL arguments
38
39           0   = < x < = 127 - numeric value
40           128 = < x < = 255 - index into variable array
41   */
42   DECLARE variable__values(128:255) FIXED BINARY(31);
43
```

NOTE The variable *table_pc* is the program counter that references locations in the array *driver_table*.

```
44   /*
45   define local variables
46   */
47
48   DECLARE table__pc FIXED BINARY(31);
49   %REPLACE max__stack BY 1000;
```

NOTE The variables *interpreter_stack* and *cur_sp* are used to save the interpreter's state when *call* actions are executed.

```
50   DECLARE interpreter__stack(max__stack) FIXED BINARY(31);
51   DECLARE cur__sp FIXED BINARY(31);
52   DECLARE (i,j) FIXED BINARY(31);
```

Figure 6   *(continued)*

NOTE The variable *test_state* is the bit that is set or cleared by the actions that have a true/false result, such as *eq* and *neq*.

```
53    DECLARE test_state BIT(1) ALIGNED;
54
55    /*
56     interpreter start
57    */
58    table_pc = 0;                  /* start program at 0 */
59    cur_sp = 0;                    /* initialize stack */
60    test_state = '0'B;            /* assume test state false */
61
```

NOTE In the main interpreter loop, the interpreter reads the unsigned byte in the driver table and uses that value as the subscript of a label array reference in a PL/I GOTO statement. Thus, the first action executed in the sample TBL program, an *assign* action, results in a branch to *case(assign_action)*, or case 10 (line 186).

```
62    /*
63     main interpreter loop
64    */
65    next_action:
66            GOTO case(RANK(driver_table(table_pc)));
```

NOTE Each action increments the *tbl_pc* variable depending on the number of arguments it processes for each action and whether the action has a branch label or a variable number of arguments. For example, the *call* action's interpreter must save the return address of the next byte following the *call* action and its arguments.

```
67    /*
68     call_action - implement a TBL call
69    */
70    case(call_action):
71
72    /* save pc of next instruction */
73
74            cur_sp = cur_sp + 1;
75            IF cur_sp > max_stack THEN CALL error(stack_error);
76            interpreter_stack(cur_sp) = table_pc + 3;
```

NOTE The function *evaluate_goto_target* (see line 272) returns the new value of *tbl_pc* based on the two-byte argument of a target label in the call (which, like a *goto* action's target label, has a two-byte displacement).

```
77            table_pc = evaluate_goto_target(table_pc+1);
78            GOTO next_action;
79
```

Figure 6   *(continued)*

```
80    /*
81     case__action - implement case action
82    */
83    case(case__action):
84
```

> NOTE The function *get__argument__value* (see line 217) returns the value of an argument, whether the argument is an immediate value (in the range 0 through 127) or a variable (in the range 128 through 255).

```
85    /* get value of argument to case on */
86
87             i = get__argument__value(table__pc+1);
88             IF i <= RANK(driver__table(table__pc+2))
89                 THEN table__pc =
90                     evaluate__goto__target(table__pc+3+(i*2));
91                 ELSE table__pc = table__pc +
92                     3 + (RANK(driver__table(table__pc+2))*2);
93
94             GOTO next__action;
95
96    /*
97     if__action - implement a branch false action
98    */
99    case(if__action):
100
101    /* perform a GOTO if the state of test__state is false */
102
103            IF ^test__state
104                THEN table__pc =
105                    evaluate__goto__target(table__pc+1);
106                ELSE
107                    table__pc = table__pc + 3;
108            GOTO next__action;
```

Figure 6   *(continued)*

```
109    /*
110     if_not action - implement a branch true action
111    */
112    case(if_not_action):
113
114    /* perform a GOTO if the state of the test_state is true */
115
116           IF test_state
117               THEN table_pc =
118                      evaluate_goto_target(table_pc+1);
119               ELSE
120                      table_pc = table_pc + 3;
121            GOTO next_action;
122
123    /*
124     goto_action - transfer control
125    */
126    case(goto_action):
127
128            table_pc = evaluate_goto_target(table_pc+1);
129            GOTO next_action;
130
131    /*
132     return action - implement subroutine return
133    */
134    case(return_action):
135
136            IF cur_sp = 0
137                THEN
138                     CALL error(stack_error);
139                ELSE DO;
140                     table_pc = interpreter_stack(cur_sp);
141                     cur_sp = cur_sp - 1;
142                END;
143            GOTO next_action;
144
```

Figure 6 *(continued)*

```
145     /*
146      add_action - implement a two address add operation
147     */
148     case(add_action):
149
150             i = get_argument_value(table_pc+1) +
151                 get_argument_value(table_pc+2);
```

NOTE   The subroutine *set_value* (see line 234) sets the value of a variable.

```
152             CALL set_value(table_pc+2,i);
153             GOTO two_arg_action_done;
154
155     /*
156      sub_action - a two-address subtract operation
157     */
158     case(sub_action):
159
160             i = get_argument_value(table_pc+2) -
161                 get_argument_value(table_pc+1);
162
163             CALL set_value(i,table_pc+2);
164             GOTO two_arg_action_done;
165
166     /*
167      equal_action - implement a test for equal
168     */
169     case(eql_action):
170
171             test_state = (get_argument_value(table_pc+1) =
172                           get_argument_value(table_pc+2));
173             GOTO two_arg_action_done;
174     /*
175      not_equal action - implement a not_equal action
176     */
177     case(neq_action):
178
179             test_state = (get_argument_value(table_pc+1) ^=
180                           get_argument_value(table_pc+2));
181             GOTO two_arg_action_done;
182
```

Figure 6   *(continued)*

```
183   /*
184    assign_action - implement an assign action
185   */
186   case(assign_action):
187           CALL set_value(
188                   table_pc+2,get_argument_value(table_pc+1));
189           GOTO two_arg_action_done;
190   /*
191    action completion routines
192   */
193   two_arg_action_done:
194           table_pc = table_pc + 3;
195           GOTO next_action;
196   /*
197    output variable routine
198   */
199   case(output_action):
200
201           i = get_argument_value(table_pc+1);
202           PUT SKIP LIST(i);
203           table_pc = table_pc + 2;
204           GOTO next_action;
205
206   /*
207    finish TBL and clean up
208   */
209
210   case(finish_action):
211
212           RETURN;
213
```

Figure 6   *(continued)*

```
214   /*
215    get__argument__value - get value of argument using table__pc
216   */
217   get__argument__value: PROCEDURE(index) RETURNS(
218                                 FIXED BINARY(31));
219   DECLARE index FIXED BINARY(31);
220
221   /* get argument value */
222
223   IF RANK(driver__table(index)) < 128
224      THEN
225            RETURN(RANK(driver__table(index)));
226      ELSE
227            RETURN(variable__values(RANK(driver__table(index))));
228
229   END get__argument__value;
230
231   /*
232    set__value - set value of an interpreter variable
233   */
234   set__value: PROCEDURE(index,value);
235
236   DECLARE (index,value) FIXED BINARY(31);
237
238   IF RANK(driver__table(index)) < 128
239      THEN
240            CALL error(inv__write__arg);
241                ELSE
242            variable__values(RANK(driver__table(index))) = value;
243
244   RETURN;
245
246   END set__value;
247
```

Figure 6   *(concluded)*

```
248    /*
249     error - output error routine
250    */
251    error: PROCEDURE(number);
252
253    DECLARE number FIXED BINARY(31);
254
255    /* declare error messages */
256
257    DECLARE messages(0:max_error_message) CHARACTER(100)
258                        VARYING STATIC READONLY INIT(
259    'Stack overflow or underflow at:',
260    'Invalid write argument at:');
261
262    PUT LIST(messages(number),table_pc) SKIP;
263
264    STOP;
265
266    END error;
267
268
269    /*
270     evaluate_goto_target - returns branch displacement value
271    */
272    evaluate_goto_target: PROCEDURE(index) RETURNS(
273                        FIXED BINARY(31));
274    DECLARE index FIXED BINARY(31);
275
276    RETURN(RANK(driver_table(index+1)) * 256
277                + RANK(driver_table(index)));
278
279    END evaluate_goto_target;
280
281    END interpreter;
```

This short introduction to TBL should prove helpful for understanding later examples of TBL programs developed for specific purposes in the compiler. In fact, two of the first three PL/I-specific phases of the front end of the PL/I compiler are written in TBL.

4

What the Front End Must Do

The job of the compiler's front end is to read the source program statements from one or more files and assign them semantic meaning. It must then build, in memory, data structures that represent this meaning in a form that will be understood by the back end. Traditionally, compilers express this semantic information in a symbol table, which describes the objects that the program manipulates, and in trees, which describe operations on those objects. In this chapter we describe our Symbol Table and trees and how they are built. We also discuss the architecture of the machine for which our compilers are written—the VAX-11—as it is seen by the front end. We assume that our readers are already somewhat familiar conceptually with the requirements for building symbol tables and trees. But before describing our implementation of them, we summarize their basic requirements.

The Symbol Table contains entries giving information about the procedures, names, and constants used in the program. The trees give an explicit, convenient-to-manipulate representation of the program's statements. For example:

```
DCL x FLOAT (51), i FIXED;
x = 3 * i - 1;
```

The Symbol Table entry for x specifies that x is a variable, has a data type of floating-point binary with a precision of 51 binary digits, and has the storage class automatic (this default PL/I storage class indicates that the storage for the variable will be allocated dynamically). Similarly, the Symbol Table entry for i specifies that i is an integer variable, is automatic, and has the default precision of 31 binary digits. The Symbol Table entry also specifies a storage location for each variable that requires storage in memory.

Figure 7 shows the tree resulting from the assignment statement. In general, the leaves of a tree denote basic data items either by referencing the Symbol Table (such as references to x and i); or by specifying immediate data (in this case, the integers 3 and 1). The other nodes specify operations on the data. The tree produced by the front end may contain operations not explicitly written in the source. Here, the tree explicitly specifies taking the value of the variable i and converting the value of the expression $3 \times i - 1$ from integer to floating point for its assignment to x.

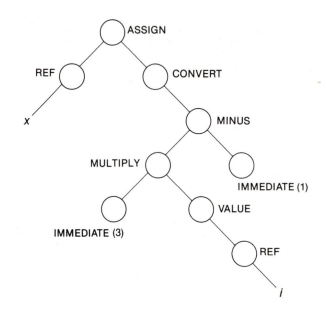

Figure 7.   A tree produced by the front end.

Parsing and Semantic Analysis

Discussions of compilers usually distinguish between parsing and semantic analysis. Parsing is the process of converting a source program to trees (or one very big tree) in accordance with a grammar. The resulting tree is not very explicit because, for one thing, the data types of expressions will be unknown at this point. Semantic analysis transforms the parsed trees into more explicit forms as required by the back end, or code generator, of the compiler. For the tree in Figure 7, the semantic analysis routine has filled in data types (not shown in the figure) and has inserted the operator that performs the conversion from integer to floating point.

Semantic analysis and parsing may be separated or combined, depending on the language being compiled and the preferences of the compiler writers. In our PL/I compiler, the front end is divided into four phases. PASS1 reads the source text, parses it, and builds an initial Symbol Table. The Symbol Table contains only information explicitly given in declarations. Thus, in our example in Figure 7, PASS1 does not set the automatic attribute in the Symbol Table entry for *i* because that attribute was not explicit in the declaration.

Following PASS1, the DECLARE phase fills in all missing details in the Symbol Table. PASS2 then performs semantic analysis a few statements at a time and calls Write Tree to transform the resulting trees into the operators of the Intermediate Language. Finally, the Storage Allocator assigns storage locations for level-one static and automatic variables and outputs the object language records necessary to allocate and initialize the static variables. The Storage Allocator phase executes after Write Tree and the Optimizer so that it need assign locations only for variables that are found to require storage (for example, an automatic variable that is never referenced will not be assigned any storage).

Because parsing is discussed in many other books, we note in Chapter 11 only the interesting differences between the approaches we took in the two compilers we have written. In Chapter 5, we discuss the specific semantics of references and procedure calls and the run-time treatment of block activation and variables.

The Symbol Table

Subsequent phases of the VAX-11 Code Generator reference and add to the Symbol Table. The Symbol Table contains much information that is used only by the front end and some that is required by the back end. Exactly how the front end builds and uses the Symbol Table is irrelevant as long as it accurately accumulates the information required. (Our Optimizer, in particular, relies on the completeness and accuracy of the Symbol Table information. The implementors of the PEARL compiler who used our common back end, however, chose not to accumulate information required by the Optimizer and did not use the Optimizer at all.)

The structure of the Symbol Table resembles the declarative and semantic structure of the source program in that its primary data structures are block nodes, symbol nodes, and token nodes. Block nodes contain information about structural program units, such as procedures, for which a separate set of declarations and temporaries is required (in PL/I and similarly block-structured languages, block nodes are required for begin blocks as well). Symbol nodes contain information about user-defined and compiler-generated variables, procedure parameters, function return values, labels, and language-specific entities such as PL/I format and file constants. Token nodes represent source program identifiers, keywords, and constants and contain the spellings of these objects.

Memory Allocation in the Symbol Table

The front end builds the nodes in virtual memory, using common utility routines. The allocation utility provides as much memory as is required for a node of a given type and returns the location of the node to the front end. Within the Symbol Table, and within the operators for the Intermediate Language, nodes are denoted by signed 15-bit *node identifiers*, each of which uniquely identifies the memory associated with a node. This identifier can be thought of as an address, and it is in fact encoded for easy transformation to a VAX-11 32-bit virtual address. The calculation is:

virtual-address = (node-identifier $\times$ unit size) + base-address

The unit size in our implementation is 16 bytes. Each type of node is allocated in terms of these units; for example, a symbol node requires 3 units, a token node 1, and so on. Using different unit sizes changes the amount of memory that can be represented. Thus, with a unit size of 16 we can represent approximately $2^{15} \times 2^4$ or 2^{19} bytes, whereas a unit size of 1 would allow a maximum addressing space of 2^{15} bytes. During compiler initialization, space for the Symbol Table is reserved with enough virtual memory to occupy 2^{15} node identifiers. As the front end requests space for nodes, memory utility routines allocate space starting at the low end (that is, with lower node identifiers) and moving to the higher. As nodes are built, the utility routines allocate the memory required to hold them.

Nodes are never allocated for the first 64 node identifiers, thus making identifiers 0 through 63 invalid and providing an excellent bug catcher. (The VAX/VMS operating system uses a similar approach to memory allocation, always reserving the first 512 bytes of the virtual address space.) Although node identifiers are limited to 15 bits, they are actually stored as positive integers in 16-bit fields. The sixteenth bit is used in fields that occur in trees and in operators of the Intermediate Language. If this bit is 1, that is, if the field is negative, the field denotes another tree or operator.

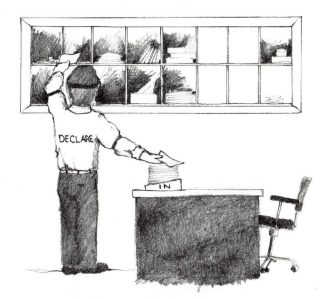

The Symbol Table is completed during PASS2, after which no more nodes are allocated. However, we have reserved enough space for all possible node identifiers so that the remainder of the Symbol Table virtual memory is available for use by PASS2 and the Local Code Generator. PASS2 uses this storage space for temporary trees during semantic analysis. The space at the upper end of the Symbol Table storage is easily allocated and deallocated by the Symbol Table memory allocation routines. Figure 8 illustrates the allocation scheme.

Denoting Symbol Table nodes using node identifiers rather than pointers is necessary if the compiler is to run on a computer with a limited address space. However, we have found the design advantageous even with the large address space available on the VAX-11. It increases performance because the Symbol Table remains in a small, localized region of compiler memory; this decreases paging during the compiler's execution. Second, this design decreases the total amount of memory required to hold the Intermediate Language representation of the program. Moreover, the 15-bit Symbol Table node identifiers are somewhat machine independent—an advantage that was crucial during bootstrapping. Of course, we do have to perform the computations to convert the node identifiers to virtual addresses, but the overhead required for these computations is inconsequential compared with the potential size of a symbol table that uses 32-bit addresses.

The number of possible node identifiers is limited to 2^{15}. Since a given node usually occupies more than one allocation unit, there are actually fewer than 2^{15} nodes. However, we have never encountered a program large enough to

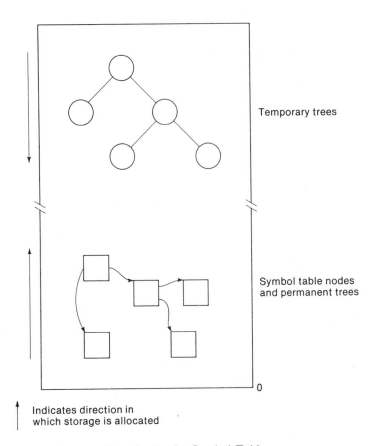

Temporary trees

Symbol table nodes
and permanent trees

0

Indicates direction in
which storage is allocated

Figure 8. Memory allocation in the Symbol Table.

overflow this space. If such a program were devised in an effort to exhaust the space, we suspect it would fail in some other compilation error before it ran out of Symbol Table space.

Block Nodes

The front end builds a block node to represent each program block, including an imaginary outer block that envelops all external procedures and variables declared outside the external procedures. This block provides program symmetry by supplying a place to which to move external declarations. Depending on the structure of the language and the implementation chosen, block nodes may also be required for other program entities. For example, the PL/I compiler builds block nodes for all begin blocks and ON-units as well as for GET and PUT statements.

The block nodes for a program are linked by node identifiers. The first block node in the chain is the node describing the imaginary outer block. Fields within a block node describe the structure of the program by indicating the lexical nesting level and specifying the parent block. Figure 9 illustrates a chain of blocks for a program with one external procedure (the outermost) and one internal procedure.

Although PL/I has both procedure blocks and begin blocks, the compiler treats a begin block as a special case of procedure block, so we can ignore the distinction between the two. The block structure of a program also defines the run-time stack requirements for each block and the scope of all variables. Thus, a block node contains accumulated information about the stack requirements, entry points, and parameters and a list of variables declared in the

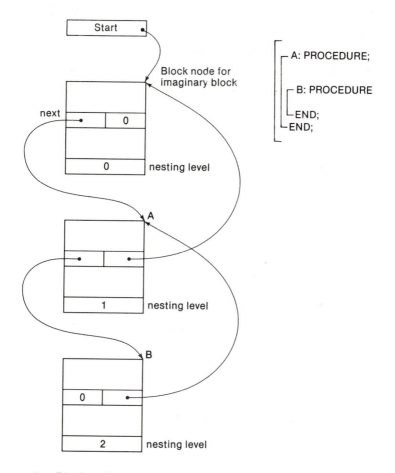

Figure 9. Block nodes.

block. The front end is responsible for filling in basic information in the block node, such as the nesting level. The back end accumulates much of the stack usage information and reference information and uses this information during optimization.

Symbol Nodes

Each block node contains a pointer to a list of variables declared in the block. The list consists of a chain of symbol nodes. A symbol node typically represents a user-defined program variable. The attributes specified in the source file declaration are encoded in the symbol node along with attributes derived by the language's default rules and information about the variable's relationship to other variables. The node describes the variable's data type and size, its storage requirements (such as automatic, static, external, or based), extent information (the size of an array or the length of a string), and so on. The extent information always indicates whether the extent is a constant size or must be dynamically evaluated at every reference. In the latter case, the extent is kept as a tree specifying how it is to be computed.

Figure 10 illustrates a chain of symbol nodes linked to a block node.

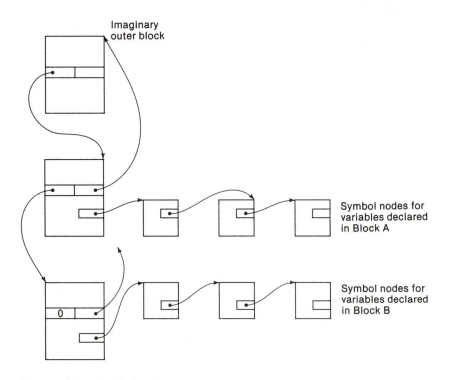

Figure 10. Symbol nodes.

In addition to variables, the front end also builds symbol nodes for such program entities as formal parameters if the block has parameters, return values if the block represents a function, and internally generated local variables, labels, or other symbols.

For certain categories of data, such as aggregates, the symbol node also contains node identifiers of additional nodes. For example, structures are represented by a chain of symbol nodes in which the first symbol node is the topmost structure member; symbol nodes for subsequent members are linked from this chain. Figure 11 illustrates a chain of symbol nodes for a structure declaration.

Array Nodes

Closely related to the symbol nodes are array nodes, shown in Figure 12, which are linked from the symbol node definition for the array declaration. The array node contains information such as the number of dimensions (our implementation allows a maximum of eight), the bounds of each dimension,

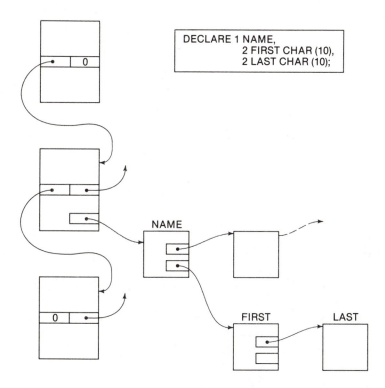

Figure 11. Symbol nodes for structure declaration.

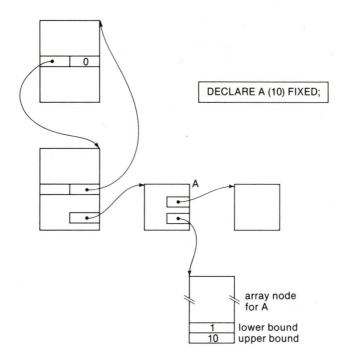

DECLARE A (10) FIXED;

array node
for A

1   lower bound
10   upper bound

Figure 12. Array nodes.

and the multipliers used to calculate the offset of a given element. As with variables in the symbol node, information in the array nodes indicates whether the bounds or extents of array elements are constant or variable. If variable, the extent is specified as a tree.

Token Nodes

Token nodes hold the spellings of objects, such as the user-specified identifiers for procedure, block, or variable names, constants, and program keywords (in PL/I, keywords are not reserved words). Each block or symbol node contains a link to the token that holds its name, if any. Each token node representing a symbol name also contains a list of all symbols with that name (linked by a field in the symbol nodes). During semantic analysis, PASS2 uses this list to match each instance of a variable name in the source program with the particular symbol it represents. In PL/I, multiple declarations of the same name are allowed as long as they can be distinguished by the language's block structure or by explicit qualification using the names of containing structures. We represent this in the Symbol Table by linking symbol nodes with the same name on a list rooted in the token node containing the name.

Token nodes may or may not be linked, depending on the requirements of the front end; however, all token nodes representing constants must be linked so that they can be found by the Storage Allocator. Figure 13 illustrates token nodes for a block node, the symbol nodes for names declared within it, and a constant token node.

Trees

A tree node specifies an operation to be performed on zero or more operands. Each operand can be another tree node, a Symbol Table node, or a nonnegative integer value. If the operation represented by the tree is one that produces a result (say, addition), the tree may occur as an operand (subtree) of another tree node.

The principal components of a tree node are fields that specify the number of operands, opcode, the operands themselves, data type, size, and size units (the bits, bytes, and so on in which the size is expressed).

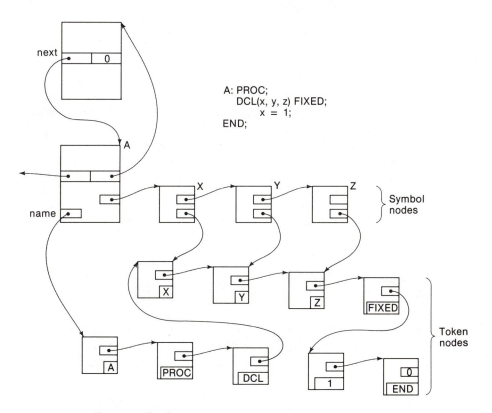

Figure 13. Token nodes.

Data type and size are present only in trees representing operations that produce results. The size is the precision of an arithmetic item, the length of a string, and so on. For string and aggregate data, the size may itself be a tree and may have associated size units. In this case, the size is determined at run time.

The rules relating opcode, operands, data type, and size of a tree node are generally the same as the rules for operators in the Intermediate Language (all discussed in more detail in Chapter 5). Frequently, however, we use the term *operator* to mean either a tree node or the entire tree. Some opcodes are reserved for use within the front end and are eliminated before getting to Write Tree. Write Tree will accept more flexible forms of some trees and transform them as required by the rest of the back end.

Tree nodes are kept in the Symbol Table (as shown in Figure 8) and denoted by node identifiers. However, an identifier that denotes a tree node is always stored as its negative (in a 16-bit field). Thus there is an easy way to distinguish operands that denote trees from those that denote other sorts of nodes or nonnegative integers.

The compiler's storage management for trees distinguishes between temporary and permanent trees. Temporary trees are needed only during semantic analysis of a statement and output of the result by Write Tree; when the latter finishes processing a statement, it frees all temporary tree nodes. To allocate a temporary tree node, the compiler simply adjusts the current limit of the space used for these nodes in the upper part of the Symbol Table. This method of storage management significantly improves the front end's performance in comparison with the common technique of individually freeing tree nodes and allocating subsequent nodes from free space lists.

Permanent tree nodes are used for the extent expressions in the Symbol Table and in other cases where semantic analysis requires that a tree be kept beyond the processing of a single statement. An example from PL/I is translating an entire DO-group:

```
DO WHILE (x(i) < 2);
         .
         .
         .
     END;
```

In the interest of efficiency, the front end of the compiler generates code for this test at the end of the loop. To do this, it has to make a permanent copy of the tree for the test expression $x(i)<2$ when it analyzes the DO statement and then use that copy when it encounters the END statement.

Permanent trees can be allocated and freed by the front end's own routines, but the memory used is not returned to the compiler's general pool until the front end has finished.

Keeping tree nodes in the Symbol Table and denoting them by node identifiers is not advantageous unless the compiler must run in a restricted address space. This design leads to cumbersome coding and is a definite compile-time performance penalty. For example, translating the statement $i=i+1$ causes PASS2 and Write Tree to make over 40 calls to the routine that obtains the address of a node; almost all of these calls are for tree node addresses. We considered changing the front end to use pointers in trees, but we decided that it would have required too many detailed changes to the front end's code.

Block Activations and Stack Management

This section describes in general how procedure calls and data addressing work on the VAX-11 and summarizes some adjustments we had to make in the compiler, mostly in the front end, to support PL/I on the VAX-11.

Most data are associated with an activation of a block. These include constant-sized automatic variables, constant-sized temporaries, procedure arguments, dynamically sized automatic variables, information about ON-units in the block, and dynamically sized temporaries (such as the result of $SUBSTR(s,m,n) \mid \mid 'ABC')$.

In addition to accessing the data of the current block activation, it may also be necessary to access variables belonging to the activation of containing blocks, as the following example shows.

```
p:  PROCEDURE(a);
        DECLARE (a,b) FIXED;
        q:  PROCEDURE;
            CALL r;
            END q;
        r:  PROCEDURE;
            a = b;
            END r;
        CALL q;
```

Here, p calls q, which calls r, which makes references to the parameter a and the automatic variable b, both of which are declared in the procedure p. These are known as *uplevel* references; to manage them, the code for r must be able to find the parent block activation, that is, the activation of the procedure p in which r is declared. Because of recursion, several activations of a single block may exist at one time, and the most recent activation (highest on the stack) need not be the parent activation required by the language definition. Fortunately, the VAX-11 architecture provides a natural starting point for managing block activations.

The Architectural Base

On the VAX-11, four registers have an architecturally specified function: Register 12, the Argument Pointer (AP); Register 13, the Frame Pointer

(FP); Register 14, the Stack Pointer (SP); and Register 15, the Program Counter (PC). The PC is used to address instructions during a program's execution. SP points to the top byte of data on the stack—the last byte of data associated with the current block activation. FP points to the last longword in a data structure known as a *call frame*. AP points to the argument list for the block activation.

The longword of data pointed to by FP is defined as the block activation's condition handler address. It contains the address of a condition handling routine for the block activation, or zero (null) if there is no condition handler for that block. When an exception occurs, the system software searches for the topmost stack frame (see below) with a nonnull condition handler address and invokes that routine to handle the exception. This tailors the condition handling mechanism to the requirements of the current block activation so that procedures written in different languages may call one another with reasonable behavior.

The four registers, PC, SP, FP, and AP, and the condition handler are all set by the VAX-11 call instructions. After a call instruction, both FP and SP point to the top of the block activation call frame, AP points to the argument list, and the condition handler address is null. The call instructions also save enough information to restore the state that existed immediately before the call; execution of a return instruction will accomplish this. This information is stored immediately above the condition handler address in the call frame (that is, just above FP). The piece of the stack from the beginning of the call frame through SP is called a *stack frame* and it is the VAX-11 realization of a block activation. Figure 14 illustrates a VAX-11 stack frame with the extended information introduced to support PL/I requirements.

The call frame is used as follows: each time a call instruction is executed, the word-size mask at the call destination is interrogated for the list of registers to save. The registers specified in the mask are then pushed onto the stack. The address of the next instruction (the saved PC), FP, AP, the current program status word, mask of saved registers, and then a null longword are pushed onto the stack. FP is loaded with the updated SP, AP with the effective address of the argument list, and PC with the destination address plus 2 (that is, the address of the first instruction past the register save mask). Because the call instructions save the previous Frame Pointer, all dynamic predecessor stack frames can be found by starting at the current value of FP.

PL/I Elaborations

The basic VAX-11 call frame, though complete in most regards, is not adequate for all the semantics of PL/I block activation. The compiler must therefore generate code to acquire the additional information. This code is executed when the block is activated but before the execution of any code that is associated with the user program. We call this code sequence a *procedure prologue.*

One of the critical pieces of information gathered during the prologue code sequence is used for uplevel addressing. A VAX-11 software convention specifies that on entry to internal procedures, register R1 contains a copy of the Frame Pointer for the block activation in which the current block is declared. This is the new block's parent pointer, and it is saved in a fixed location in the stack frame. When it generates code for the procedure, the Local Code Generator uses the parent pointer in R1 and the saved parent pointers in containing block activations to construct a set of temporaries containing the Frame Pointers for all ancestor block activations. Any uplevel data reference will be based on one of these temporaries. This set of pointers is called a *display*. Because uplevel references may be made to arguments, the value of AP is also saved in a fixed location in the stack frame.

For condition handling, PL/I generates prologue code to set the stack frame's condition handler to a PL/I-specific run-time routine. Another fixed location in the stack frame points to a linked list of ON-unit descriptors for ON-units established in the block. This list is initially empty; an entry is added

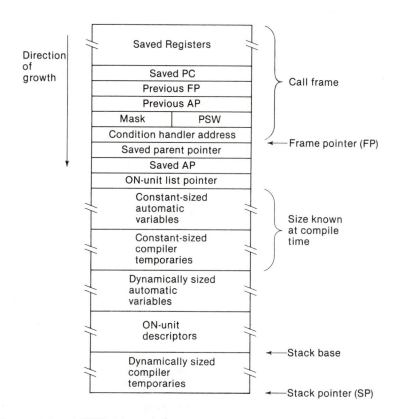

Figure 14. A VAX-11 stack frame.

each time an ON statement is executed (and deleted by a corresponding REVERT statement). Storage for the entries is allocated by extending the stack frame as needed.

Nondynamic local (that is, automatic) storage is allocated by a simple subtraction of the size of the needed space from the value of SP; the code to do this is also in the prologue.

In general, a dynamically sized temporary cannot be allocated until the moment it is needed. To allocate such a temporary, the compiler simply extends the stack. Freeing these temporaries is much trickier. One method, freeing them at the end of a statement, is unsatisfactory because it could allow temporaries to accumulate, unfreed, when statements do not reach their ends (as when a function invocation terminates with a GOTO). Because the span of a dynamic temporary is never more than a statement, we use the opposite approach: the Local Code Generator maintains a special temporary called the *stack base*, or the value the stack pointer should have at the beginning of a statement when there are no more dynamic temporaries in the stack. If any dynamic temporaries are used in a statement, the Local Code Generator resets SP to equal the stack base just before allocating the first temporary. Thus the stack frame will never contain dynamic temporaries produced by more than one statement. Freeing dynamic temporaries in this way is simpler (and much more efficient) than freeing them at the end of a statement.

Figure 14 illustrated the complete layout of a PL/I stack frame along with the basic VAX-11 call frame information. The stack frame is built in a procedure's prologue code at run time in the following order:

1. Extend the stack by the number of longwords required to hold the necessary prologue values and uplevel display information (saved parent pointer and so on), all constant-sized automatic variables, and all constant-sized temporaries. (The total number is known at the end of local code generation.)

2. Set the ON-unit list pointer to null and set the condition handler address to the PL/I-specific routine.

3. Save AP and the parent pointer.

4. Generate the complete set of ancestor pointer temporaries (the display).

5. For each dynamically sized automatic variable, compute its size, round the size up to longwords, and allocate space for the variable by extending the stack. The variable's address is saved in a compiler-generated automatic variable (which occupies part of the space allocated in step 1).

6. Set the stack base equal to the current value of SP.

In contrast, to leave a block we simply execute the VAX-11 return instruction. The run-time routine implementing GOTOs that transfer control out of the current block executes the return instruction for each block activation terminated by a GOTO. This ensures proper restoration of the registers and stack in the block activation that is the target of the GOTO.

Optimizations

The overhead in setting up a PL/I procedure can be substantial. However, the compiler reduces the overhead by checking for the usage of various language features and by generating only the prologue code that is necessary. In particular:

- The parent pointer is passed in R1 to a procedure only if it or one of its subprocedures needs it.

- The parent pointer is saved in a fixed stack frame location only if a subprocedure needs it.

- The AP is saved in a fixed location only if a subprocedure needs it (that is, if the subprocedure makes an uplevel reference to a parameter of this procedure).

- The condition handler address and ON-unit list are set only if the procedure contains an ON statement.

- The stack base temporary is introduced only if the procedure requires dynamically sized temporaries.

General optimizations in the back end further reduce overhead. These optimizations include the replacement of automatic variables by register temporaries and global register assignment. Thus, each display pointer is treated as a separate temporary and is assigned to a register on the basis of its own usage. For many procedures, all variables and temporaries end up in registers, no stack storage is used, and there is no overhead beyond the hardware call and return instructions.

5

The Intermediate Language

In the compiler's Intermediate Language, a program is represented by a linear sequence of operators. These operators are similar to the tree nodes used in PASS2 and Write Tree. The Intermediate Language is used for the output of Write Tree and the input of the Local Code Generator. When the Optimizer runs, it transforms the Intermediate Language from Write Tree into a more compact version that will run faster. We think of the Intermediate Language as the backbone of the compiler's design because all work in the front end is directed to expressing the program in it and all work in the back end is directed to translating it into an executable program.

The Intermediate Language in the bootstrap compiler defined the interface between a single PL/I front end and multiple back ends, these being implemented on a variety of computers. The Intermediate Language described here defines the interface between multiple front ends, each for a different language, and a single back end. The language has evolved to accommodate this change in aim, and it has also evolved to better support some of the compiler's optimizations. However, this evolution affected only details of the the Intermediate Language; its general structure has remained the same.

In the first part of this chapter, we discuss considerations in the design of any such intermediate language and suggest the range of operators it must include. In the second part of the chapter, we provide some details about our use of the Intermediate Language to solve one of the most complex aspects of the design of any compiler—the manner in which it resolves references to data and passes data from one procedure to another.

Design Considerations

The basic components of an operator are the same as those of a tree node (although the actual representation is more compact): operands, operand count, opcode, data type, size, size units, and offset units (which are present only for operators representing references). Figure 15 is a simplified illustration of the structure of an operator node.

Each operator contains an identifier, a negative integer value that is unique within a block. Other operators that reference this operator, either as an operand or as a size, specify it by this identifier. In addition, the operator contains a reference count specifying the number of times the result of that operator is used as an operand or size in a subsequent operator. This information tells the Local Code Generator, which processes operators sequentially, when it has encountered the last use of an operator.

The general form of the Intermediate Language allows flexibility in engineering both front and back ends. The specific choice of operators shapes the TBL-driven code generation and defines the target for semantic analysis and Write Tree. Fine details of the language affect semantic analysis, Write Tree, the Optimizer, and the Local Code Generator.

Many compilers simply use trees as the intermediate language, in which case the entire program is kept as one big tree. Others use triples or quads, operators that have precisely three or four operands, respectively. In a triple, the operands are *operator, operand, operand.* In a quad, a third operand is added, a destination. All intermediate forms of the programs using triples or quads are forced to these rigid (though regular) structures. As a result, several triples or quads may be required in cases when our Intermediate Language needs only a single operator.

Variable-length operators (sometimes called *n*-tuples) are far more flexible than triples or quads and have two distinct advantages over trees. First, the order in which operations are performed is explicit. Second, they are space efficient and can be processed sequentially in a small amount of working storage.

The operators in an intermediate language must satisfy two requirements. First, they must express the basic constructs of either a machine architecture or the general rules for programming languages, or of both. Thus, an intermediate language has to have operators for such constructs as addition, assignment, procedure calls, and branches. Second, the set of operators must be

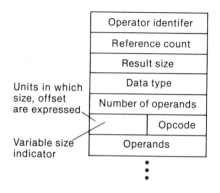

Figure 15. An operator node.

capable of expanding to handle specific operators that may be required for a single source language. The latter requirement can be handled in either of two ways. The first is to provide for the addition of operators to the language. For example, we introduced an operator called ASSIGN_REPEAT to implement the PL/I assignment

```
array-name = scalar ;
```

to assign the given scalar value to each element of the given array.

The other method for implementing a language-specific construct is to expand it during semantic analysis into a series of existing operators, in a sort of subroutine. If an intermediate language has an adequate basic set of operators, this type of expansion can accommodate almost all language-specific constructions. (This is what the PEARL implementors did.)

All operators—including language-specific ones—are ultimately interpreted by individual TBL routines in the common back end. Thus, we frequently found it easier to introduce a language-specific operator and to do the expansion in TBL.

In general, we tried to make the front end and the back end as distinct as possible. Except when TBL routines are introduced to process language-specific operators, the back end knows almost nothing about the semantics of the programming language. By the time the back end sees the program, it has been reduced to a canonical representation in the Intermediate Language that conveys just the right amount of information. For example, the front end makes all addressing computations explicit primarily so that the Optimizer can work on them. Whenever we have compromised the distinction between the front end and the back end, we have done so in the interests of optimization.

Summary of Operators

The Intermediate Language is best and most simply described by a presentation of its operators. We have categorized the operators according to related functions. In the subsections that follow, we introduce all the operators by name but describe only those whose functions are not self-explanatory (such as mathematical and logical operators) or that are not described elsewhere in this book.

Statement Identification Operator

The front end must precede all operators for a given source statement with the STATEMENT operator, which identifies the line number in the source program of the statement. This information preserves the program's lexical order and is used both to write the listing file and to provide line numbers for debuggers.

Reference Operators

Four operators—CONSTANT, IMMEDIATE, VALUE, and REF—are used to reference data items. The REF operator denotes a variable's address (that is, the storage containing its value); while the others denote the actual value itself. In its simplest form, the REF operator's only operand is the node identifier of the symbol node representing a variable.

A CONSTANT operator has a single operand, the identifier of the token node containing the constant whose value the CONSTANT operator represents. The constant token can be either in its original source form or in the machine's internal representation. In general, the compiler delays changing the constant to the internal representation until absolutely necessary.

The IMMEDIATE operator has no operands in the normal sense. It denotes a value that is stored immediately in the operator. We use the operand count field in the node to specify the amount of space required to hold the value.

The VALUE operator denotes the value of a variable. Its operand is always a REF operator that specifies the address of the variable whose value is to be taken. For example, to reference the value of the variable i the Intermediate Language requires:

```
-32    REF(i)
-33    VALUE(-32)
```

In a later section, we expand on the requirements for specifying references and discuss the PARAM_PTR and ADD_OFFSET operators; these operators denote the addresses of parameters and offsets within the storage of aggregates or strings, respectively.

Program Structural Operators

Structural operators such as BEGIN, ENTRY, PROCEDURE, and BLOCK_END let the front end define the block structure of a program to the back end. The structural operators define the limits of blocks and the primary and secondary entry points of procedures.

The END_OF_PROLOGUE operator delimits the end of operators for a procedure's prologue code generated by the front end. (This is discussed in Chapter 4.) The operators between the ENTRY operator and the END_OF_PROLOGUE operator represent the procedure's prologue code.

Procedures with multiple entry points require the execution of all the prologue code when any of the entries is used. To avoid duplicating the prologue at each entry point, the prologue code is gathered in a special subroutine delimited by the SAVE and EXIT operators. This sequence does not represent a block activation. A BRANCH_SAVE operator, inserted at each entry point, "calls" this special subroutine to set up the prologue.

Assignment and Definition Operators

Assignment is accomplished by the ASSIGN operator. All elements of an array may be assigned the same scalar value with the ASSIGN_REPEAT operator mentioned above.

The SETS operator lets the front end give special information to the back end. It provides a way for the front end to specify that a variable has been modified in cases that the back end might not be able to detect. We discuss this operator in Chapter 7.

Program Control Operators

The Intermediate Language contains the usual program call operators: CALL invokes a procedure; CALL_BEGIN, a begin block; CALL_FUNCTION, a function; CALL_FUNCTION_STORAGE, a function whose return value is returned to storage rather than to a register; and RETURN specifies a return from any of these.

The branch operators include GOTO, BRANCH, BR_FALSE, BR_TRUE, BR_EQ, BR_NE, BR_GT, BR_GE, BR_LT, BR_LE, and BR_SWITCH, which is used to set up computed branches to elements in a label array or a case construction. The significant difference between the GOTO operator and the branch operators is that a GOTO operator may transfer control to a label in another block or to a label variable, whereas branch operators must have labels in the current block as destinations.

Loop control is accomplished with a special sequence of operators that must be specified in a particular order: LOOP_TOP, LOOP_BODY, and LOOP_BOTTOM. Two operators are of special use in loops and loop control. These are ADD_COMPARE_AND_BRANCH, which can be used to increment a control variable, compare it with a limit variable, and consequently either continue or exit the loop, and SAVE_RESULT, which preserves the initial value of a limit variable. The SAVE_RESULT operator and its related INCREMENT_USAGE operator are described in Chapter 6; the loop control operators, in Chapter 7.

The LABEL operator defines both source program labels and compiler-generated labels. It accepts a subscript operand to permit implementation of label arrays.

Logical and Mathematical Operators

The relational and logical operators supported by the Intermediate Language consist of EQ, GE, GT, LE, LT, and NE, which produce Boolean results, and AND, NOT, OR, and XOR, which perform operations on bit strings.

The mathematical operators are: ABS, ACOS, ADD, ATAN (including ATAND and ATANH), CEIL, COS (including COSD and COSH), DIV (with a special DIVIDE for PL/I), LOG (including LOG2 and LOG10), MAX, MIN, MINUS, MULTIPLY, PLUS, SIN (including SIND and SINH), SUBTRACT, and TAN (including TAND and TANH).

The mathematical operators require that the operands be of the same data type; conversions are handled by the CONVERT and CONVERT_UNITS operators.

Memory Allocation

Three operators control the allocation and deallocation of run-time storage. ALLOC_AUTO allocates stack space for dynamic extents and automatic variables; ALLOC_MEM allocates heap storage. The FREE operator frees memory allocated for heap storage.

Error-Handling Operators

Special operators for error control are the ERROR operator, which generates an error signal, and the RANGE operator, which implements run-time checking of array bound specifications.

Operators Produced by the Optimizer

A number of operators in the Intermediate Language are present to perform specific optimizations. Most of these are introduced by the Optimizer. For example, the ASSIGN_REGTEMP operator indicates that a variable is a candidate for assignment to a register. The Optimizer also detects loop addressing of array elements by increments of one and introduces the AUTO_DECREMENT and AUTO_INCREMENT operators to speed up the addressing. It introduces USE and ADDR_BASE operators, as required, in the optimization of references. These are all described in Chapter 7.

Language-Specific Operators

A number of operators exist to perform functions specific to PL/I. Some actually map to PL/I built-in functions; these include the string functions CONCAT, COPY, LENGTH, and TRANSLATE, and the RANK, SIGN, BOOL, and BYTE functions. These functions can easily be adapted for use by other front ends. The ON and SIGNAL operators implement PL/I's error signaling and condition handling.

Completing the list of language-specific operators are the bit-field operators we added during our implementation of the C compiler and included in a subsequent release of PL/I: EXTRACT (Extract Sign-Extended Field), EXTRACTZ (Extract Zero-Extended Field), INSERT (Insert Field), SHIFT (Shift Signed Value), and UDIV (Unsigned Division).

Data Types of Operators

Many operations within the VAX-11 Code Generator depend on the data type and size of an operand. The data types supported by the VAX-11 Code Generator reflect the VAX-11 architecture and some generally useful data types defined in the PL/I language (such as varying-length strings). We expect that most language-specific data types can be easily mapped onto the VAX-11 Code Generator's basic data types. However, for historical reasons, the VAX-11 Code Generator also supports PL/I-specific data types (such as offset and format) and makes some distinctions meaningful only in PL/I (such as between floating-point decimal and floating-point binary). In our discussions here, we generally ignore the PL/I-specific details.

The basic data types supported are:

- The arithmetic data types integer, decimal, and floating point (the PL/I-specific data types offset and pointer are treated as integers by the back end)

- Character strings and varying-length character strings

- The bit data types bit and bit-aligned.

The VAX-11 Code Generator supports both scalar and aggregate data of these types, but operations on aggregates are limited. In general, aggregate operations must be expanded by the front end.

Most data types come in more than one size. For some types, the size must be a constant, that is, known to the compiler's front end. For others, the size may be variable, that is, computed in some way during program execution. The following list summarizes the data types we have implemented and the way in which we represent their sizes.

- Integers are constant sized in sizes of byte (8 bits), word (16 bits), or longword (32 bits). Signed integers are represented in two's complement form.

- Decimal numbers are constant sized. The size is the number of digits, which must be less than or equal to 31. The data is packed into $p/2 + 1$ bytes, where p is the number of digits. In operators, both the size and scale factor (number of fractional digits) are packed into the size field.

- Floating-point data are constant sized: longword (precision 24), quadword (precision 53), or octaword (precision 113).

- Character data may have either a constant or a variable size. The size (or length) is the number of bytes in the string.

- Varying-length character data may be constant or variable in size. The size is the maximum length of the string. The data occupies $size + 2$ bytes of storage. The first two bytes hold a word-sized integer giving the string's current length.

- Aligned bit data may be constant or variable in size. The size is the number of bits in the string. The data occupy $(size + 7)/8$ bytes. When the data have a value, any fill bits will be zero.

- Bit data may be constant or variable in size. The size is the number of bits in the string. The data occupy exactly $size$ bits, and the storage of data may begin at any bit location. Thus bit data cannot be "addressed" by a VAX-11 address (which always denotes a byte location in storage).

In references to aggregate data, the size field of the respective REF or VALUE operator specifies the total storage size occupied by the data.

References to Data

As we have noted, a VALUE operator must be inserted whenever an operation uses (or may use) the value of a variable. Consider the simple declaration and reference:

```
DECLARE (i,j) FIXED BINARY(31);
     i = j;
```

To assign the value of the variable *j* to *i*, we need the operators:

```
-30    REF(j)
-31    REF(i)
-32    VALUE(-30)
-33    ASSIGN(-31,-32)
```

The treatment of the VALUE operator in the Intermediate Language permits the Optimizer to distinguish systematically between uses of a variable that require its value and uses that require only its location. For example, assignment to a variable, *x*, will not prevent the Optimizer from detecting the equivalence of two occurrences of *ADDR(x)* and eliminating one of them. It is interesting to note that the VALUE operator appears explicitly in the BLISS language as the dot (.) operator. (The only exception to the rule for inserting VALUE operators is in passing a variable by reference as a procedure argument. The Optimizer understands this special usage.)

A VALUE operator, *v*, denotes the value of the referenced variable at the point where it occurs in the operator sequence. Suppose a later operator that uses *v* (that is, that has *v* as an operand) is separated from *v* by other operators. None of these operators is allowed to modify the value of the variable referenced by *v*. Thus the Local Code Generator is not required to capture the value of *v* in a temporary. Sometimes it is necessary for the front end to capture explicitly the value of a variable; this case is discussed in the next chapter.

A REF operator tree denotes the storage of a variable or part of a variable (as in a substring of a string). The most general form of a REF operator has three operands, listed below. Usually some of the operands are null or implied, and the most common REF operators (as in the example above) contain only the first operand. The operands are:

1. The symbol node identifier of the variable being referenced
2. The offset within the variable's storage (this operand may be null)
3. A base pointer for the variable.

Before describing these operands and some of their properties, uses, and pitfalls, we discuss some comparatively simple declarations and the REF operators that must be generated for them. We have seen a simple reference in the example above. Here is an array variable and a reference to one of its elements:

```
DECLARE A(100) FLOAT BINARY(24);
        a(5) = 10;
```

To specify the offset of the array element 5 from the beginning of the array, we introduce operators to compute the offset. The operators are:

```
-49    IMMEDIATE(16)
-50    ADD_OFFSET(-49,0)
-51    REF(a,-50)
```

Here we have an easy case, since both the array element reference and the element size are known values. The integer value, 16, referenced in the ADD_OFFSET represents the element size of four bytes multiplied by the element position. Later in this chapter we discuss some of the trickier details of calculating offsets and multipliers when (as commonly happens) the element references are specified as variables.

The next example requires a base pointer for a reference:

```
DECLARE c CHARACTER(10) BASED(p);
        c = 'string';
```

Here, p is a pointer. The operators for this reference are:

```
-55    REF(p)
-56    VALUE(-55)
-57    REF(c,0,-56)
```

Thus, we must first reference the pointer, obtain its value, and use this base pointer as the third operand in the reference to c. The last case illustrates an array reference made with a variable and a base pointer:

```
DECLARE b(100) CHAR(1) BASED(p);
        b(i) = 'e';
```

The operators for this reference are:

```
-61    IMMEDIATE(-1)
-62    REF(i)
-63    VALUE(-62)
-64    ADD_OFFSET(-61,-63)
-65    REF(p)
-66    VALUE(-65)
-67    REF(b,-64,-66)
```

First, we reference i (operator –62) and obtain its value (–63). This value is referenced in the ADD_OFFSET operator, which needs both the base bias (expressed in the IMMEDIATE operator, –61) and the element offset. Then, we have a reference to p (–65), we take its value (–66), and we have a resulting REF that has all three operands.

Some Properties of REF Operators

A REF operator node always has a data type and size. Usually, these are the same as the data type and size of the respective VALUE operator specifying the REF operator, but they can be different. For example, in a REF operator denoting a varying-length string, the size gives the maximum length of the string; in the corresponding VALUE operator, the size gives the current length of the string. Not all uses of a REF operator require knowledge of its type and size (as when we reference it to obtain its address, as for p in the example above), but the redundant information is normally harmless. However, if the size is a tree in one of these cases, the front end replaces it with zero to avoid a pointless computation at run time. For references to entire arrays and structures, the size may be in units of bits, bytes, and so on. The units are specified in a field in the operator node.

REF operators may also be used to reference labels, file constants, and other forms of named data. Some of these (such as a PL/I file constant) are variables as far as the back end is concerned. Others (such as labels) will eventually be recognized as special cases. In this book, we ignore the complications of handling these data types.

The Symbol Node Operand

The first operand of a REF operator is the identifier of the symbol node representing the variable referenced by the REF operator. Thus, the Optimizer considers an assignment to the REF operator to be an assignment to the symbol node; this fact governs common subexpression recognition and the removal of invariant computation from loops.

A complication in references occurs when variables are not distinct objects bearing no relation to each other. In fact, variables can share storage in various ways; we call such variables *aliased*. Thus, an assignment to one of these variables may modify another variable in a program, as in this example taken from PL/I:

```
DECLARE a FIXED BINARY;
DECLARE b DEFINED(a);
        b = 1;
```

The assignment to b modifies a, which has the same storage.

The Optimizer divides variables into various classes according to how they can overlap. The most difficult cases to deal with belong to the aliased class. The front end must mark a symbol node as aliased if the variable shares storage with other variables in some way that we cannot always predict. In the example above, the front end could mark *a* and *b* as aliased. This is the safe thing to do, but it unnecessarily inhibits optimization. The front end itself can see that a reference to *b* is really a reference to *a*, so it generates a REF opera-tor whose first operand is *a*. This does not occur immediately, however. First, PASS2 generates a four-operand REF tree node whose first operand is *b* and whose fourth is *a*. Write Tree then makes *a* the first operand when it pro-cesses the tree. Both *a* and *b* are kept in the REF tree node during semantic analysis so that any error messages about the REF tree node will use the name *b* from the original source text.

The PL/I front end does the same thing for constructions such as *ADDR(x)->y*. This will translate into a REF operator for *x*, which will not be marked as aliased. Unions (structures in the C language in which data declara-tions explicitly define variables whose storage is to be overlaid) are handled in a similar way.

The Offset Operand

The second operand in a REF operator specifies an offset within an array, structure, or string. The offset has units (such as bits and bytes) that depend on the properties of the data aggregate. For example:

```
DECLARE a(0:9) FIXED BINARY(31);
DECLARE 1 s,
          2 x BIT(3),
          2 y BIT(13);
        a(2) = BINARY(s.y);
```

The reference *a(2)* has an offset of two in units of longwords. The reference *s.y* has an offset of three in units of bits.

Here is another example:

```
DECLARE s CHARACTER(10);
        SUBSTR(s,k,1) = 'A';
```

The SUBSTR reference results in a REF operator whose offset operand has the value *k*-1 bytes.

During semantic analysis, the offset operand of a REF operator is developed as a general tree, the only restriction being that its value must be a longword integer. Write Tree changes this tree to a more restricted form that facili-tates optimal code generation. In the Intermediate Language, the offset operand (if present) must be an ADD_OFFSET operator. This operator has two operands: the first, an IMMEDIATE operator, specifies a constant offset in bytes; the second (if present) is a longword-valued operator that specifies a variable offset. This variable offset is expressed in units of bits, bytes, and so on and can actually be a constant (that is, it can be specified by an IMMEDIATE operator) if the offset is a bit offset not divisible by eight.

The Base Pointer Operand

The base pointer operand is required for references to data that must be located through other items, such as variables that share storage and procedure parameters. In the latter case, the base pointer is specified using the PARAM_PTR operator, which has two operands: the identifier of a block node in the Symbol Table and a positive integer such that the value of

```
PARAM—PTR(b,n)
```

is the address of the nth parameter of block b. In the current block activation, this is the $(nth+1)$ longword in the argument list pointed to by AP. If b is a parent block of the current block, the saved AP in b's stack frame points to the argument list, and one of the display temporaries in the current block activation points to b's stack frame.

The base pointer of a REF operator referring to a variable, x, is generated as follows:

1. If x is static, there is no base pointer; the base address can be considered zero.

2. If x is a constant-sized automatic, the REF operator does not contain a base pointer. Instead, the Local Code Generator provides either the current frame pointer or a display temporary as the REF operator's base pointer.

3. If x is a dynamically sized automatic variable, the base pointer is a VALUE operator that specifies the value of the local variable in which x's address was stored during the procedure prologue. (The REF operator denoted by this VALUE operator will fall into case 2, above.)

4. If x is a parameter, the base pointer operand will be either a PARAM_PTR operator or a VALUE operator denoting an address in a descriptor. (We are ignoring the complications that can arise with multiple-entry-point procedures.)

5. If x is a based variable, the base pointer operand will be a pointer-valued operator representing the base pointer expression from the source program. For example, in the reference $f(3)->x$, the operand will give the value of $f(3)$.

The Complete Address Denoted by a REF Operator

In the Intermediate Language (leaving aside operand specifiers for VAX-11 instructions and the mechanics of code generation), the storage location denoted by a REF operator is determined as follows:

1. Take the value of the base pointer operand, explicit or implied, as explained above.

2. For static and automatic variables in which the base address was implied, add the location assigned by the Storage Allocator for the variable if it is a level-one variable. If the symbol node in the REF operator is the node identifier of a structure member, obtain the location from the Symbol Table of the containing level-one structure.

3. Add the constant byte offset.

4. Add the variable offset, changing its units to bytes if not already in bytes.

This process gives the byte address of the referenced storage and can usually be represented by a single VAX-11 operand specifier. A REF operator with a variable bit offset cannot incorporate the offset directly in the operand specifier. Instead, the Local Code Generator must insert special instructions to extract and insert data beginning at the specified bit offset from the byte location.

Computation of Offsets and Extents

Determining the correct offset for a variable reference is one of the front end's more complicated jobs. An offset may depend on a string length or array bound that is specified as an expression. The extent expressions for automatic variables can be evaluated in the procedure's prologue, and the values can be saved. The extents of based variables must be evaluated each time the variable is referenced. Consider the following:

```
n = 3;
BEGIN;
        DECLARE 1 a,
                  2 b CHAR(n),
                  2 c CHAR(8);
        DECLARE 1 x BASED (ADDR(a)),
                  2 y CHAR(n),
                  2 z CHAR(4);
        n = 5;
        a.c = x.z;
```

The offset of *a.c* is 3 bytes; the offset of *x.z* is 5 bytes.

The extents of parameters may be specified as asterisks, in which case the extent is determined by the actual argument passed to the procedure. The extent value is passed in a descriptor (in some texts, these are called "dope vectors") associated with the parameter. If an offset depends on the extent, the tree for the offset will include a VALUE operator whose operand is a REF operator denoting the appropriate field in the descriptor.

To manage this, the DECLARE phase builds a permanent tree for each nonconstant extent expression. Evaluation of the tree at any point in the block after the prologue will yield the extent value. For extents of an automatic variable, *a*, the tree will denote the value of a compiler-generated variable, *t*. DECLARE also builds trees to save the original extent value in *t*, to allocate storage for *a*, and to save *a*'s address in another compiler-generated variable. The PASS2 phase emits these trees so that the evaluation will be executed as part of the procedure's prologue code.

DECLARE also builds trees representing the multipliers and virtual origins of an array (explained below) and the offset of a structure member from the beginning of a level-one structure. PASS2 then incorporates these trees as required to build a complete tree for the offset. This tree also contains the trees for index values or substring positions specified in the reference. This is illustrated in the following example:

```
DECLARE 1 s BASED (p),
          2 a CHAR(n),
          2 b FIXED,
          2 c CHAR(8);
SUBSTR(s.c,k,1) = 'A';
```

For this reference, PASS2 generates a REF operator whose offset operand (in bytes) is the tree corresponding to $(n+4)+(k-1)$, $n+4$ being the structure member offset built by DECLARE. After being processed by Write Tree, the offset operand is an ADD_OFFSET operator whose second operand is a tree for $n+k$.

Calculating the offset of an element in an *n*-dimensional array uses multipliers whose values are determined as follows:

multiplier(n) = element_size
multiplier(k) = (high_bound(k+1)−low_bound(k+1)+1)×multiplier(k+1)

Thus, for a two-dimensional array (which we usually think of in terms of rows and columns), *multiplier(1)* is the row size. The multipliers have units: bits, bytes, and so on. Normally, all the multipliers have the same units, and these are natural to the size of the array (such as longword units for longword integer data). In this case, the first multiplier is 1, rather than the element size.

Given the multipliers, the offset of an array element can be expressed as:

$$\sum \text{multiplier}(k) \times [\text{index}(k) - \text{low\_bound}(k)], \quad k = 1, \dots n$$

This can be rewritten as

$$\left[\sum \text{multiplier}(k) \times \text{index}(k) \right] - \text{virtual\_origin}$$

where

$$\text{virtual\_origin} = \sum \text{multiplier}(k) \times \text{low\_bound}(k)$$

This form is more efficient when the virtual origin is constant or when it needs to be computed only once, as with an automatic array. Our PL/I compiler uses the virtual origin method in most cases. If the offset units are not bits, the virtual origin for the offset may be combined with the array's address (that is, the address of its first element) to give a virtual base address. In this case, the offset operand tree will compute only

$$\sum \text{multiplier(k)} \times \text{index(k)}$$

Using the virtual origin this way can introduce overflow. Consider:

```
DECLARE A(2**20:2**20+3,2**20:2**21-1) FIXED BINARY(31);
```

The array *a* has *multiplier(2)* equal to 1, *multiplier(1)* equal to 2^{20}, multiplier units that are longword, and a total of 2^{22} elements. However, the virtual origin is

$$\text{virtual\_origin} = 2^{20} * 2^{20} + 2^{20}$$

which causes overflow on a 32-bit computer. Fortunately, experience with the VAX-11 FORTRAN compiler suggests that this is not a problem in practice.

Procedure Calls

Our next topic is the relationship between a PL/I procedure call and the hardware call instruction and argument list. The hardware call instructions (mentioned in Chapter 4) set AP to the address of an argument list. This list is a block of $n+1$ longwords. The first longword contains the value n. Longword $k+1$ specifies the *k*th argument of the procedure call. This can be an actual value (say the integer 5), the address of a variable or constant, or the address of a descriptor describing a variable or constant.

The key Intermediate Language operator is the CALL operator, which has $n+1$ operands. The first operand specifies the procedure entry point to be called; the remaining operands specify the longwords in the argument list (excluding the argument count). The Local Code Generator emits instructions to push a longword onto the stack for each operand and then to execute a VAX-11 call instruction. The call instruction pushes the argument count onto the stack and then executes the rest of the hardware procedure call. Return from the procedure automatically removes the argument list from the stack. The following subsections discuss the operands of the CALL operator in more detail.

The Entry Point Operand

The entry-point operand is a value-producing operator whose data type is entry. In the general case, this value has two components: the address of a procedure entry point and the frame pointer for the parent block activation.

(This general case arises from PL/I usage, which permits both entry variables and entry parameters.) Usually, the entry-point operand is a VALUE operator; the operand of the VALUE is a REF operator denoting the entry-point constant, that is, the entry point's symbol node. The Local Code Generator provides the parent frame pointer if it is needed.

The Argument Operands

An argument operand can be a REF, BUILD_STRUCTURE, ARG_VAL, or other value-producing operator whose size is less than or equal to a longword. In the first two cases, the Local Code Generator pushes an address onto the stack. For an ARG_VAL, it pushes the actual value. This usage does not arise in standard PL/I, but it is implemented in our compiler to enable us to conform to the VAX-11 calling conventions. It is also the normal method for passing arguments in C.

In standard PL/I, all procedure arguments are passed by reference, that is, the actual argument passed to the procedure is a variable (not a value), and a reference to the parameter is a reference to this variable. This is not as simple as it may sound. Consider the following:

```
p: PROCEDURE (a);
      .
      .
      .
END p;
CALL p(arg);
```

If *arg* is a variable reference whose data type and size exactly match those of *a*, then *arg* is passed directly to *p*. A reference to *a* within *p* denotes the same storage as *arg*. In this case the argument operand in the CALL operator is the REF operator for *arg*.

If *arg* is not an exactly matching reference, it is treated as an expression whose value is to be passed. The value is converted to *a*'s data type (if necessary) and assigned to a dummy variable, which is passed to *p*. In the Intermediate Language, the dummy variable is represented by an ARG_VAL operator whose single operand is the converted value. The Local Code Generator creates a temporary in storage for the ARG_VAL operator and assigns the value to it. The ARG_VAL operator produces the address of this temporary, and this address is pushed onto the stack. Expressions, label constants, entry constants, and file constants are also passed in this way.

If associating the parameter *a* with an actual argument requires more than passing an address, then the address of a descriptor is passed. In the Intermediate Language, the argument operand of the CALL operator is a BUILD_STRUCTURE operator, with a variable number of operands. The first operand specifies the size in bytes of a storage temporary. The remaining operands occur in pairs (*displacement, value*), where *displacement* is a byte displacement within the temporary and *value* denotes the value to be stored at that displacement. (If the value is a REF operator, it is the address that is stored.) In this way, the construction of an elaborate descriptor is represented by a single tree. The BUILD_STRUCTURE operator is also used to build the elaborate data structure passed to the run-time routine that implements the PL/I OPEN statement.

Descriptors are required in PL/I in the following cases:

1. The parameter is a string whose length is specified as * (or is an aggregate containing such a string).

2. The parameter is an array whose bounds are specified as * (or is a structure containing such an array).

3. The parameter is an unaligned bit string (or is an aggregate composed entirely of such strings).

In the third case, the descriptor contains a base address (in bytes) and an offset in bits; the combination gives the location of the first bit in the data. Array descriptors contain upper and lower bounds, multipliers, and the virtual origin as well as the address of the array. String descriptors contain the address and length of the string. In addition, the descriptor contains codes that specify a descriptor class and data type. These are not needed by PL/I but are specified as part of the VAX-11 calling conventions to facilitate interlanguage calls.

The address in a descriptor can be the address denoted by either a REF operator or an ARG_VAL operator. If the BUILD_STRUCTURE operator denotes a variable being passed by reference (in the PL/I sense), the variable's symbol node identifier is stored in the BUILD_STRUCTURE operator's size field. The purpose of this ad hoc device is to enable the Optimizer to identify easily the variables passed by reference in a CALL operator.

Returned Value of a Function

It is a VAX-11 convention that function values of suitable data type are returned in register R0 or the register pair R0 and R1. A function call of this type is represented by a CALL_FUNCTION operator, which differs from a CALL operator only in returning a result. If the data type is one whose size is too large for a double register (such as a 16-byte floating-point number) or if the data type is not natural for use in registers (such as a character string), then the function value is returned in storage provided by the calling routine. The address of this storage is the first argument in the argument list. In this case, the front end generates a CALL_FUNCTION_STORAGE operator whose second operand (or first argument) is null, and the Local Code Generator allocates the temporary and pushes its address onto the stack.

Procedure Arguments in the Bootstrap Compiler

The treatment of argument passing described above conforms to the VAX-11 calling conventions that facilitate calls between procedures written in different languages. The bootstrap compiler treated descriptors differently. The descriptor was passed as an extra argument and did not contain the data's address. If a bit offset was needed, the item in the argument list was the address of a pointer/offset pair, and the Local Code Generator had to separate the two components. Thus a descriptor of data with constant extents was itself constant. This treatment works perfectly well on a VAX-11; we did not in fact change it until several months after we completed the bootstrap.

6

Writing and
Reducing Trees

Write Tree is a procedure that accepts a tree and either returns a "reduced" tree or writes it out, transforming the tree to a sequence of operators. While writing out the tree, it collects information about the usage of variables, labels, and so on and stores this information in the Symbol Table for use by the Optimizer and Local Code Generator.

Reducing a tree entails transforming it to a semantically equivalent tree that satisfies all the requirements of the Intermediate Language. The reduced tree may be larger than the original, but it is always in a form that appears more desirable for code generation or global optimization.

Write Tree performs many functions, most of them simple in themselves but all related by a complicated recursive control flow. In this chapter we discuss what Write Tree does and our motivation for making it part of the common back end. Two topics are covered in detail: the optimization of integer expressions and the differences between the trees used in the front end and trees in the strict mathematical sense of the term.

The Evolution of Write Tree

In the bootstrap compiler, Write Tree was a simple subroutine that transformed a tree into Intermediate Language operators representing exactly the same tree. The tree nodes contained reference counts, just like the operators, and the reference counts were also used in storage management for trees. A tree node was placed on a free list (one list for each size of node) when its reference count was decremented to zero. PASS2 had to spend a fair amount of time incrementing and decrementing reference counts and allocating, initializing, and freeing tree nodes. The only tree optimizations done in PASS2 concerned integer expressions, and these were not applied in all contexts where they were called for.

After considering the performance of PASS2, the possibilities for tree optimization, and the Optimizer's need for usage information, we decided to delete reference counts from trees and to expand Write Tree into a separate, substantial procedure with a coroutine relationship to PASS2. Our primary motivation was to have a better place to collect usage information and perform tree optimizations. We could have implemented these features in

PASS2, but PASS2 was already complicated enough. Moreover, we expected that a change in the storage management of tree nodes would improve performance. This proved to be the case, and the technique we now use (as described in Chapter 4) is more efficient. Even with Write Tree doing a lot of new work, the combined execution time of PASS2 and the new Write Tree is much less than that of their counterparts in the bootstrap compiler.

Two other considerations influenced the decision to make Write Tree a separate routine. The first was our growing interest in a common back end. By making Write Tree separate, we could put more functions in the common part. This seemed especially important in regard to collecting usage information and processing REF operators, functions that might (and did) change frequently as the Optimizer developed. Also, by collecting usage information after preliminary optimizations performed by PASS2 and Write Tree, we had more precise information and hence better optimization later in the compiler.

The second consideration was the desirability of separating optimizations related to the Intermediate Language and VAX-11 hardware from PL/I-specific semantic details. For example, in PL/I the precision of arithmetic expressions must be computed exactly according to the language standard's rules; an integer variable declared as FIXED BINARY(15), when added to another variable of FIXED BINARY(15), must yield a result of FIXED BINARY(16). The exact PL/I precision must be maintained within PASS2, and it is also relevant to code generation for some language-specific operators. On the other hand, the VAX-11 hardware requires only that we distinguish among byte, word, and longword integers; so Write Tree optimizes integer expressions on this basis, ignoring the PL/I precision.

Initially, our new Write Tree dealt only with the new tree management, collection of some usage information, and conversion of constants. The routine was structured as a large case table based on the tree node's opcode. This worked well enough, but many subroutine calls (and jumps to small pieces of code) resembled the style of a TBL program. For this reason, when we reorganized Write Tree we used TBL. The amount of TBL is modest compared with that in the Local Code Generator or in PASS1, but it neatly organizes the application of the many rules used within Write Tree.

Write Tree and the language-specific front end interact as coroutines but in a very simple arrangement. In the VAX-11 PL/I compiler, Write Tree interacts with PASS2. Each routine has an internal state. For example, each routine maintains its own current source line number for diagnostic messages. PASS2 is the master routine. Its first action is to initialize its own state and call an initialization entry in Write Tree. Then PASS2 reads operators, builds trees from them, and translates the trees until it has processed a group of one or more source statements. At this point, PASS2 calls Write Tree which writes out the group of trees and returns. This process of reading operators and writing trees continues until the entire program is processed. Then

PASS2 calls a routine to finish the processing of usage information collected by Write Tree. This routine is considered to be a part of Write Tree, although syntactically it is a free-standing procedure.

At a few points during Write Tree's execution, it may call certain routines that are logically part of PASS2, for example, to free permanent tree nodes after Write Tree has processed the end of a DO-group. This is the closest we get to a true coroutine call.

Most of the functions incorporated in Write Tree could be done by a separate pass running between PASS2 and the Optimizer. The coroutine arrangement leads to simpler code and better compiler performance. However, with a restricted address space, the coroutine approach might make the total code size of PASS2 combined with Write Tree too great.

Write Tree itself normally initiates tree reduction, but in a few cases the front end invokes Write Tree to reduce a tree during semantic analysis. For example, PASS2 calls Write Tree with the trees for the TO and BY options of a DO statement to see if they reduce to IMMEDIATE operators, that is, to constants.

Overview of Functions

The following list provides a reasonably complete picture of Write Tree's functions. Write Tree:

1. Writes out trees, assigning operator identifiers sequentially within each program block and calculating the correct reference count for each operator.

2. Reduces REF operators from the flexible form allowed by Write Tree to the restricted form required by the Intermediate Language. In doing so, Write Tree performs the following optimizations:

   - Separates the constant part of an offset expression from the variable part (described in the section "Collection of the Constant Part of an Offset").

   - If a REF operator has an offset in units of bits, divides the constant part into a byte offset (the first operand of the ADD_OFFSET operator) and a remaining bit offset, which is incorporated in the second operand of the ADD_OFFSET operator. This split is optimized with respect to the special properties of the bit field instructions.

   - When a nonbit variable offset is present, Write Tree checks the units of the offset against the natural VAX-11 context of the REF operator's data type. (For example, it checks that a longword integer REF operator has an offset in longwords.) If they do not match, Write Tree tries to change the units without cost to get a match. For example, if a longword REF operator has a byte offset of $16 \times i$, Write Tree changes this to a longword offset of $4 \times i$. In most cases, the front end will have already arranged that the offset will be in natural units, but arrays of structures can generate unnatural units. For example, in

   ```
   DECLARE 1 s(20),
               2 a FLOAT BINARY(53), /* quadword */
               2 b FIXED BINARY(31), /* longword */
               2 c CHARACTER(8);     /* bytes    */
   ```

   after offset collection, $a(i)$, $b(i)$, and $c(i)$ will all have a variable offset of $20 \times i$ with units in bytes. This is fine for c, but it cannot be changed to a quadword offset for a, because 8 does not divide evenly into 20. However, the offset for b will be changed to $5 \times i$ in units of longwords.

3. Marks the symbol node of each variable in accordance with the variable's usage in emitted operators as follows:

   - Marks the node's *referenced* attribute if it occurs in any REF operator.

   - Marks the *uplevel* attribute if a REF operator specifying the variable is emitted in any subblock of the block of declaration.

   - Marks the *requires_storage* attribute if a REF operator specifying the variable is such that the variable must be in storage even though that is not implied by the variable's own data type. For example, in

```
DECLARE i FIXED BINARY,
        s CHARACTER(4) BASED(ADDR(i));
        s = 'j';
```

the assignment generates a character-string assignment to *i* and this operation requires that the variable be in storage.

4. Accumulates usage information for each block for the Optimizer and the Local Code Generator:

   • Marks a block node as having dynamically allocated automatic storage if it detects an ALLOC_AUTO operator in that block.

   • Marks a block node as having stack temporaries if it emits any operator that produces a nonconstant-sized result (excluding REF or VALUE operators).

   • Marks a block node as using the AP (Argument Pointer) if it writes out a PARAM_PTR operator specifying the block. If this operator is emitted in a subblock, the block node (of the parameter) is also marked as *save_ap*, meaning that the value of AP must be saved in its fixed stack frame location for access by the subblock. (If AP is not required for argument passing, it can be used as a general register.)

   • Determines the block's display level. Each REF operator denoting an automatic variable has a display level. (This is the difference between the current block's nesting level and the nesting level of the block in which the REF operator's variable was declared.) The display level of a PARAM_PTR operator is determined in a similar way. The block's display level is the maximum of all such REF operators and PARAM_PTR operators emitted in the block.

   • Marks the block as *save_parent_pointer* if a subblock has a display level extending above this block. This block's parent pointer will be saved in its fixed stack frame location so that the subblock can access it.

   • Marks the block as *needs_parent_pointer* if it has a display level greater than zero or if *save_parent_pointer* is set. A procedure call to an internal procedure passes a parent pointer only if this attribute is set in the procedure's block node.

   • Marks a block as *has_local_on_unit* if an ON-unit in the block does a GOTO to a label in the block. (This is the worst sort of ON-unit for optimization.)

   • Marks the block as *flush-on-call* if calls to external procedures, procedure parameters, or entry variables can result in uplevel references to variables, labels, or procedures in this block. This can occur if an internal procedure name is passed as a parameter or assigned to an entry variable. (This attribute has special significance to the Optimizer and is described in Chapter 7.)

5. Marks the symbol node of each label in accordance with its usage as follows:

   - Marks the label *alias* if the label is assigned to a label variable or passed as a parameter.

   - Marks the label *used_in_comparison* if the label is used in a comparison operator (say, EQ, NE, or LE) or is aliased.

   - Marks the label *uplevel* if it is the target of a GOTO operator in a subblock.

6. Counts the approximate number of nodes and edges in the flow graph. The Optimizer uses these numbers to determine the amount of storage required for its data structures.

7. Reduces a GOTO operator to a BRANCH operator if the target is a label in the current block.

8. Reduces a reference to a subscripted label with a constant subscripted expression—such as GOTO LAB(3*7)—to a reference to the specific scalar label.

9. Converts CONSTANT and IMMEDIATE operators (of any data type) used in floating-point, binary-integer, or bit contexts (with a length less than or equal to 32) to IMMEDIATE operators of the correct data type. (The difference between these operators is that CONSTANT operators are references to ASCII tokens and IMMEDIATE operators hold the encoded binary representation of a value.) This ensures that all frequently occurring cases of constant conversion are done at compile time. Moreover, the result is in a form (as an IMMEDIATE operator) that can participate in further reductions, such as arithmetic reductions (described in the next section). Converting constants at this point also ensures the best possible numeric result (within the language's constraints) for floating-point constants. Consider a constant without an exact binary representation such as:

```
x = 3.14159...E0;
```

where *x* is a FLOAT BINARY(24), that is, a longword. If the constant were converted to an internal quadword or octaword representation earlier in the computation (say, during lexical analysis) and subsequently converted to a floating-point longword, accuracy could be lost as a result of the double conversion. (Depending on the method used, the loss occurs due to premature truncation of fractional digits or double rounding.) A MINUS operator whose operand is an integer or floating-point constant reduces to an IMMEDIATE operator in the same way.

10. Replaces IMMEDIATE operators not acceptable to the back end with CONSTANT operators. Write Tree always performs this replacement after the conversion described in step 9.

11. Reduces integer expressions (discussed in detail in the next section).

12. Reduces short bit logical expressions involving constants. For example,

    x AND '0'B

    reduces to the equivalent of ′0′B.

13. Reduces comparison operators (such as EQ, NE, and LE) whose operands are constants.

14. Reduces BR_TRUE, BR_FALSE , and relational branch operators in line with steps 12 and 13 above.

15. Reduces RANGE operators (the workhorse of subscript-range checking) when the test value and one or both limits are constants.

16. Reports any errors detected during reduction. For example, Write Tree can detect division by zero as it performs reductions.

One important traditional tree reduction, the short-circuiting of the evaluation of Boolean expressions, is not in the list above. The bootstrap compiler included a form of this optimization. Before we developed Write Tree, we replaced this algorithm with the more general algorithm now used in the compiler. Although coding Boolean optimization in the Optimizer was not convenient (because of the linear representation of trees on entry to the Optimizer), getting the general algorithm into the compiler quickly was well worth the trouble.

Reduction of Integer Expressions

Write Tree performs several optimizations on integer expressions built from the basic operators ADD, SUBTRACT, MULTIPLY, and DIVIDE. The most obvious optimization is evaluating an operator whose operands are constants (sometimes referred to as "constant folding"). In this context, being a constant can simply mean being an IMMEDIATE operator. But constants in the source program are not so easily dealt with. In PL/I, integer constants have the data type fixed decimal and an exact decimal precision (for example, the constant 01 would have a precision of two). This information must be saved until the back end knows exactly how the constant will be used. Therefore, integer expressions coming into Write Tree contain many CONVERT operators that convert operands from decimal to integer. The code that reduces such operators not only converts decimal CONSTANT operators but also evaluates expressions in which all of the operands are decimal integer constants.

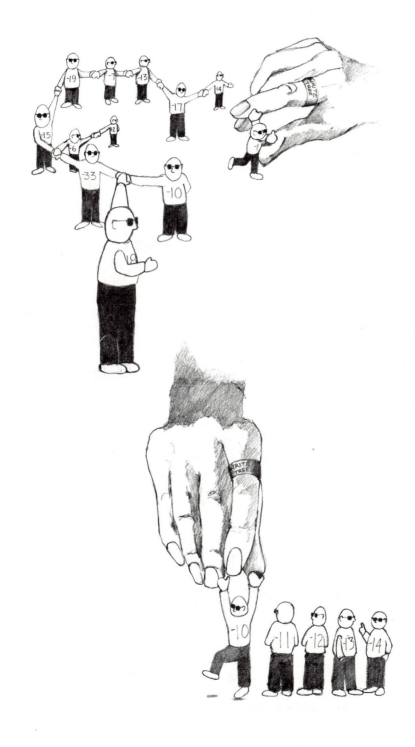

Write Tree also applies the following identities to simplify integer computations:

```
x - 0 = x
0 - x = -x
0 * x = x * 0 = 0
1 * x = x * 1 = x
x / 1 = x
0 / x = 0 (x ^= 0)
```

Opportunities to apply these identities arise mostly in the trees that PASS2 builds for offsets.

Conversion of Integer Expressions

The fact that integers come in three sizes on the VAX-11 creates interesting situations. An integer ADD operator and its two operands coming into Write Tree all have a data type of integer, and each is byte-, word-, or longword-sized. These sizes need not be the same for all three, but each operand size must be less than or equal to the size of the result of the ADD operator. The compiler must produce instructions that will convert each operand to the result size, if needed, then add them using signed integer addition in the result size.

To convert an operand to the result size, Write Tree inserts the CONVERT operator in the operator file. In the bootstrap compiler, the conversion was performed in the back end; the Local Code Generator added the conversions and the Peephole Optimizer reduced them. In what we feel is a better arrangement, given the VAX-11 architecture, Write Tree inserts the CONVERT operators and the Optimizer detects redundant ones and removes them from the operator file.

In some cases, however, the conversion can be avoided without changing the program's behavior. Suppose x and y are integer variables with a precision of 15, and consider the following:

```
x = x + y;
```

By PL/I rules, the expression $x+y$ has a precision of 16; hence, the result size of its ADD operator is longword. Literal translation of this statement would yield the following intermediate instructions:

```
CVTWL    x,temp1
CVTWL    y,temp2
ADDL3    temp1,temp2,temp3
CVTLW    temp3,x
```

These instructions convert x and y from word to longword, add them using longword addition, and convert the result back to word. In this case the size conversions are unnecessary; the same result can be produced by:

```
ADDW3    y,x,x
```

This instruction will overflow only if the CVTLW instruction in the preceding fragment also results in an overflow. To eliminate the unnecessary conversions, Write Tree changes the result size of the ADD operator for $x+y$ to word.

This sort of precision reduction applies to SUBTRACT and MULTIPLY operators and also when the operands and target are byte sized. For integer DIVIDE operators, precision is adjusted in a different way: the result size is set to the maximum of the two operand sizes to produce the correct arithmetic result.

Collection of the Constant Part of an Offset

The reductions described above are performed on all integer expressions. Another important optimization is currently performed only on expressions that occur as the offset operand of a REF operator. This is the collection of a constant part. Consider:

```
DECLARE x(1:100) FIXED;
        int = x(3*(i-5));
```

Here, the offset operand of the REF operator is the tree for $(3 \times (i\text{-}5)\text{-}1)$, which is equivalent to $3 \times i\text{-}16$. The latter expression is simpler, and the offset of -16 will materialize as a byte displacement of -64 in an operand referencing $x(3 \times (i\text{-}5))$, so the only explicit calculation required is the multiplication $3 \times i$.

Collecting the constant part of an offset in this way also increases the chances that the Optimizer will detect a redundant expression and therefore eliminate it. This example

```
x(2*i) = x(2*(i+1)) + x(2*(i-1))
```

will yield three REF operators, with ADD_OFFSET operators specifying different byte displacements, but all with $2 \times i$ as the variable part of the offset. Again, the fact that the constant byte displacement can be incorporated in the operand specifier of an instruction means additional code improvement as a result of constant collection. The following is typical code for the preceding statement (unless the autoincrement optimization occurs; see Chapter 7):

```
ADDL3   i,i,R3
ADDL3   4(R2)[R3],-12(R2)[R3],-4(R2)[R3]
```

The only possible problem with rewriting an arithmetic expression in this way is that overflow may occur. For example, if x has the value 2^{30}, then $4 \times (x\text{-}2^{30})$ is 0 but $4 \times x$ will overflow. However, if we know a suitable bound for the expression, we can rewrite it without causing overflow. Suppose a and b are constants. We can test in Write Tree to see if $ABS(a \times b) < 2^n$. Suppose further that in some way we know that $ABS(a \times (x+b)) < 2^n$. If so, it follows that $ABS(a \times x) < 2^{(n+1)}$. This means that for any value of $n \leq 30$, we can change $a \times (x+b)$ to $(a \times x) + (a \times b)$ without causing overflow on a VAX-11. If $n < 30$, the rule can be recursively applied to a subexpression. For example, if n is 29, then we know that $ABS(a \times x) < 2^{30}$. If x is actually the expression $z + c$, we can write $a \times x$ as $a \times z + a \times c$.

For offset collection in our compiler, we make the assumption that all offsets are less than 2^{28} in magnitude. For an offset within a given variable, this will be true if the variable's size does not exceed 2^{28} in the units for the offset. The total VAX-11 address space contains 2^{32} bytes, but this is divided into four equal regions; each contains 2^{30} bytes, and a variable must be allocated entirely within a region. Therefore the maximum possible size of a variable is 2^{30} bytes. Thus, for an array of longword integers or single-precision floating-point numbers, all offsets must be less than 2^{28} in longwords.

We consider the bound of 2^{28} reasonable for all data types, and it does allow Write Tree to collect constant offsets from trees of some complexity. The bound could be sharpened greatly for offsets within variables declared with constant sizes or for expressions whose magnitudes can be bounded based on the values of constants and the exclusive use of word- and byte-sized variables. We did not, however, do this.

Although Write Tree collects the constant part of an integer expression only for an expression that occurs as a REF operator's offset, it could do so for any integer expression whose value is known to be less than 2^{30} in magnitude. Thus any expression assigned to a byte- or word-sized variable or used as a string length could be collected. It does not seem sensible, however, to collect something as simple as $5 \times (i+1)$ unless one knows (or suspects) that it also occurs in an offset expression. Changing $5 \times (i+1)$ to $5 \times i + 5$ in an ordinary expression still requires addition, and the expression is farther from that in the original program.

When a Tree Is Not a Tree

As we have described things so far, Write Tree accepts a list of trees and writes them out in order. We have not said what order means for the subtrees of a tree, and we have talked about trees as though they really are trees in the strict mathematical sense of the term. That is, we have implied that:

1. A tree node is either the root of a tree or else it occurs as a subtree of exactly one other tree node.

2. The only trees related to a particular tree node are its parent (if it is not a root node) and its subtrees (size and/or operands).

In fact, the order in which things are written out can be important, and the structures used in PASS2 and Write Tree are not always as simple as trees. A tree node may occur more than once; indeed the same node can occur in distinct trees. Also, a tree node may be adorned with lists of trees to be written out before or after the node itself.

In this section, we discuss some of the circumstances that lead to deviations from purity in our tree structures and we explain what Write Tree does when it encounters these deviant structures.

Common Subexpressions and DAGs

In expanding certain source language constructions, the front end may generate a tree in which the same subexpression occurs more than once. Consider:

```
DECLARE (j,k) FIXED BINARY;
DECLARE s CHARACTER(10);
SUBSTR(s,j+k)   = '';
```

The REF operator generated by PASS2 for the SUBSTR reference has for its size operand the tree representing *11-(j+k)*. Its offset operand is the tree representing *(j+k)-1*. The subexpression *(j+k)* occurs in both operand subtrees, as illustrated in Figure 16.

The correct technical term for this sort of structure is *directed acyclic graph,* and the abbreviation *DAG* is used in compiler theory literature. The literature related to the use of DAGs in compilers is extensive, so we should explain why DAGs are not discussed as such in this book. There are two reasons. First, in almost all places in the front end and Write Tree, the tree-like structures that we use are treated as though they were trees in the strict sense. Second, the theoretical work based on DAGs does not have much rel-

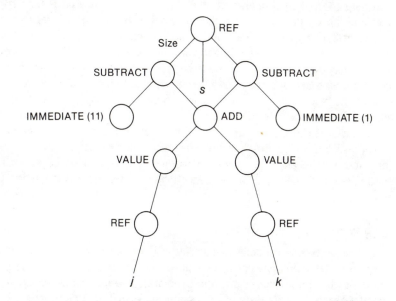

Figure 16. A tree (DAG) containing a common subexpression.

evance to our compiler. The normal use of a DAG in compiler theory is to represent the operations to be performed in a block of code (usually called a "basic block") in which no control-flow operators occur. The DAG does not specify a complete ordering for performing the operations; instead it gives the order relations that must be satisfied to produce a correct interpretation of a program. Much of the theory involves determining a compatible, complete ordering that is optimal according to some measure related to local code generation and register allocation.

By the time we get to code generation and register allocation in our common back end, we have imposed a complete ordering on the operators. DAGs are no longer visible, although they could be reconstructed. In Write Tree, the appropriate DAGs are not available. The list of trees given to Write Tree is not related to the division of a program into basic blocks. A common subexpression tree node may actually occur in trees separated by a control flow operator. Even if Write Tree had a list of trees corresponding to a basic block, it would have to assemble them into a rather conservative (overly restrictive) DAG because information about aliasing of variables is not yet complete. (Write Tree itself collects this information as it scans the entire program.) Write Tree could treat each tree after reduction as a DAG and try to write out the nodes in an optimal order. However, it simply writes subtrees out in left-to-right order, first the size, then operand one, and so on. We have not felt any pressure for optimization here, perhaps because of the VAX-11's generous number of registers.

Returning to the actual operation of Write Tree, we note that it correctly handles multiple occurrences of a tree node anywhere in the list of trees given to it by PASS2. (The occurrence of a tree node in more than one list—that is, in distinct calls to Write Tree—is only allowed for SAVE_RESULT operators, which are discussed later.) A tree node is written out only at its first occurrence, along with any subtrees not already written. Subsequent occurrences increment the reference count of the corresponding operator. If reduction of a tree modifies it or has no effect at all, the tree is marked reduced and will not be reduced if it occurs again. However, if reduction replaces a tree (for example, replaces $x+0$ with x), the tree is not marked reduced. Thus the replacement can take place at every occurrence of a tree. This occasionally leads to better code because further reductions may depend on the particular context.

Explicit Side Effects

Many language constructions that produce a result can have side effects. For example, a function invocation may have the side effect of modifying parameters or global (external) variables. Even such a simple operation as integer addition may have the side effect of causing overflow. In general, these natural side effects can be ignored by the front end and Write Tree. (A compiler that uses DAGs, however, may have to take account of such side effects when constructing the DAGs.) There are other cases where the front end needs to generate operators that explicitly accomplish the side effect. An example from PL/I is subscript range checking. When this compiler option is enabled, PASS2 generates a RANGE operator whose operands are the subscript value and the high and low bounds. This operator does not produce a result, but it will cause a run-time exception (or an error message from Write Tree) if the subscript value is out of bounds.

PASS2 generates the RANGE operators for a particular subscripted array reference while generating the REF operator. Where should it put the RANGE operators? If it emits them as they are generated (that is, if it puts them on the list of trees for the next invocation of Write Tree), they may end up far from the REF operator. Indeed, the REF operator might be eliminated entirely by optimization, leaving only the RANGE operators.

Language definitions seem to allow great flexibility in the placement of side-effect code, but we feel that it is best placed close to the code for the main construction: that is, the RANGE operators for subscript checking should be close to the REF operator that uses the subscripts. To accomplish this, we have included a pretree field and a posttree field in tree nodes. Each can denote a tree or a list of trees. If a tree node *x* contains a nonnull pretree field, the trees denoted by it are written out before *x* and its subtrees. The RANGE operators for a REF operator go on a list denoted by the REF operator's pretree field.

If a tree node *x* contains a nonnull posttree field, its contents are written out after *x* and its subtrees. For an example of using the posttree field, we turn to the C language, a language rich in explicit side effects. The operator ++ used as a postfix operator means "increment the value of a variable after taking its value." Thus, in

```
y = i++;
```

i is incremented but *y* is assigned the value of *i* before the incrementation takes place. Figure 17 shows the tree we produce for *i*++. The SAVE_RESULT operator captures the value of *i* before it is modified by the ASSIGN operator. Use of the posttree field ensures that the operators are emitted in the correct order. Note that although the REF operator for *i* could be equivalent to another (and thus eliminated by the Optimizer), two distinct VALUE operators are required. Otherwise we would violate the Intermediate Language rule that at all points where a particular VALUE operator is used the referenced variable must have the same value. One must be careful about this when doing elaborate semantic expansions in the front end.

Capturing Values

If it is necessary to hold the value of a variable over a span of code that might modify the variable, a SAVE_RESULT operator is used. This use has al-

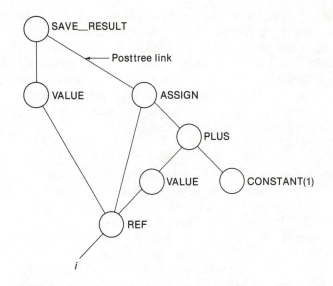

Figure 17. A tree representing i++.

ready been illustrated from the C language, as shown in Figure 17. In PL/I, the SAVE_RESULT operator may be needed to save the values of the increment and limit variables in a DO-loop. For example:

```
m = 2;
n = 20;
DO i = 1 TO n BY m;
        m = 1;
        n = 0;
        .
        .
        .
        END;
```

This loop means

```
DO i = 1 TO 20 BY 2;
```

that is, the assignments to *m* and *n* inside the loop are required to have no effect on the loop-increment and loop-limit values.

In the DO-loop case, we put the identifier of the SAVE_RESULT operator in the LOOP_BOTTOM operator so that the captured reference will be saved for the duration of the entire loop and will be released when the LOOP_BOTTOM operator is processed. Because a loop can contain an arbitrary amount of code, the SAVE_RESULT operator may occur in the trees processed by more than one call to Write Tree. This has two consequences. First, the

SAVE_RESULT operator has to be a permanent tree node rather than a temporary tree node. It is explicitly freed when it occurs in the LOOP_BOTTOM operator for the DO-loop. Second, instead of incrementing the operator's reference count at each occurrence of the SAVE_RESULT, Write Tree emits an INCREMENT_USAGE operator. This intervention keeps the reference count correct without violating the principle of local processing of trees and operators in Write Tree.

In the Intermediate Language, the operand of a SAVE_RESULT operator must be a VALUE operator with a constant size. Write Tree allows more flexibility: the operand may be any value-producing operator with a constant size. The various cases are handled as follows, where x is the SAVE_RESULT operator's operand after reduction:

Case 1: x is a VALUE operator, as in the case of a SAVE_RESULT operator, discussed above.

Case 2: x is a CONSTANT or IMMEDIATE operator. At each occurrence, the SAVE_RESULT operator is replaced by a CONSTANT or IMMEDIATE operator that is reduced and written in the normal way.

Case 3: x is any other value-producing operator. Each occurrence of x is replaced by the identifier of the operator for x. (No reduction is possible at these occurrences.) INCREMENT_USAGE operators are emitted for x just as they would be for a SAVE_RESULT operator.

Flow analyses by the Optimizer may detect that a SAVE_RESULT operator is unnecessary if the variable's value does not change in the SAVE_RESULT operator's span. If so, the Optimizer then eliminates the SAVE_RESULT operator. As a consequence, the front end can generally introduce a SAVE_RESULT operator wherever it might be needed without worrying about details.

In PL/I, it is also necessary to capture the reference for the control variable of a loop. For example:

```
p = ADDR(y);
DO p->x = 1 TO 10;
        p = q;
```

Because the assignment to p must not affect the loop control, the offset and base pointer of the reference (or its entire address) are captured, and a new reference is made with the same symbol nodes and the captured offset and base pointer. Capturing references could be done instead in the Local Code Generator, but that approach is not advantageous when index variables and pointer variables can be held in registers.

7

Global
Optimization

Although we use the name *Optimizer* to refer to a specific phase of the VAX-11 Code Generator, program and code optimization are by no means restricted to this phase. The Optimizer is, however, the phase in which we perform the classic global optimizations, which include the removal of invariant expressions from loops, elimination of common subexpressions, and propagation of values. All these involve analysis of the program, followed by the removal, shortening, or rearrangement of statement operators or expressions. This chapter describes how we perform these optimizations on the Intermediate Language and how the Optimizer selects local variables that are candidates for assignment to registers and performs certain optimizations that are targeted for specific features of the VAX-11 instruction set.

We agree with those (Aho and Ullman, among others) who find the term code improvement more accurate than optimization. Few programs can ever be fully optimized; but a compiler can be developed so that the code it generates is continually better. Each improvement in the code generates new possibilities for further improvement. Ideas for improvement come from close scrutiny of the code generated, from the application of data collected for one purpose to another purpose, and at times from simple wishful thinking. Once begun, a commitment to optimization can become an obsession never to be laid aside. Even in the conclusions we draw at the end of this chapter, we suggest areas in which we could further optimize our code.

Background: Engineering an Optimizer

The Optimizer was neither designed nor implemented all in a piece. The bootstrap compiler contained an optimization phase, but we had no specific goals for improving it. Because that compiler was designed to run on machines with a limited address space, its optimizer did not collect the potentially large amounts of data needed to obtain detailed information about program flow and variable use. Moreover, this optimizer operated within a limited range of operators in the program and did not adequately handle PL/I complications like lexically nested procedures (occurring within the text of other procedures). The optimizations it performed were common subexpression elimination, removal of invariant computations from loops, partial optimization of Boolean branches, and replacement of selected patterns of operators with equivalent but shorter patterns.

Our development of the Optimizer phase started just after we had written the new Register Allocator, which had a comprehensive algorithm for allocating registers for temporaries representing the results of operators. It seemed clear that we could apply the same allocation method to local variables and that the payoff from doing so would be high. We therefore added data collection facilities to Write Tree to determine which variables were candidates for holding in registers. Then, we extended the Optimizer to select up to 32 variables per block from these candidates and perform data flow analysis over all the operators in each block. The analysis gave the Register Allocator the freedom to assign different instances of a variable to different registers in cases where it was advantageous to do so.

The next areas we targeted for code improvement were Boolean branches and what we call *result incorporation*. The optimization of Boolean branches is nothing more than short-circuiting the evaluation of a Boolean expression as soon as the final result can be determined. We replaced the original algorithm with one that optimizes more cases. Our version of result incorporation takes advantage of the availability, on the VAX-11, of both two- and three-operand forms of many instructions. This optimization combines an assignment operator with the operator computing the value that gets assigned, and thus replaces two-operand operators followed by ASSIGN operators with a single three-operand operator.

When we had completed work on these three optimizations, we looked for additional ways to use the flow graph constructed for register assignment. At this stage of development, we essentially threw the flow graph away when register assignment was complete. We had continued to use the old algorithms to eliminate common subexpressions and to remove invariant values from loops. Thus, our next step was to use the flow graph to eliminate common subexpressions. While rewriting this routine, we changed the algorithm from an *n*-squared algorithm to a linear one. The result was a faster and more comprehensive subexpression eliminator.

Lastly, we replaced the routine that removed invariant values from loops. Our prime considerations in reworking this routine were twofold: to use a layout for loop code that takes maximum advantage of the VAX-11 architecture, and to change the algorithm so that it conformed to the PL/I standard. Changing the algorithm required modifying the front end so that we would always have a safe place to move the invariant computations of a loop.

This modification was the last improvement we made to the Optimizer before releasing the first version of the VAX-11 PL/I compiler. It was a very good Optimizer; but while trying to discover ways to improve the generated code further, we realized that we had already collected the information necessary to do value propagation (sometimes called "copy propagation" or "subsumption") for variables that were selected as candidates for assignment to registers. Value propagation, as we implement it, is simply the elimination of local variables not required for the correct execution of the program.

A final optimization we implemented is one we had thought about doing for some time: the improvement of array addressing within loops. The Optimizer moves the base address of an array (the address of the first element addressed in the initial trip through the loop) outside the loop if the array is being addressed through the control variable of the loop. This optimization, an addressing *strength reduction,* allows us to use the autoincrement and autodecrement addressing modes of the VAX-11; these addressing modes are both faster and shorter than the conventional context-index mode used in most other VAX-11 compilers. (Few other machine architectures provide context indexing at all.)

We are very pleased with the results of our optimization. The original optimization phase consisted of approximately 1,500 lines of PL/I source code and required approximately 12K bytes for the program as compiled by the PL/I bootstrap compiler. Our Optimizer consists of approximately 6,000 lines of source code, requires approximately 24K bytes (as compiled by our latest PL/I compiler), and runs much faster.

Underlying Concepts and Assumptions

The rules and assumptions applied during optimization provide a framework for understanding the program and the ways in which it can be improved. The application of a specific set of rules to the elements of a program results in:

- Understanding what a variable is, when its value is defined, and when that definition is consumed

- Being able to calculate the furthest backward point in a program to which an operator can be moved

- Knowing the ways in which nonsequential program flow may possibly alter the modification of variables, and being able to devise a mechanism for recording and dealing with this flow.

What Is a Variable?

A variable is a data entity that is manipulated by the program being compiled. In the source program, a variable is declared and given a name and a set of attributes. The front end of a compiler inserts this name and these attributes in the Symbol Table and directs all references to the variable to the Symbol Table. In the Intermediate Language, we subsequently access the variable's attributes in the Symbol Table by using REF operators. The structure of the Symbol Table and the manner in which variables' attributes are recorded reflect the scope of the variables in the source program.

Definition and Use

A reference to a variable can mean one of two things: a definition of the variable or a use of its value. In terms of the Intermediate Language, a *definition* (or *definition point*) is the occurrence of an operator that modifies the value of a variable. The Optimizer knows what these operators are and uses its knowledge to keep track of places in the program where a variable is defined. An obvious example of a definition of a variable is an assignment such as:

```
x = 5;
```

In a less obvious example, a variable is specified as an argument passed by reference in a call:

```
CALL invert(x);
```

The Intermediate Language also includes an operator, SETS, which lets a front end tell the Optimizer about definitions the latter could not otherwise detect. For example, our PL/I compiler's WRITE statement has an option called RECORD_ID_TO, which causes the internal identifier of the record being written to be returned to a specified variable. The Optimizer has no way of discerning that this variable is modified by the operation. Thus, the front end must follow the operators expressing the write operation with a SETS operator that specifies that the previous operator represents a definition point for the specified variable. (We could have made the Optimizer know about this case and other special cases; however, we wanted the Optimizer to be as language independent as possible.)

Use of a variable in a reference is merely a reference to its current value. In the Intermediate Language, there are only two ways to represent a use of a variable—its occurrence as an operand of a VALUE operator or its occurrence as an operand passed by reference in a CALL operator. Both of the following examples show the use of a variable, *x*:

```
y = x;
z = comp(x);
```

The second use of *x* is also a definition, since the occurrence of a variable passed by reference in a call always represents both a use and a definition.

The Limit of an Operator

During both removal of invariant expressions from loops and elimination of common subexpressions, the Optimizer constantly calculates the limit of an operator to determine whether an optimization can be performed, such as whether it is safe to move a given operator outside a loop or to combine operators. The *limit* of a given operator is defined as the operator identifier of the most recent definition point of any of its operands. The Optimizer performs the limit computation recursively, computing the limits of the operands and then of the operands of the operands, until all the leaves of the tree have been traversed. The Optimizer then uses the resulting limit value to determine how far backward on the flow path in question the operator can be moved. Consider the following program fragment and resultant Intermediate Language representation:

Source Program Fragment

```
p = b + c;
b = b + 1;
q = b + c;
```

Intermediate Language Operators

```
-50    REF(p)
-51    REF(b)
-52    VALUE(-51)
-53    REF(c)
-54    VALUE(-53)
-55    ADD(-52,-54)
-56    ASSIGN(-50,-55)


-57    REF(b)
-58    REF(b)
-59    VALUE(-58)
-60    IMMEDIATE(1)
-61    ADD(-59,-60)
-62    ASSIGN(-57,-61)


-63    REF(q)
-64    REF(b)
-65    VALUE(-64)
-66    REF(c)
-67    VALUE(-66)
-68    ADD(-65,-67)
-69    ASSIGN(-63,-68)
```

In this example, the ASSIGN operator –56 is a definition point of p, –62 is a definition point of b, and –69 is a definition point of q. During the elimination of common subexpressions, the Optimizer attempts to combine the two references to the expression $b+c$ by changing the ADD operator –68 to a reference to the previous (identical) ADD operator, –61. This proves to be impossible, however, because in computing the limit of ADD –68 the Optimizer finds that the limit is –62, the last definition point of one of its operands, b. Thus,

16-Jan-79

1. allocate symbol node and clear
   location(s)

2. use ~~arg~~ field for link to next symbol

3. use value (w) field to store symbol number
   allocated, external Symbols are distinguished from
   declared external symbols by zero token
   id field

4. the cons-at bit is set to indicate
   the external ~~has been~~ referred to.

5. the ext-at bit is set to indicate the
   symbol is an external

6. block node index set to outer block

the farthest point backward in the program to which ADD –68 can be moved is –62, which is not far enough backward to encompass the ADD operator –61.

Classes of Variables

Although the Optimizer has precise information about variable definition in some cases (such as the ASSIGN operator), it cannot, in general, know whether it has complete and explicit information about all the definition points of a variable. A good example is the case of a procedure that has declared an external variable. Each time the procedure calls an external procedure, the external variable might be modified by some action within the external procedure. The Optimizer cannot know whether it actually was modified because that information is not available at compile time. The same type of situation occurs with a variable whose address has been assigned to a pointer (that is, has been aliased). To cope with these problems we have classified variables as follows:

- *External class.* A variable that is defined or referenced in modules that are not a part of the current compilation.
- *Static class.* A variable that has the static (as opposed to automatic) attribute. A variable in this class must retain its value across block activations, including recursive activations of the current block.
- *Uplevel class.* A variable that is referenced from a block contained in its block of declaration (a lexically nested block).
- *Alias class.* A variable that may be modified by something that we cannot know about in the current compilation, in particular, one that may be referenced elsewhere by some other name. Parameters that are passed by reference as well as based variables are in this class, since we have no way of knowing whether they might be modified under some other name.
- *Ordinary class.* A variable that is not a member of any of the other classes. In general, these are the variables for which we can exactly determine all definition points.

The Optimizer maintains a record of the last explicit definition point for all variables. The last explicit definition point is represented as the identifier of the operator that last defined the variable. In addition, the Optimizer records the last definition point for each of the classes external, static, uplevel, and alias in what we call *class definition points.* The last definition point for any of these classes is the most recent point in the program at which any variable belonging to that class was assigned a value. When the Optimizer computes the limit of an operator, it also considers class definition points. For example, the limit of a reference to an aliased variable is the most recent explicit defini-

NOTES: FEB-8

Ⓞ Externals can be split out from aliased variables as follows.

1. An assignment to an external variable that is not aliased only defines a definition point for that variable.

2. all externals calls set a definition point for external variables

3. an aliased external variable acts just like all other aliased variables

Don must remove alias bit in pass2 from variables that are not aliased.

tion of the variable itself or the most recent definition point of the alias class, whichever is more recent.

Rules for Determining Definition Points

An explicit definition point of a variable occurs when an operator directly or indirectly assigns a value to the variable. This occurs as a result of any of the following events:

- An ASSIGN operator specifies the variable as the target of the assignment.
- The variable is specified as the argument of a CALL operator and is to be passed by reference.
- The variable is specified as the operand of a SETS operator.
- The variable is used as the control variable of a loop in an ADD_COMPARE_AND_BRANCH operator.

Explicit class definition points occur when any variable belonging to the class is assigned a value as a result of any of the above. However, class definition points also occur as a side effect of assignment to variables of other classes according to the following rules:

- A definition point for any variable of the alias class is also a definition point for the uplevel, static, and external classes. This rule is necessary when an external, static, or uplevel variable is passed to a procedure by reference and the target procedure may address the variable either directly by name or indirectly via the parameter list.
- A definition point for a variable of the external, static, or uplevel class is also a definition point for the alias class. This follows from the case above (that is, when a variable is referenced both directly by name and indirectly via the parameter list).
- All procedure and function calls are definition points for the alias, external, and static classes. This rule is necessary because the information needed to determine exactly what variables are and are not modified is either not computed (we do not do interprocedural analysis) or is not available at compile time (in the case of calls to external procedures).
- All procedure and function calls to internal procedures or from blocks that have the *flush-on-call* attribute are definition points for the uplevel class. This rule is necessary because internal procedures may directly address uplevel variables by name.

A block with the flush-on-call attribute is a block in which a call to an external procedure could result in a call back into a contained internal procedure because the entry constant of the internal procedure has been assigned to an entry variable or has been passed by reference to another procedure. An example of a program containing such a construct is:

```
flush: PROCEDURE;
DECLARE ecalc ENTRY (ENTRY),
        a(10) FLOAT BINARY(24);
        CALL ecalc(icalc);
            .
            .
            .
        RETURN;


icalc: PROCEDURE;
DECLARE i FIXED BINARY(31);
        DO i = 1 TO 10;
            a(i) = i;
            END;
        RETURN;
        END;
END;


ecalc: PROCEDURE (routine);
DECLARE routine ENTRY;
        CALL routine;
        RETURN;
END;
```

Along with these rules for definition points of classes of variables, the following rules are required for definition points in structure and procedure parameters:

- A definition point for any member of a structure constitutes a definition point for all containing structures.

- A definition point for an entire structure constitutes a definition point for all members of the structure.

- A definition point for any element of an array is considered to be a definition point for the entire array.

- A definition point for an entire array is considered to be a definition point for all elements of the array.

- Whenever a variable is passed by reference in a procedure or function call, that reference constitutes a definition point for the variable.

All of this information and the formalization of these rules are extremely important in computing the limit of an operator. This critical information lets us perform optimizations across longer spans of the program (for example, across branches and procedure calls) and has increased our ability to optimize aggregates.

Structure and Control Flow in the Optimizer

The front end of a compiler is responsible for producing a linear representation of a program by passing trees to Write Tree. The Optimizer is an optional phase of the compiler that is responsible for performing reductions on this linear form (the operator file) in a machine-independent fashion.

Before the optimization process begins, the Optimizer scans the entire Symbol Table. For each variable, whether it be external, static, automatic, or scalar or an aggregate, the Optimizer assigns a definition point number and stores this number in the variable's symbol node. It subsequently uses this number throughout optimization as an index into arrays that contain information about variables, such as the array that contains the most recent definition point of each variable. Figure 18 illustrates the order in which the Optimizer performs optimizations on the program. The Optimizer scans the linear program representation to segregate the program into procedure and begin blocks and performs optimizations on each individual block.

For each block, the Optimizer constructs an array of pointers (the pointer array) to the operators in that block and a position array that is indexed by the negated values of the operator identifiers. The pointer array is itself indexed by the position array; the value in the position array is the index of the respective pointer to the operator in the pointer array. Figure 19 illustrates these

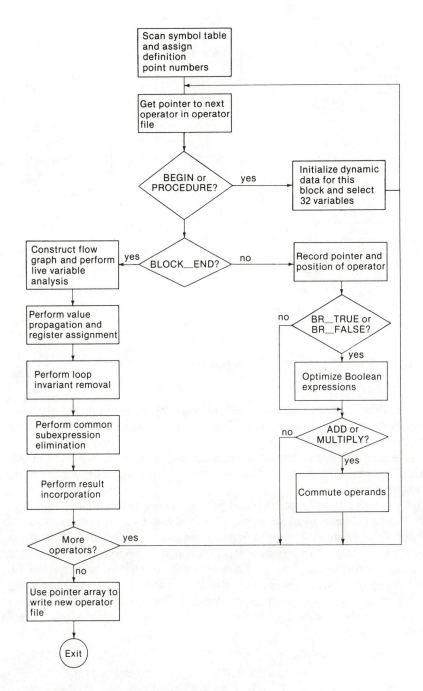

Figure 18. Sequence of optimizations.

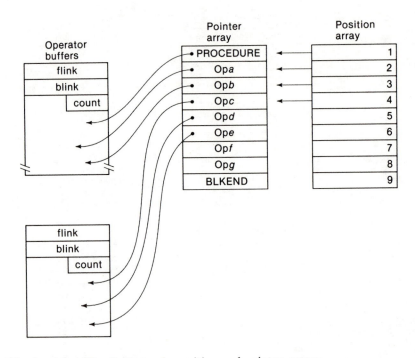

Figure 19. The Optimizer's position and pointer arrays.

arrays. The Optimizer makes several passes over the operator file, the exact number depending on the optimizations it is performing. Once it has built the pointer and position arrays during the first scan, it uses only these arrays in subsequent scans and locates specific operators (when it needs to modify them) by using the position array to locate the corresponding pointer in the pointer array.

As it constructs the position and pointer arrays, the Optimizer optimizes Boolean conditional expressions and performs various small reductions on the Intermediate Language. (For example, it commutes the operands of MULTIPLY and ADD operators to a canonical form for common subexpression elimination so that expressions such as $a+b$ and $b+a$ will be found to be equivalent.) It selects up to 32 variables as candidates for assignment to registers based on their usage within the program and builds a flow graph of the block. After completing the flow graph, the Optimizer performs its optimizations in the following order:

1. Value propagation

2. Assignment of automatic variables to register temporaries

3. Removal of invariant expressions from loops

4. Elimination of common subexpressions

5. Result incorporation.

Any of these optimizations can be suppressed at compile time by individual command options. Although users of the compiler rarely suppress individual optimizations (and our compiler requires suppression of few optimizations—notably value propagation and the computation of disjoint lifetimes—in order to do interactive debugging), we found it useful while isolating bugs in the Optimizer to be able to be selective about which optimizations were being done.

Throughout its execution, the Optimizer records removal or reordering of operators so that it can write out the final optimized form of the operators in the correct lexical order. For operators that it eliminates, it zeros its pointer in the pointer array. For operators that it moves, the Optimizer moves the corresponding pointer in the pointer array and updates the respective element in the position array to signify the new pointer position; thus, the pointer array is constantly shuffled during the removal of invariant expressions. Finally, when it has processed all the blocks in the program, the Optimizer uses the resultant pointer array to write the optimized set of operators into an internal file that will be read by the Local Code Generator.

In the remaining sections of this chapter, we discuss in detail each optimization we implemented in this phase of the VAX-11 Code Generator. We describe the optimizations and the data collection procedures in the order the Optimizer executes them. Figure 18 provides a guide to how these pieces fit together.

Selecting Variables for Assignment to Registers

The Optimizer does not actually assign variables to registers. Final selection and assignment of variables to specific hardware registers does not occur until after code generation and is performed by a distinct phase of the compiler, the Register Allocator. The Optimizer scans the Symbol Table, selecting up to 32 variables as candidates for assignment to registers. (The number of variables is not arbitrary. We felt that, given a 32-bit architecture with 16 registers, 32 was a reasonable number if as a result of the computation of disjoint lifetimes we could use the same register for more than one variable. Moreover, using 32 variables lets us perform efficient bit-string operations on sets representing the variables we selected.)

The Optimizer determines which variables are eligible by making some specific tests. If more than 32 variables in the block meet the test, it chooses those that are more frequently referenced by looking at the reference information accumulated by the front end. To be eligible, the variable must be:

- One of the data types floating point, integer, bit aligned (and less than or equal to 32 bits), pointer, offset, or file

- Scalar
- Referenced
- Automatic.

A variable is ineligible if it does not meet all these conditions, or if Write Tree has set the attribute *requires_storage* in the variable's symbol node. Write Tree sets this attribute if the variable's address has been taken or is used in some peculiar way, for example as the operand of a SUBSTR (substring) function.

(In the current version of the compiler, being passed by reference or being uplevel addressed does not automatically make a variable ineligible for register assignment, as was the case in the first version. After the first version was released, we realized that if we could segregate uses of a variable—that is, if we could tell whether over some period it was not being passed by reference or being uplevel addressed—we could put it in a register during the times when it was safe to do so. We were able to accomplish this by letting the Optimizer delay its decision about the variable's eligibility until after it has built the flow graph. To do this, the Optimizer constructs a 32-member set signifying which variables that are candidates for register assignment are also uplevel addressed at some point in the program. We refer to this as the *uplevel set*. The Optimizer sets the *requires_storage* attribute for these variables so that the Storage Allocator phase will allocate memory for them in the stack frame. While it is building the flow graph, the Optimizer also sets the *requires_storage* attribute for variables passed by reference.)

As it selects variables by using these criteria, the Optimizer assigns them numbers from 1 to 32. It uses these numbers thereafter to access information about the variables stored in various arrays (such as an array containing the symbol node identifiers of the 32 variables) and as an index into various bit arrays (such as various sets required for data flow analysis). It stores the assigned number in the variable's symbol node and sets the *register_temporary* attribute in the symbol node to indicate that the variable may be assigned to a register.

Optimizing Boolean Branch Expressions

The optimization of Boolean branch expressions (sometimes called "Boolean minimization") occurs during the initial scan of the operators. We wanted to perform this optimization as early as possible because the resultant introduction of different branch operators into the file will modify the flow graph of the program. This optimization modifies the computation of Boolean branches so that the generated code will at run time evaluate only as much of the expression as is needed to determine the final result.

The Optimizer tests for seven specific code patterns and performs a specific optimization for each. The patterns are

1. *NOT a*
2. *a OR b*
3. *NOT (a AND b)*
4. *a AND b*
5. *NOT (a OR b)*
6. *x RELATION y*
7. *NOT (x RELATION y)*

where *a* and *b* are Boolean expressions and *x* and *y* are arithmetic expressions. The following code fragment and generated operators illustrate the first pattern listed above:

Source Program Fragment

```
IF NOT a
    THEN conditional statements
```

Intermediate Language Operators

```
-50    REF(a)
-51    VALUE(-50)
-52    NOT(-51)
-53    BR_FALSE(label1,-52)
-54         .
            . conditional statements
            .
-70    LABEL(label1)
```

This code sequence specifies that the conditional statements be executed if *a* is false. Thus, we can modify the operators so that the conditional statements are not executed if *a* is true. The following set of operators shows how the Optimizer replaces operators –52 and –53 with a single operator:

```
-50    REF(a)
-51    VALUE(-50)
-52    BR_TRUE(label1,-51)
-53         .
            . conditional statements
            .
-70    LABEL(label1)
```

The second pattern optimizes the OR case shown in the following code fragment and generated operators.

Source Program Fragment

```
IF a OR b
    THEN conditional statements
```

Intermediate Language Operators

```
-50    REF(a)
-51    VALUE(-50)
-52    REF(b)
-53    VALUE(-52)
-54    OR(-51,-53)
-55    BR—FALSE(label1,-54)
-56       .
             . conditional statements    .
          .
-70    LABEL(label1)
```

This code sequence specifies that the conditional statements be executed if *a* or *b* is true. Thus, we can modify the operators so that the conditional statements are executed if *a* is true or so that the conditional statements are not executed at all if *a* is false and *b* is also false. The optimized set of operators is as follows:

```
-50    REF(a)
-51    VALUE(-50)
-52    BR—TRUE(label2,-51)
-53    REF(b)
-54    VALUE(-53)
-55    BR—FALSE(label1,-54)
-56    LABEL(label2)
-57       .
             . conditional statements
          .
-70    LABEL(label1)
```

The third pattern can be optimized with a similar modification, by removing the NOT operator and substituting BR_TRUE operators for each occurrence of a BR_FALSE operator, and vice versa. Thus, the conditional statements are executed if *a* is false, or they are not executed at all if both *a* and *b* are true. The fourth and fifth patterns can be treated similarly.

The sixth pattern is used to optimize relational operators such as EQ (equal), GT (greater), and so on. The following code fragment illustrates the operators generated for relational expressions.

Source Program Fragment

```
if x RELATION y
        then conditional statements
```

Intermediate Language Operators

```
-50    REF(x)
-51    VALUE(-50)
-52    REF(y)
-53    VALUE(-52)
-54    RELATIONAL_OPERATOR(-51,-53)
-55    BR_FALSE(label1,-54)
-56      .
         . conditional statements
         .
-70    LABEL(label1)
```

This code sequence specifies that the conditional statements be executed if the relationship between *x* and *y* is true. We can therefore optimize the operators by replacing the relational operator that is followed by a **BR_FALSE** operator (−54 and −55 above) with an inverse relational branch operator as follows:

```
-50    REF(x)
-51    VALUE(-50)
-52    REF(y)
-53    VALUE(-52)
-54    INVERSE_RELATIONAL_BRANCH(label1,-51,-53)
-55      .
         . conditional statements
         .
-70    LABEL(label1)
```

The seventh pattern is optimized in the same way as the sixth except that a relational branch is used instead of an inverse relational branch.

All Boolean branch optimizations are performed recursively so that each transformation opens new opportunities for further optimization. Consider the following code fragment and intermediate code:

Source Program Fragment

```
if (a OR b) AND (c AND d)
    then conditional statements
```

Intermediate Language Operators

```
-50    REF(a)
-51    VALUE(-50)
-52    REF(b)
-53    VALUE(-52)
-54    OR(-51,-53)
```

```
-55    REF(c)
-56    VALUE(-55)
-57    REF(d)
-58    VALUE(-57)
-59    AND(-56,-58)
-60    AND(-54,-59)
-61    BR_FALSE(label1,-60)
-62         .
            . conditional statements
            .
-70    LABEL(label1)
```

The first pattern selected for optimization is pattern (4), an AND operation. We replace the AND (–60) and the BR_FALSE (–61) with two BR_FALSE operators, because the conditional statements will not be executed if either operand of the AND (–60) is false. The operators resulting from this optimization are (note the insertion of the BR_FALSE (–55) before the REF of *c*):

```
-50    REF(a)
-51    VALUE(-50)
-52    REF(b)
-53    VALUE(-52)
-54    OR(-51,-53)
-55    BR_FALSE(label1,-54)
-56    REF(c)
-57    VALUE(-56)
-58    REF(d)
-59    VALUE(-58)
-60    AND(-57,-59)
-61    BR_FALSE(label1,-60)
-62         .
            . conditional statements
            .
-70    LABEL(label1)
```

We have now created the opportunity to apply further optimization to the operators –55 and –61. The completely optimized set of operators is:

```
-50    REF(a)
-51    VALUE(-50)
-52    BR_TRUE(label2,-51)
-53    REF(b)
-54    VALUE(-53)
-55    BR_FALSE(label1,-54)
-56    LABEL(label2)
-57    REF(c)
```

```
-58    VALUE(-57)
-59    BR_FALSE(label1,-58)
-60    REF(d)
-61    VALUE(-60)
-62    BR_FALSE(label1,-61)
-63      .
           . conditional statements
           .
-70    LABEL(label1)
```

We now skip evaluation of *b* if *a* is true and proceed immediately to evaluate *c*. If *c* is false, we exit the sequence entirely.

Constructing the Flow Graph

A flow graph, in visual terms, shows us what happens in the program and as such is similar to a flowchart. However, because it is constructed according to well-defined rules developed to chart possible control flow, it enables us to describe formally the relationship and flow of control among the various units of a program.

To build a flow graph, the Optimizer simply scans the operators for a given block and generates graph nodes and list entries describing the relationships among the nodes. (In some books, these nodes are called "basic blocks." To avoid confusion with procedure and begin blocks in our text, we call them *nodes*.) When this graph is complete, each node represents a sequence of instructions that will always be executed in their entirety if at all. Moreover, each node can be entered at only one place in the control flow, although it can have more than one place at which it exits.

We defined a very basic set of rules for constructing the flow graph. These are:

- There is an initial node from which all other nodes can be reached. This node is generated mostly for convenience and provides a place from which all flow paths emanate.
- A label is the start of a node.
- A conditional branch is the end of a node. The operator following the conditional branch is the start of a new node even though it may not be a label (since control can fall through the test).
- A procedure or function call is the end of a node. The operator following the procedure or function call operator is the start of a new node even though it may not be a label (since control normally returns from the called procedure or function).
- An unconditional branch is the end of a node. Unconditional branches include Intermediate Language operators for returning from a proce-

dure, for signaling an error condition, and for resignaling an error, and the obvious case of the GOTO operator.

Generally, for each new node that it generates the Optimizer constructs two edges. The edges represent the flow of control from the previous node to the new node. One edge is inserted in the successor list of the previous node, the other in the predecessor list of the new node. Two edges are also generated for the target node of a conditional or unconditional branch. These edges are entered in the predecessor and successor lists of the previous and target nodes, respectively. Figure 20 illustrates successor and predecessor edges for a flow graph whose nodes represent some basic programming constructions.

The rules listed above for generating edges do not allow for the generality required to optimize languages that have such concepts as label variables, multiple entry points to a procedure, and exception handling. Thus, in developing the flow graph logic for analyzing PL/I programs we had to introduce rules that allowed us to represent—and safely optimize—a program containing these more complex constructs. We also had to introduce two fictitious nodes that let us represent hidden or unknown flow, such as uplevel GOTO statements and aliased labels. These nodes are called the *uplevel* and *alias nodes*. The extended rules are:

- An alternate entry point is the start of a new node; its immediate predecessor is the initial node. Thus, we can represent that control flowing into the block at any of its entry points must come through the initial node.
- A call to an external procedure has an additional successor node: the alias node.
- A call to an external procedure from a procedure with the *flush-on-call* attribute has an additional successor node: the uplevel node.
- A call to an entry variable has both the uplevel and alias nodes as additional successors.
- A call to an internal (contained) procedure has both the alias and uplevel nodes as additional successors.
- A block that contains a condition handling routine (such as a PL/I ON-unit) with an uplevel GOTO into the containing block has an additional successor to its initial node: the uplevel node.
- A CASE or SELECT statement has a successor node that is generated for the label array.
- A label constant assigned to a label variable or passed to a called procedure heads a node that has the alias node as an additional predecessor.

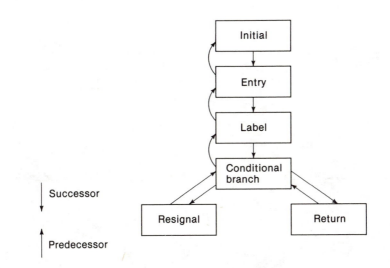

Figure 20. Successors and predecessors.

- A label constant that is uplevel addressed (that is, referenced by an uplevel GOTO) heads a node that has the uplevel node as an additional predecessor.
- A subscripted label constant heads a node that has the node generated for the label array as an additional predecessor.
- A GOTO with a label variable as its target has the alias node as a successor.

Collectively, these rules permit construction of a flow graph for any language. Figure 21 illustrates what the flow graphs would look like for a few of these more complicated cases.

These rules do not allow us to model exactly the control flow in a program. They do, however, enable us to construct a conservative model in which the representation will always allow us to perform correct, albeit not all possible, optimizations.

Collecting Use and Definition Information

While scanning the operator file to build the flow graph, the Optimizer collects the use and definition information for each variable selected as a candidate for assignment to a register. The information is collected for each node and includes:

- A *use* set, containing a true value for each variable whose value was used in the node before it was assigned a value.

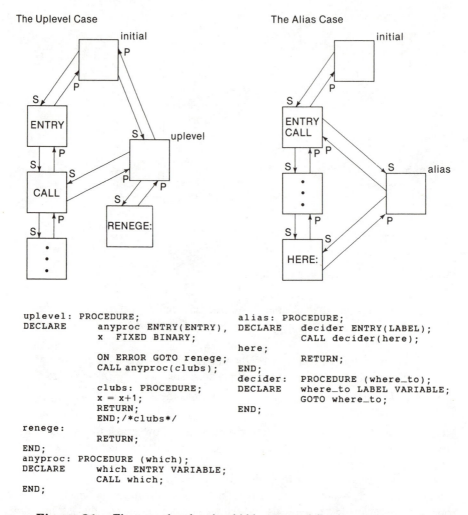

Figure 21.   Flow graphs charting hidden control flow.

- A *def,* or definition, set, containing a true value for each variable that was assigned a value before its value was used in the node.

- A *ref,* or referenced-by-address, set, containing a true value for each variable that was either (1) passed by reference within the node or (2) is uplevel addressed and the node contains either a call to an internal procedure or a call to an external procedure and the containing block has the *flush-on-call* attribute. This set signifies variables that must have a memory address within that node.

- A *use-definition* list for each variable, containing the operator identifiers of the operators in the node that either reference or define the variable's value.

The respective set member and list for a specific variable are determined from the number assigned when the variable was selected as a candidate for assignment to a register. Each set is maintained in a 32-bit variable, or bit vector.

What We Keep in a Node

Conceptually, a node represents a distinct sequence of instructions in a program. Each node holds information about a consecutive set of Intermediate Language operators. The compiler's data structure summarizing the information collected to represent a node contains:

- The operator identifiers of the first and last operator in the node (the *id_first* and *id_last* identifiers).

- A listhead for a list of all nodes in the graph that may precede the node (the predecessor list).

- A listhead for a list of all the nodes in the graph that may follow the node (the successor list).

- Set variables *(use, def, in, out,* and *ref)*, used for collecting data flow information about the variables selected as candidates for assignment to registers.

- Thirty-two listheads for the use-definition lists for each of the variables selected as candidates for register assignment. These lists contain the identifiers of all operators in the node that represent either a use or a definition of the respective variable.

- A Boolean variable, used during various graph analyses to determine if the node has been visited or not.

There are set variables and use-definition lists in each node in the graph. That is, each node of the graph carries all necessary information about each of the 32 variables that are candidates for assignment to registers. Figure 22 summarizes the information in a flow graph node.

Special Cases of Data Collection

To collect use information for the *use* set, the Optimizer scans the operator file forward looking for the occurrence of VALUE operators whose operands are REF operators referring to variables selected for register assignment. That is, if x is a variable that is a candidate for assignment to a register, the Optimizer looks for sequences of operators like the following:

```
-88    REF(x)
-89    VALUE(-88)
```

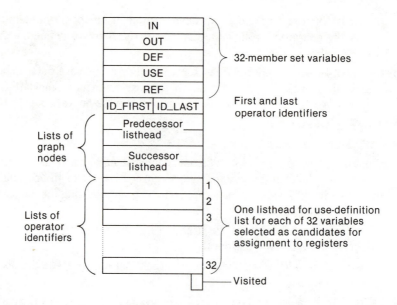

Figure 22. Data in a flow graph node.

Collecting definition information for this set entails special processing of assignment, call, and looping operators.

To obtain use information for a given variable, the Optimizer interrogates the *def* set with the variable's assigned number. If the respective member of the *def* set is false, then the respective member of the *use* set is set true; that is, the value of the variable was used in the node before it was assigned a value. The operator identifier of the VALUE operator is inserted in the appropriate list of references within the current node.

Collecting definition information entails explicit treatment of the different types of assignment operators. In each case, the Optimizer interrogates the respective member of the *use* set with the variable's assigned number. If the respective member of the *use* set is false, then the respective member of the *def* set is set true; that is, the value of the variable was defined in the node before it was used.

Loop control and call operators specifying variables passed by reference indicate both uses and definitions of their operands. In a loop control operator, the control variable is used, augmented, and then assigned a new value. The Optimizer detects the usage of the control variable in a loop control operator when it scans the operator for VALUE operators. Call operators, however, must be treated specially. If the call is to an internal procedure or from a procedure that has *flush-on-call* set, then the call is considered to be an implicit use of the values of all uplevel-addressed variables selected as candidates for register assignment. The Optimizer replaces the *ref* set with the union of the *ref* set and the *uplevel* set, thus signifying that all uplevel variables must be in memory during the execution of the node. Then the Optimizer replaces the *use* set with the set formed by taking the union of the *use* set and the intersection of the complement of the *def* set and the *uplevel* set, thus signifying that all variables that are uplevel-addressed and have not been defined in the node before being used are considered to have been used in the node before being defined.

The Optimizer scans each operand of the CALL operator to determine whether it is a reference to a variable selected for register assignment. For each such reference, it sets the *requires_storage* attribute in the variable's symbol node and sets its respective member true in the *ref* set. If the respective member in the *def* set is false, then the respective member in the *use* set is set true. Variables that are passed by reference must be in memory during execution of the node.

Assignment and loop control operators are also inserted in the appropriate list of references within the current node. The operator identifiers of these operators are inserted in the use-definition lists.

Computing the Depth-First Order

To use the completed flow graph, the Optimizer uses *depth-first ordering* as a systematic way to visit the nodes in the graph. Depth-first ordering is the reverse of the order in which the nodes were last visited in preorder traversal, and thus the Optimizer can use it to visit nodes both from the root of the graph to its outermost levels, and vice versa. The algorithm for computing depth-first order, shown in Figure 23, is taken directly from Aho and Ullman's *Principles of Compiler Design.*

Figure 24 illustrates a flow graph and indicates the depth-first ordering of the nodes in the graph.

After constructing the graph, the Optimizer first performs live variable analysis and adds this information to the nodes in the graph.

Live Variable Analysis

Live variable analysis enables the Optimizer to determine which values of variables are valid at each node in the graph. The value of a variable is said to be *live* at a point in the graph if that value is used before it is defined along some flow path emanating from the specified point in the graph. Otherwise, the value is considered to be dead because there is no further use.

Live variable analysis requires the solution of two data flow equations. The equations are solved only on the candidates for register assignment; their solutions employ the *use* and *def* sets that were collected during the building of the flow graph for a procedure or begin block.

Figure 23. Computing the depth-first order.

```
FOR index = all nodes in the graph;
        node(index).visited = FALSE;
        END;
CALL compute_depth_first(1);
        .

        .

        .

Compute_depth_first PROCEDURE(new_node) RECURSIVE;
        node(new_node).visited = TRUE;
        FOR next_node = each successor of node(new_node);
                IF node(next_node).visited = FALSE
                        THEN CALL compute_depth_first(next_node);
                END;
        depth_order(index) = new_node;
        index = index - 1;
        END;
```

The information derived from the calculations tells the Optimizer which values are live on entrance to a node and which are live on exit from a node. These two sets are called the *in* and *out* sets, respectively. The *in* set represents those variables whose values are valid on entry to a node. The *out* set represents those variables whose values are live on exit from the node. The formal equations used to calculate these sets are shown in Figure 25.

Intuitively, we can see the following relationships between the *in* and *out* sets:

- A variable's value is valid coming in to a node if it is used before being defined in that node.
- A variable's value is valid coming out of a node if it comes in to any of that node's successors.
- A variable's value is valid coming in to a node if it comes out of the node and is not defined before being used within the node.

Live variable analysis represents a backward flow problem: the Optimizer must compute what values come in to the successors of a node before it can compute its *in* and *out* sets. It therefore examines the nodes in the graph in depth-first order and computes both the *in* and *out* sets iteratively until there are no changes in the computed *out* sets. The algorithm for these computations, also taken directly from Aho and Ullman, is shown in Figure 26.

Figures 27 through 29 illustrate the operators, flow graph nodes, and the solution of the data flow equations on the variables in the following simple program:

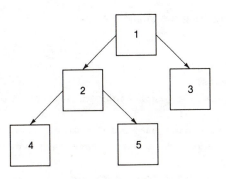

Depth-first order = 4, 5, 2, 3, 1

Figure 24. Nodes in depth-first order.

```
check: PROCEDURE (y);
DECLARE (x,y) FIXED BINARY;
    IF y > 0
        THEN x = 1;
        ELSE x = 2;
    y = x;
    RETURN;
END;
```

Figure 27 illustrates the operators; horizontal lines indicate the divisions between the nodes.

Figure 28 shows the flow graph nodes for this program.

Figure 29 shows the solutions of the data equations and the values of the bit vectors for the variable *x* in the program.

Value Propagation and Register Assignment

After performing live variable analysis for all nodes in the graph, the Optimizer begins individual processing of the variables selected as candidates for assignment to registers. First, the Optimizer computes a *region* or *subgraph*

Figure 25. Equations for live variable analysis.

OUT(node) = ∪ IN(successor-nodes)

IN(node) = OUT(node)—DEF(node) ∪ USE(node)

∪ indicates set union
— indicates set difference

Figure 26. Computing the in and out sets.

```
changes = TRUE;
DO WHILE (changes);
    changes = FALSE;
    FOR loop_index = graph nodes in depth-first order;
        new_out = null;
        FOR next_node = each successor of node(loop_index);
            new_out = new_out ∪ node(next_node).in;
            END;
    IF new_out ^= node(loop_index).out
        THEN DO;
            changes = TRUE;
            node(loop_index).out = new_out;
            node(loop_index).in = new_out -
                                node(loop_index).def ∪
                                node(loop_index).use;
        END;
    END;
END;
```

Figure 27. Operators divided into nodes.

1		check: procedure(y);	Node 1
-33	0	STATEMENT(1)	
-33	0	PROCEDURE(174,169)	
-34	0	ENTRY(CHECK)	Node 2
-35	0	END_OF_PROLOGUE	
2			
3		declare (x,y) fixed binary;	
4			
5		if y > 0	
6		then x = 1;	
-36	0	STATEMENT(6)	
-37	1	PARAM_PTR(y)	
-38	1	REF(y,0,-37)	
-39	1	VALUE(-38)	
-40	1	IMMEDIATE(0)	
-41	1	GTR(-39,-40)	
-42	0	BR_FALSE(195)	

Figure 27 *(concluded)*

-43	1	REF(x)	Node 3
-44	1	IMMEDIATE(1)	
-45	0	ASSIGN(-43,-44)	

7		else x = 2;

| -46 | 0 | STATEMENT(7) |
| -47 | 0 | BR(199) |

| | | | Node 4 |

-48	0	LABEL(195)
-49	1	REF(x)
-50	1	IMMEDIATE(2)
-51	0	ASSIGN(-49,-50)

| | | | Node 5 |

| -52 | 0 | LABEL(199) |

8		y = x;

-53	0	STATEMENT(8)
-54	1	PARAM—PTR(y)
-55	1	REF(y,0,-54)
-56	1	REF(x)
-57	1	VALUE(-56)
-58	0	ASSIGN(-55,-57)

9		return;

| -59 | 0 | STATEMENT(9) |
| -60 | 0 | RETURN |

10	end;

| -61 | 0 | STATEMENT(10) |
| -62 | 0 | BLOCK—END(169) |

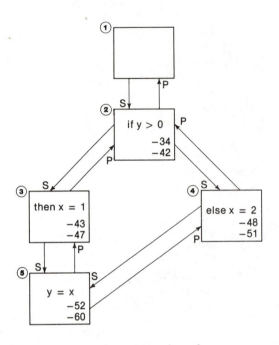

Figure 28. The flow graph of a program's nodes.

for the *instance* or a *discrete lifetime* of a variable. Then it attempts value propagation; failing that, it assigns the variable to a register temporary. If the value of the variable can be propagated over the entire region, there is no need to assign the variable to a register because value propagation effectively eliminates the particular instance of the variable from the program. If the variable's value cannot be propagated, the Optimizer assigns it to a register. The assignment is accomplished using an operator we invented specifically for this purpose: ASSIGN_REGTEMP, for Assign Variable to Register Temporary. After introducing an ASSIGN_REGTEMP for the variable into the operator file, the Optimizer replaces all references to the variable within the region with references to the ASSIGN_REGTEMP operator.

In the next subsections, we discuss how the Optimizer defines an instance of a variable, how it computes regions within the program, how it determines whether a variable's value can be propagated, and some of the mechanics of the ASSIGN_REGTEMP operator.

Computing the Instance of a Variable

An instance of a variable is defined by a set of interconnected graph nodes. The nodes at the tails of successor edges in the graph have the variable live on exit (its value comes out of the node) and the nodes at the heads of succes-

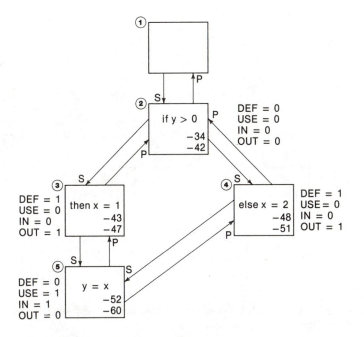

Figure 29. Bit vectors for live variable analysis.

sor edges in the graph have the variable live on entrance (its value comes in to the node). The set of nodes that form the instance or discrete lifetime of the variable is called a region. Consider the following program fragment:

```
IF y < 0
    THEN RETURN;

x = 5;
IF y = 2
    THEN DO;
    x = x + 1;
    RETURN;
    END;

x = y;
IF x > 4
    THEN x = x + 1;
    ELSE x = x - 1;
```

Assume that this program has a single variable, *x*, that is a candidate for assignment to a register. Figure 30 illustrates the flow graph for this program fragment. The first assignment shown above, *x*=5, occurs in node 2.

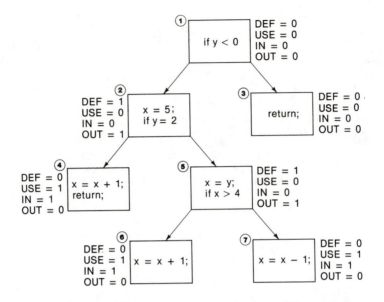

Figure 30. Flow graph for a program containing a register temporary.

Two regions in the graph describe discrete lifetimes of the variable. One is the set of nodes 2 and 4; the other is the set 5, 6, and 7. Nodes 1 and 3 do not use or define the variable's value and thus are not part of a region.

The Optimizer computes regions by examining nodes in reverse depth-first order, starting with the initial node. For each node, it computes the set of variables that are used, defined, or that come out of the node. Using the bit vectors that correspond to these sets, we express this computation as:

use_or_def = def(node) ∪ use(node) ∪ out(node)

(We include the *use* and *out* sets, even though they might not be expected to play a part in this computation, in order to take into account programs that use the value of a variable before the variable is defined.)

The Optimizer now scans the resulting set, looking for true entries. If there are none, it simply moves to the next node in reverse depth-first order. The bit number of a true entry specifies the index into the array of symbol node identifiers for variables selected for assignment to registers. It is also used to interrogate members of the *in* and *out* sets of subsequent nodes.

Finding a true entry signals the start of a region for a discrete instance of a variable. The current node becomes the first node in the list of nodes that form the region, and the true entry is cleared in the *use_or_def* set. The minimum and maximum operator identifiers are recorded from the current node, a Boolean variable called *cycles* is initialized to false, and a Boolean variable called *referenced* is initialized from the variable's member (specified by the bit number) of the current node's *ref* set. The Optimizer also initializes a set called *node_visited,* a bit vector that has a member for each node in the graph for the block. The bit vector is initialized so that the only true member is the one corresponding to the first node in the region.

If the value of the variable comes out of the current node, then the Optimizer searches all the successors of the current node. Each time it finds a successor that the variable's value comes in to, the Optimizer performs the following operations:

1. Adds that successor node to the region list

2. Sets true its member in the *node_visited* set

3. Updates the minimum and maximum operator identifiers to keep track of the minimum and maximum identifiers in the region

4. Computes the union of all members of the *ref* sets for the variable across the region in *referenced*

5. Checks the graph for cycles (any backward branch along any flow path in the region)

6. If a cycle is detected, indicating a backward branch in the region to a node that has already been visited, sets the variable *cycles* to true.

Next, the Optimizer searches the predecessors of each successor node that was added to the region list for nodes that the variable's value comes out of. Both predecessors and successors are searched recursively until no more can be added to the region list. During this recursive search, the Optimizer continually interrogates the respective member in the *node_visited* set to ensure visiting each node only once during the recursive search.

As it adds each node to the region list, the Optimizer sets the respective *in, out, def,* and *use* members false for the variable in question. This ensures that the node will not also be added to another region for the same variable. Figure 31 illustrates a subgraph list for the variable *x,* whose operators and flow graphs are shown in Figures 27 through 29.

Value Propagation

Very simply, value propagation is the elimination of local variables by replacing references to them with references to their assigned values. As an example,

```
a = b;
c = a;
```

can be reduced to

```
c = b;
```

without losing meaning. (We could do this for any automatic variable that does

NOTES: 19-MAR-80   Pg 1

Computing the list of nodes that are sure to
be executed.

1. Compute the dominators of all the nodes in
   the loop

2. Starting at the bottom of the loop construct
   the list of dominators backward to the loop
   ~~body~~ node. If the loop ~~body~~ node does not
   dominate the loop bottom node, then there
   is no flow of control to the end of the loop
   and the loop is ignored.

3. Starting with the node headed by the
   loop ~~body~~ operator repeat the following
   algorithm

   a. Scan the current block backward
      starting at the position indicated
      by the operator of last operator in the
      block and attempt to remove invariants.
      The scan is continued backward ~~until~~
      until the starting operator id of the block
      is greater than the operator id of
      the operator under consideration.

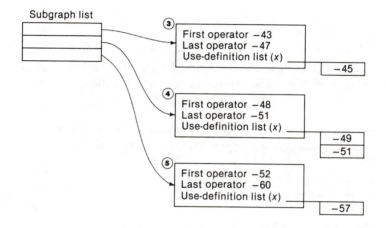

Figure 31. A subgraph for a variable selected for assignment to a register.

not require storage—not just the candidates for register assignment—but we do not do so because we think that 32 is a realistic number of variables. Furthermore, we would have to collect all the flow graph information about all the extra variables as well.)

After completely isolating a region, the Optimizer has the following information about it:

- A list of the nodes in the region
- The minimum and maximum operator identifiers that lexically define the region
- Whether there are cycles in the region
- Whether the value of the variable must be in memory for any part of the region.

If the variable must be in memory, then it is not eligible for either value propagation or assignment to a register. The original REF operators are left in place and the *requires_storage* attribute is set in the variable's Symbol Table node so that the Storage Allocator will allocate storage for the variable even though its *register_temporary* attribute is also set. (Registers do not have memory addresses, and a propagated value would have to be explicitly materialized in memory by the addition of an operator.)

The Optimizer next computes the following information:

- The operator identifier of the last definition within the first node of the region
- Whether multiple definitions exist within the region (multiple definitions in the first node do not count)

- Whether there is a data type mismatch among uses and definitions of the variable (as when a variable is the target of a PL/I UNSPEC built-in function, in which a variable is interpreted as a bit string).

Using this information, the Optimizer determines whether value propagation can be performed. The determination is made using the following test:

```
IF
    the first node in the region contains the minimum
    operator identifier (that is, it is lexically first)
    AND
    the first entry in the use-definition chain points
    to an assignment operator
    AND
    the compiler option DEBUG=SYMBOLS is not selected
    AND
    no type mismatch is detected
    THEN
    value propagation can be performed
```

The rules underlying this test are as follows:

- The first node in the region must contain the lexically first occurrence of the value to be propagated, because a propagated value must have an operator identifier that is greater than all its uses. (In the operator file, all operands must appear lexically before the operator that uses them; because the operator identifiers are negative, the operand identifiers therefore have higher numeric value.)
- The existence of an assignment operator indicates that there is a value to be propagated.
- A user debugging a program needs to be able to display the values of all variables so we must not eliminate any of them.
- The maintenance of data type information is necessary to preclude later generation of erroneous code.

Value propagation can always be performed on the first node in the graph up to the last definition point within that node, as long as all the tests listed above hold true. If other nodes in the region contain definitions of the value, or if there are cycles and the value being propagated is not a constant, then value propagation ends at this point.

As values are propagated, the Optimizer removes entries from the use-definition lists. If values can be propagated over the entire region, there will be no references or assignments left in the region. However, if the value of a variable cannot be propagated or is only partially propagated, the remaining

Notes: 13-Nov-8∅   Pg'

Value propagation Rules

1. Value propagation can always be performed
   on the first basic block of a slice. The
   last definition is not propagatable unless)
   1. there are no other definitions in the slice
      i.e. definitions = false

   2. the last assignment operand is an integer
      and there are or are not cycles in the
      graph

   this implies a variable that holds the
   index of the last definition

   cycles is computed by search successor and
   search predecessor and occurs when the
   graph loops back on itself.

2. if value propagation cannot be performed
   on the entire slice, then the generation
   of an assign register temp must be performed.

references to the variable can be assigned to a register temporary. Figure 32 illustrates operators before and after value propagation.

Assignment of Variables to Register Temporaries

If the Optimizer cannot propagate the value of a variable that has been selected as a candidate for assignment to a register, it takes all the information it has about the variable and writes this into the operator file using an ASSIGN_REGTEMP operator. This operator tells the Local Code Generator to create a temporary to hold the value of the variable; we call this temporary a *register temporary,* or a *T-reg.*

The first step in assigning variables to T-regs is to find a free operator identifier that lexically precedes the minimum operator identifier of the region. The Optimizer can easily locate free operator identifiers by looking for null pointers in the pointer array. There are 32 null pointers to start with (initially reserved by the front end). As value propagation and register assignment proceed, more and more operator identifiers become available as the Optimizer eliminates reference operators.

Figure 32.   Effect of value propagation on operators.

Before optimization	Initial transformation	After value propagation
5 x = y;	5 x = y;	5 x = y;
-37 STATEMENT(5)	-37 STATEMENT(5)	-37 STATEMENT(5)
-38 REF(x)		
-39 PARAM_PTR(y)	-39 PARAM_PTR(y)	-39 PARAM_PTR(y)
-40 REF(y,0,-39)	-40 REF(y,0,-39)	-40 REF(y,0,-39)
-41 VALUE(-40)	-41 VALUE(-40)	-41 VALUE(-40)
-42 ASSIGN(-38,-41)	-42 SAVE_RESULT(-41)	-42 SAVE_RESULT(-41)
6 z = x*2;	6 z = x*2;	6 z = x*2;
-43 STATEMENT(6)	-43 STATEMENT(6)	-43 STATEMENT(6)
-44 REF(z)		
-45 REF(x)		
-46 VALUE(-45)	-46 USE(-42)	
-47 IMMEDIATE(2)	-47 IMMEDIATE(2)	-47 IMMEDIATE(2)
-48 MULTIPLY(-46,-47)	-48 MULTIPLY(-46,-47)	-48 MULTIPLY(-42,-47)
-49 ASSIGN(-44,-48)	-49 USE(-48)	
7 RETURN(z);	7 RETURN(z);	7 RETURN(z);
-50 STATEMENT(7)	-50 STATEMENT(7)	-50 STATEMENT(7)
-51 REF(z)		
-52 VALUE(-51)	-52 USE(-49)	
-53 RETURN(-52)	-53 RETURN(-52)	-53 RETURN(-48)

An ASSIGN_REGTEMP operator has the following operands:

- The first operand contains the Symbol Table node identifier of the variable whose value is to be held in a T-reg. The symbol node identifier is obtained by indexing the array of symbol node identifiers using the bit number of the variable that was determined when the *use_or_def* bit vector was scanned.

- The second and third operands are negated operator identifiers of the minimum and maximum operator identifiers of the region and thus define the lexical span of the program over which the value must be retained in the register.

- The fourth operand is zero. We do not use this operand but have reserved it for future use by compilers that want to use it to hold a register number (say to provide explicit register assignment).

After allocating the operator node and setting the operands in the ASSIGN_-REGTEMP operator, the Optimizer sets its identifier to that of the free operator and fills in the corresponding position in the pointer array with the address of the allocated ASSIGN_REGTEMP operator.

Next, the Optimizer examines the use-definition lists of all nodes in the region, replacing the operand in each VALUE operator that references the variable with a reference to the new ASSIGN_REGTEMP operator. Similarly, all targets of assignments and all ADD_COMPARE_AND_BRANCH operators are replaced with the operator identifier of the ASSIGN_REGTEMP operator. The Optimizer decrements the reference count of the REF operators previously used as operands as it replaces the references; if a reference count reaches zero, the Optimizer releases the operator by zeroing its pointer in the pointer array, thus freeing its operator identifier for use with an ASSIGN_REGTEMP operator. This process continues until all regions of the graph have been explored. Figure 33 illustrates the operators from Figure 27 after introduction of the ASSIGN_REGTEMP operator. The ASSIGN_REGTEMP introduced with an identifier of −2 is referenced in operators −45, −51, and −57. Its span is set to include all the nodes containing these three operators. Previous REF operators (−43, −49, and −56) denoting the variable have been removed.

Loop Invariant Removal

The purpose of loop invariant removal is to move outside of a loop all invariant computations that lie on a path of certain execution in the loop. To explain how the Optimizer performs this, we must review both the manner in which the Intermediate Language represents loops and our concept of the limit of an operator; we must also describe the computation of dominators. At this point in the compilation, the Optimizer also uses the information it now

Figure 33. Operators changed by assignment of locals to registers.

1		check: procedure(y);

-33	0	STATEMENT(1)
-1	0	PROCEDURE(174,169)
-2	3	ASSIGN__REGTEMP(x,43,60,0)
-34	0	ENTRY(CHECK)
-35	0	END__OF__PROLOGUE

2		
3		declare (x,y) fixed binary;
4		
5		if y > 0
6		then x = 1;

-36	0	STATEMENT(6)
-37	1	PARAM__PTR(y)
-38	1	REF(y,0,-37)
-39	1	VALUE(-38)
-40	1	IMMEDIATE(0)
-41	1	BR__LE(195,-39,-40)
-44	1	IMMEDIATE(1)
-45	0	ASSIGN(-2,-44)

7		else x = 2;

-46	0	STATEMENT(7)
-47	0	BR(199)
-48	0	LABEL(195)
-50	1	IMMEDIATE(2)
-51	0	ASSIGN(-2,-50)
-52	0	LABEL(199)

8		y = x;

-53	0	STATEMENT(8)
-54	1	PARAM__PTR(y)
-55	1	REF(y,0,-54)
-57	1	VALUE(-2)
-58	0	ASSIGN(-38,-57)

Figure 33 *(concluded)*

9		return;
-59	0	STATEMENT(9)
-60	0	RETURN

10	end;	
-61	0	STATEMENT(10)
-62	0	BLOCK__END(169)

has to see if conditions are right for an additional optimization, a strength reduction in which an addressing computation is replaced by a shorter, faster computation.

Loop Representation in the Intermediate Language

The general form of a loop is shown in Figure 34. This representation of loops lets the Optimizer move all invariant computations to a point just preceding the LOOP_TOP operator. The operands of the LOOP_BOTTOM operator are the identifiers of all operators whose values are being held until the end of the loop. (This includes the invariants that were removed from the loop as well as the SAVE_RESULT operators described in Chapter 6.)

It is important to remember that the limit of an operator is the identifier of the most recent definition point of any of its operands. In invariant removal, if the limit of an operator lies within a loop, the operator (or one of its operands) is defined within the loop and therefore cannot be invariant.

Computation of Loop Dominators

When the Optimizer enters its loop invariant removal phase, it first computes the dominators for the entire flow graph. A *dominator* of a node in the graph is a node that is always executed prior to execution of the node being dominated. The algorithm (derived from Aho and Ullman) used to compute the dominators of the nodes in the graph is shown in Figure 35. For each node in the graph, there exists a set of all other nodes which dominate the given node.

Scanning the Operators to Remove Invariants

The Optimizer performs loop invariant removal in a single forward pass through the operators. During this scan, it computes definition points for variables and the limits of all operators that are considered immovable (such as DATE and TIME operators). The limits of these operators are their respective identifiers. At the same time, the Optimizer looks for the loop control operators. When it encounters a LOOP_TOP operator, it saves the current loop status and initializes variables to hold the new loop state. When it encounters the

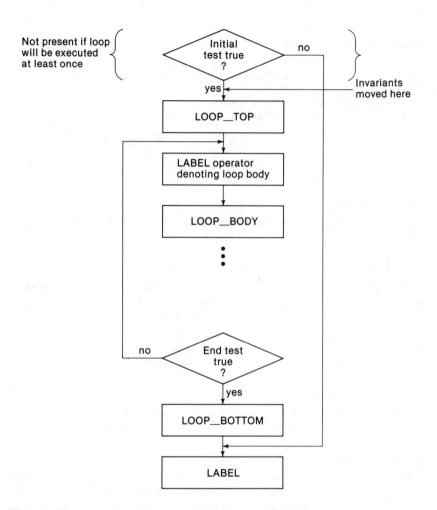

Figure 34.   Intermediate Language representation of loops.

bottom of a loop, it does a backward scan within the loop, computing the limits of all the operators inside the loop to see if they can be moved outside it.

Because the scan is occurring backward, entire trees of operators may be moved. For each operator that it moves, the Optimizer increments the operator's reference count and adds its identifier to the list of operands of the LOOP_BOTTOM operator so that its value will be held until the end of the loop. When the backward scan is complete, the state of the next outer loop is unstacked and the forward scan resumes. This procedure guarantees scanning from the inner loops outward. When it encounters nested loops, the Optimizer always examines and removes invariants from the innermost loop outward, thus allowing invariants to migrate to the farthest possible outward

Figure 35. Computation of loop dominators.

```
FOR index = all nodes in the graph;
    node(index).dominators = set of all nodes;
    END;
node(1).dominators = set of initial node;
changes = TRUE;
DO WHILE (changes);
    changes = FALSE;
    FOR next_node = all graph nodes in depth-first order;
        new_dominators = node(next_node).dominators;
        FOR last_node = each predecessor of node(next_node);
            new_dominators = new_dominators ∩
                                node(last_node).dominators;
            END;
        new_dominators = new_dominators ∪ set of next_node;
        IF new_dominators ^= node(next_node).dominators
            THEN DO;
                changes = true;
                node (next_node).dominators = new_dominators;
                END;
        END;
    END;
```

point. Only nodes within the loop that are certain to be executed if the loop is executed are considered for removal of invariant computations. This set of nodes (called *exit dominators*) is computed by taking the intersection of the dominators of all nodes in the loop that cause control to leave the loop and the node that contains the LOOP_BOTTOM operator. In other words, it is the set of nodes that dominate all exits from the loop (those that are sure to be executed before any exit from the loop can occur).

The Optimizer visits all nodes in the loop, starting with the LOOP_BODY node. It scans each node backward, checking first for array references that can be changed to based references with constant offsets (this is a shorter address specifier than for context indexing) and, second, for invariant computations. An invariant computation must also lie within a node that is contained within the exit set (the set of exit dominators) before the computation is considered for removal from the loop. The entire operator tree of the invariant computation is moved to a point just before the LOOP_TOP operator. As the Optimizer moves the tree, it shuffles pointers in the pointer array and updates the position array. Array references that can be replaced are changed to a based reference, which is the base address of the array that was previously moved when the LOOP_BOTTOM operator was discovered (see below). This process continues until all loops in the block have been examined. When one loop is finished, the forward scan continues.

Autoincrement and Autodecrement Addressing

After scanning a loop forward and just before beginning the backward scan, the Optimizer generates AUTO_INCREMENT and AUTO_DECREMENT operators, if possible. These Intermediate Language operators are produced by the Optimizer in an attempt to reduce the addressing requirements of arrays that are referenced in loops. The Optimizer determines that this optimization is possible if all of the following are true:

- The loop control variable has a data type of integer.
- The loop increment is +1 or −1.
- The loop control variable is not reassigned within the loop.
- There is an array reference of the form $a(i)$ in the loop compare node (the node within the loop that contains the end test) and the loop increment is +1 (or the same reference occurs in the loop body node and the increment is −1), and i is the control variable of the loop. This test ensures that the variable reference lies on a path of certain execution for each complete loop iteration and that the reference is either the first or the last reference to the variable within the loop.
- The array, $a,$ has a data type of floating point, integer, or pointer.
- The offset units of the variable offset match the context of the reference.
- The array has not already had its base address moved outside the loop.

If all these requirements are met, the Optimizer moves the base address of the array reference out of the loop and makes the actual reference to an AUTO_INCREMENT or AUTO_DECREMENT operator. This process can be thought as a special invariant removal in which the address of the first element of the array to be accessed is moved out of the loop. In reality, it is an addressing mode strength reduction in which the addressing mode normally used to access successive array elements (indexed) is replaced by a shorter and faster addressing mode (autoincrement or autodecrement).

The Optimizer selects the candidate reference operators by scanning forward from the first node in the loop (if the loop increment is −1) or backward from the loop-compare node (if the loop increment is +1). The direction of the scan reflects the way in which the VAX-11 autoincrement and autodecrement addressing modes work.

Autodecrement is a predecrement and therefore must occur on the first reference to the array within the loop. Autoincrement is a postincrement and therefore must occur on the last reference to the array within the loop. Each trip through the loop causes successive elements of the array to be addressed in either a forward or backward direction. Only one reference to a specific array will be converted to one of these operators. All other references to the same array within the loop are replaced with a reference to the base address that was moved out of the loop, since it is the base address that is automatically incremented or decremented. The result is a further address strength reduction for the references that were not the first or last within the loop. The following example uses the autodecrement case:

```
autodec: PROCEDURE(sum);

DECLARE   i FIXED BINARY(31),
          a(0:100) FLOAT BINARY(24),
          sum FLOAT BINARY(24);

          DO i = 99 TO 1 BY -1;
          sum = sum + a(i-1) * a(i+1);
          END;

END;
```

In this example, the array *a* is indexed with a loop increment of –1. The operators generated by the front end for this program would be as shown in Figure 36.

Figure 36. Operators for an array indexed within a loop.

1		autodec: procedure(sum);
-33	0	STATEMENT(1)
-33	0	PROCEDURE(175,170)
-34	0	ENTRY(AUTODEC)
-35	0	END__OF__PROLOGUE
2		
3		declare i fixed binary(31),
4		a(0:100) float binary(24),
5		sum float binary(24);
6		
7		do i = 99 to 1 by -1;
-36	0	STATEMENT(7)
-37	1	REF(i)
-38	2	IMMEDIATE(99)
-39	0	ASSIGN(-37,-38)
-40	0	LOOP__TOP(1,-38)
-41	0	LABEL(210)
-42	0	LOOP__BODY(1)

Figure 36 *(concluded)*

8		sum = sum + a(i-1) * a(i+1);

-43	0	STATEMENT(8)
-44	1	PARAM__PTR(175,1)
-45	1	REF(sum,0,-44)
-46	1	PARAM__PTR(175,1)
-47	1	REF(sum,0,-46)
-48	1	VALUE(-47)
-49	1	IMMEDIATE(-4)
-50	1	REF(i)
-51	1	VALUE(-50)
-52	1	ADD__OFFSET(-49,-51)
-53	1	REF(a,-52)
-54	1	VALUE(-53)
-55	1	IMMEDIATE(4)
-56	1	REF(i)
-57	1	VALUE(-56)
-58	1	ADD__OFFSET(-55,-57)
-59	1	REF(a,-58)
-60	1	VALUE(-59)
-61	1	MULTIPLY(-54,-60)
-62	1	ADD(-48,-61)
-63	0	ASSIGN(-45,-62)

9		end;

-64	0	STATEMENT(9)
-65	2	REF(i)
-66	1	VALUE(-65)
-67	1	IMMEDIATE(-1)
-68	1	IMMEDIATE(1)
-69	0	ADD__COMPARE__AND__BRANCH(-65,-66,-67,-68,210)
-70	0	LOOP__BOTTOM(1)
-71	0	LABEL(214)

10		end;

-72	0	STATEMENT(10)
-73	0	BLOCK__END(170)

NOTES: 28-OCT-80 Pg 1

Removing base addresses from loops

(revised) The loop top operator of a loop must identify
the control variable of the loop. The control
variable should only be identified for loops
whose initial value is known and its by
value is 1. The forms a monotonic increasing
or decreasing control variable value.

There must be no definition point of the control
variable within the loop other than at the
increment/decrement test operator (i.e. at
the add compare and branch operator). This
can be easily ascertained by recording the
id of the add compare operator in the
loop bottom operator.

Only addresses of connected arrays may be
removed from loops. For now only consider
one dimensional arrays so that double
removal from loops is never performed.

As the Optimizer scans the operators forward, it is interrupted by the LOOP_BOTTOM (−70). The occurrence of this operator causes the Optimizer to start scanning the loop body beginning at the first node in the loop (−42) in order to look for possible candidates for conversion to AUTO_DECREMENT operators. The first array reference it encounters is the MULTIPLY (−61), which refers to the value *a(i−1)*. Because all criteria for conversion to an AUTO_- DECREMENT operator are met, the REF (−53) is converted to an AUTO_DECRE- MENT operator. To do this, the Optimizer generates an ADDR_BASE operator that refers to the original REF operator (−53). Then it removes the variable part of the ADD_OFFSET operator referenced by this REF and adjusts the constant part so that it refers to the next to last element of the array. The variable part is no longer needed because it is a reference to the loop control variable. The ADDR_BASE, REF, ADD_OFFSET, and IMMEDIATE operators are resequenced (that is, their identifiers are changed) and the resulting operator tree is moved outside the loop. (See the operators with identifiers 49, 50, 51, and 52 in the optimized operators shown in Figure 37; the positive identifiers represent the loop invariant values.) The first time through the loop, the VALUE operator (−53) will refer to *a(98)*, the second time to *a(97)*, and so on.

Whenever a base address is moved out of a loop, the Optimizer makes an entry in a table listing references that have been removed from the loop. Further attempts to remove a reference to the same array will fail. Thus, when the VALUE operator (−60) is discovered, it will not be converted to an auto- decrement reference because the array *a* has already had its base address moved outside the loop.

The Optimizer uses the same table information during its backward scan of the loop to remove invariant computations. At this time, it transforms other references to the same array to references to the ADDR_BASE operator. The array reference must be identical in form to the original reference; only the constant part can be different. The Optimizer adjusts the constant part of the ADD_OFFSET operator of such a reference and eliminates the variable part (the reference to the loop control variable). Thus, the REF (−60) to the value of *a(i+1)* will be converted to a based reference to the ADDR_BASE operator (52). The ADD_OFFSET operator is modified so that its constant part is 8 (that is, two elements forward in the array from the base address), and the variable reference to the loop control variable *i* is eliminated.

Figure 37 shows the optimized operators (the AUTO_DECREMENT operator is at identifier −53). The generated code follows in Figure 38.

Common Subexpression Elimination

The purpose of eliminating common subexpressions is to remove redundancy in the operators. Thus, this optimization includes not only the removal of common subexpressions but also removal of any operator that is equivalent

Figure 37. Introduction of autodecrement addressing.

1		autodec: procedure(sum);

-33	0	STATEMENT(1)
-1	0	PROCEDURE(175,170)
-33	5	ASSIGN__REGTEMP(i,34,69,0)
-34	0	ENTRY(autodec)
-35	0	END__OF__PROLOGUE

2		
3		declare i fixed binary(31),
4		a(0:100) float binary(24),
5		sum float binary(24);
6		
7		do i = 99 to 1 by -1;

-36	0	STATEMENT(7)
-38	2	IMMEDIATE(99)
-39	0	ASSIGN(-33,-38)
49	1	IMMEDIATE(396)
50	1	ADD__OFFSET(-49,0)
51	1	REF(a,-50)
52	3	ADDR__BASE(-51)
68	2	IMMEDIATE(1)
67	2	IMMEDIATE(-1)
55	1	IMMEDIATE(8)
58	2	ADD__OFFSET(-55,0)
46	1	PARAM__PTR(175,1)
47	3	REF(sum,0,-46)
-40	0	LOOP__TOP(1,-38)
-41	0	LABEL(210)
-42	0	LOOP__BODY(1)

8		sum = sum + a(i-1) * a(i+1);

-43	0	STATEMENT(8)
-48	1	VALUE(-47)
-53	1	AUTO__DECREMENT(a,0,-52)
-54	1	VALUE(-53)
-59	1	REF(a,-58,-52)
-60	1	VALUE(-59)
-61	1	MULTIPLY(-54,-60)
-63	0	ADD(-48,-61,-47)

Figure 37 *(concluded)*

9		end;

```
-64            0    STATEMENT(9)
-66            1    VALUE(-33)
-69            0    ADD_COMPARE_AND_BRANCH(-33,-66,-67,-68,210)
-70            0    LOOP_BOTTOM(1,-47,0,-58,-67,-68,-52)
```

10		end;

```
-72            0    STATEMENT(10)
 73            0    BLOCK_END(170)
```

Figure 38. Optimized code using autodecrement addressing.

1	autodec: procedure(sum);

```
AUTODEC:
        .entry  AUTODEC,<r2>
        movab   -404(sp),sp
```

2		
3	1	declare i fixed binary(31),
4	1	a(0:100) float binary(24),
5	1	sum float binary(24);
6	1	
7	1	do i = 99 to 1 by -1;

```
        movzbl   #99,r2
```

NOTE   The address of *a(99)* is computed outside the loop and held in Register 1.

```
        moval    -08(fp),r1
    vcg.1:
```

8	2	sum = sum + a(i-1) * a(i+1);

NOTE   The element *a(i-1)* is addressed by the autodecrement reference –(R1). The element *a(i+1)* is addressed by the based reference 8(R1).

Figure 38 *(concluded)*

```
mulf3    -(r1),08(r1),r0
addf2    r0,@04(ap)
```

9	2	end;

```
sobgtr   r2,vcg.1
```

10	1	end;

```
ret
```

to another. For example, if the Optimizer detects REF or VALUE operators that are absolutely equivalent, it removes the redundant operator and updates references to it.

Eliminating common subexpressions really involves two distinct steps: path formation, followed by redundancy elimination. The objective is to scan the graph in depth-first order, develop the longest unique backward flow path, and then scan that path forward, looking for redundant computations. Consider the flow graph in Figure 39 and the three indicated unique backward flow paths through the nodes.

Paths start only with nodes that have not already been visited. (Initially, all nodes are marked "not visited.") Once started, however, a path may include nodes previously visited. A node is considered to have been visited if it was included in a previous path list.

Optimization for the paths shown in Figure 39 would occur in reverse order; that is, nodes 1, 2, 3, and 4 in path 1 would be optimized in that order; nodes 1, 2, 3, and 5 in path 2, in that order; and 1, 2, and 6 in path 3, in that order. As the Optimizer scans the operators in the nodes in a flow path, it tries to reduce identical value-producing operators to a single operator. (Only operators with fixed-length results are eligible for this optimization because operators whose results are variable length must be allocated on the stack.)

As it considers each value-producing operator, the Optimizer computes its limit and a hash table index. The limit is as described for loop invariant removal and is the operator identifier of the most recent operator that defined a value upon which the current operator depends. The Optimizer computes the hash table index by adding the operator opcode to the sum of its operands and truncating the value to the size of the hash table.

The hash table index is used to select a list of operators that could contain an equivalent operator (this is the only list that can contain an equivalent operator). Because the list is in LIFO order, the first operator is the one most recently put in the table; so sorting occurs in ascending order of operator

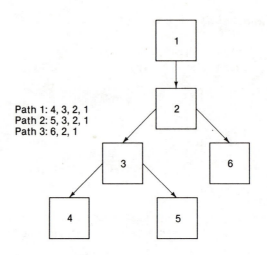

Path 1: 4, 3, 2, 1
Path 2: 5, 3, 2, 1
Path 3: 6, 2, 1

Figure 39. Determining unique backward flow.

identifier, with the most negative at the front of the list. By comparing the limit of the current operator with the operator identifier of the next entry in the list, the Optimizer can immediately tell whether a match is possible without examining any more entries in the list.

For a match to exist, the operators must match bit for bit on operands, data type, size, and opcode. Moreover, the operator identifier of the matching operator must be less than the limit of the current operator (that is, it lexically follows the limit).

If a match occurs, the Optimizer replaces the current operator with a USE operator. This operator signifies that its value is really the value produced by a previous operator, an operator already on the list. The reference count of the current operator is added to the reference count of the operator in the list. The reference counts of all the operands of the current operator are decremented; if the count goes to zero, the Optimizer deletes the operands by zeroing their respective entries in the pointer array. If a match does not occur, the operator is entered in the appropriate hash list in LIFO order. A mismatch is considered to have occurred if the operator identifier of the next entry in the list is greater than the limit of the current operator (that is, it lexically precedes the limit).

In addition, if the node that is currently being scanned has been scanned previously, the Optimizer computes the hash indexes of the operators and enters the operators directly in the hash table in LIFO order; the Optimizer already knows that there are no identical operators or it would have already found one. Consider the program fragment

```
p = a + b;
q = a + b;
```

and its corresponding operators:

```
-20   1     REF(p)
-21   1     REF(a)
-22   1     VALUE(-21)
-23   1     REF(b)
-24   1     VALUE(-23)
-25   1     ADD(-22,-24)
-26   0     ASSIGN(-20,-25)

-27   1     REF(q)
-28   1·    REF(a)
-29   1     VALUE(-28)
-30   1     REF(b)
-31   1     VALUE(-30)
-32   1     ADD(-29,-31)
-33   0     ASSIGN(-27,-32)
```

At the point in the scan just past the first ASSIGN (–26), the hash table and its entries might appear as shown in Figure 40 (the ASSIGN operator is not in the hash table because the hash table contains only value-producing operators).

The next operator is:

```
-27   1     REF(q)
```

Suppose this operator hashes to index 5 in the hash table. There is no limit for REF operators that do not reference any values, because the reference yields

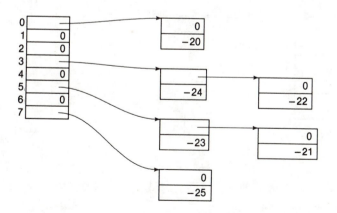

Figure 40. Hash table for eliminating common subexpressions.

only the address of the variable which is constant. Thus we have a value-producing operator with a limit of 0 and a hash index of 5.

The Optimizer now starts searching the list whose listhead is at position 5 in the hash table. The operator identifier of the first operator (–23) is less than the limit, so it compares the operators. The comparison fails, so it moves to the next entry in the list. The operator identifier is –21, which is also less than the limit, so the Optimizer compares the operators. The comparison again fails, so it tries the next entry in the list and finds the list is empty. Thus, the Optimizer must insert the current operator at the head of the list. The result is the modified hash table shown in Figure 41.

The next operator is:

```
-28     1     REF(a)
```

The hash index is computed and turns out to be 5. The scan starts with –27 and finally finds a match at –21, which is an identical operator. The –21 operator is changed to:

```
-21     2     REF(a)
```

That is, its reference count is incremented. The current operator is changed to:

```
-28     1     USE(-21)
```

This operator signifies "the value of this operator is really operator –21." Because the Optimizer has already identified the operator –28 as being identical to another and therefore one it can eliminate, it does not have to add a new entry to the hash table.

The next entry is:

```
-29     1     VALUE(-28)
```

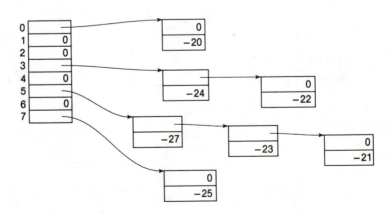

Figure 41. Modified hash table.

Remember that the limit of a value of a variable is the identifier of the operator that last explicitly or implicitly assigned a value to the variable. Because we are dealing with a small program fragment, we will assume that the assignment to *p* did not implicitly cause an assignment to *a* or *b* and that therefore their limits are before the program fragment.

First, the Optimizer replaces the USE operator reference with a reference to its operand, which is –21. Thus, the VALUE operator becomes

```
-29    1    VALUE(-21)
```

with a limit that is greater than –21. As before, the Optimizer computes a hash index, which turns out to be 3. Searching the list, the Optimizer finds that operator –22 matches; thus, –29 becomes:

```
-29    1    USE(-22)
```

The Optimizer continues the process until it ends up with the operators:

```
-20    1    REF(p)
-21    1    REF(a)
-22    1    VALUE(-21)
-23    1    REF(b)
-24    1    VALUE(-23)
-25    2    ADD(-22,-24)
-26    0    ASSIGN(-20,-25)
-27    1    REF(q)
-33    0    ASSIGN(-27,-25)
```

The thoroughness of this removal algorithm increases as the lengths of the flow paths increase; that is, the more nodes that can be looked at in a single path, the better. In most programs, control flow is most often altered in structured ways. Therefore, the Optimizer extends the flow paths if, during backward flow analysis, it recognizes the traditional programming constructions:

- IF-THEN
- IF-THEN-ELSE
- CASE.

Figure 42 illustrates the flow graphs for these constructs.

To build the backward flow path, the Optimizer uses the following rules:

1. If the backward flow is unique, it inserts the positive value of the node number in the flow path list.

2. If the backward flow is nonunique, it inserts the negative value of the node number in the flow path list.

3. A flow path always starts and ends with a positive node number.

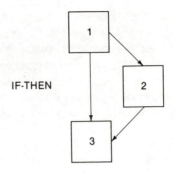

IF-THEN

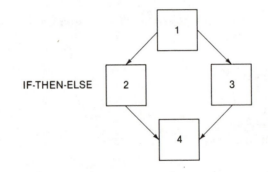

IF-THEN-ELSE

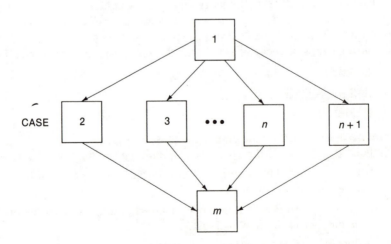

CASE

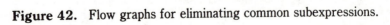

Figure 42. Flow graphs for eliminating common subexpressions.

Thus, the three special cases yield the following paths:

path 1 = 3, −2, 1
path 2 = 4, −3, −2, 1
path 3 = m, −n+1, −n, . . . , −3, −2, 1

These paths are, of course, scanned in reverse order.

To process these more complicated backward flow structures, we introduced additional data structures:

- An array to save the definition point array
- An array to save the hash table, which is really a set of list heads of LIFO lists
- A set variable to record which variables have been defined
- Four variables to save the alias, uplevel, static, and external class definition point values and four corresponding Boolean variables that indicate whether these classes have been defined.

When it first scans a flow path forward (that is, the list of nodes), the Optimizer clears the definition point array, the hash table, the limit array, the last node number, and the definition points for the alias, uplevel, static, and external class variables. It then begins examining nodes in order, making the following decisions:

1. If the next node number is positive and the last node number was also positive, then the previous node was on a unique backward flow path and the next node can be optimized using the current values of the pertinent variables (that is, it removes common subexpressions as described above).

2. If the last node number was positive and the next node number is negative, then the previous node is on a nonunique backward flow path from the next node. This represents a transition from a unique flow to a nonunique flow. The Optimizer saves the definition point array and the hash table, sets the entire *def* set to false, and saves the *alias, uplevel, static,* and *external* class variables. In effect, it saves its current state so that it can tell what changed. Using the current values, it optimizes the node.

3. If the last node number was negative and the next node number is negative, then the next node also represents a nonunique backward flow path. The Optimizer resets the definition point array and the hash table, using the information saved when decision 2 occurred, and then optimizes the node.

4. If the last node number was negative and the next node number is positive, then the next node again represents unique backward flow. The Optimizer scans the set that signifies which variables were defined

within the nonunique flow region. Each true variable represents a definition that occurred in the nonunique region; therefore, the Optimizer sets its corresponding entry in the definition point array to the starting operator identifier of the next node. The Optimizer then resets the hash table from the saved information and optimizes the node.

An IF-THEN-ELSE construct can serve as an example for the rules above. The flow graph is shown in Figure 43.

The flow path in this example is 1, –2, –3, and 4. In scanning the nodes and eliminating redundant operators, the Optimizer would apply these rules:

1. Rule 1 (positive to positive) is applied to node 1: initialize the state variables and optimize the node.

2. Rule 2 (positive to negative) is applied to node 2: save the current state variables and optimize the node.

3. Rule 3 (negative to negative) is applied to node 3: restore the state to what it was at the end of node 1 and optimize node 3.

4. Rule 4 (negative to positive) is applied to node 4: restore the hash table to its state following the optimization of node 1, set definition points for variables that were defined in the nonunique backward flow region, and optimize node 4.

During these steps, the hash table reflects only those operators that are eligible for comparison and hence removal if they are found to be equivalent. In this example, the operators in node 4 are eligible for comparison only with the operators in node 1. Even if there were redundant operators in nodes 2 and 3, those nodes would already have been optimized by the time node 4 is scanned.

The fact that the hash table is built in LIFO order makes it convenient to ensure that operators not eligible for comparison are removed from the list. When the Optimizer has completed processing in node 1, all its operators exist on the hash table in LIFO order. Before starting on node 2, the Optimizer saves the hash table. During the scanning of node 2, it keeps adding operators —always in LIFO order. When it starts on node 3, it simply restores the saved hash table so that it again contains only the operators that were in it when processing of node 1 was finished. Effectively, it trimmed the list of any operators added during processing of node 2. It does the same thing again when it starts on node 4. The Optimizer continues building backward flow paths and optimizing them until no more paths can be constructed. At that point it goes on to the next optimization.

Although this algorithm does not find all possible common subexpressions, it does find all those that occur within structured flow paths; because a large percentage of programs consist of these paths, the technique works extremely well.

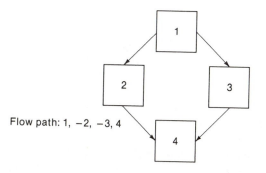

Flow path: 1, −2, −3, 4

Figure 43. Removing common subexpressions in an IF-THEN-ELSE flow.

Result Incorporation

The purpose of result incorporation is to eliminate the allocation of unnecessary temporaries. This optimization is possible on the VAX-11 because the architecture of the machine provides both three- and two-address forms of most machine operations. Result incorporation combines an assignment operator with the operator producing the value that gets assigned, thus eliminating the assignment operator and the need to generate a temporary to hold the intermediate result. Result incorporation could be done much earlier in the compiler, but in that case the Optimizer would have to provide special-case tests for a multitude of different kinds of assignment operators. Moreover, some common subexpressions would not be recognized. On the other hand, doing this optimization later, during local code generation, would require a lot of extra temporaries to hold the intermediate results.

The Optimizer performs result incorporation by making a single forward scan through the array of pointers to operators. The objective is to discover assignment operators referencing value-producing operators that have a reference count of one (operators that produce values used only once, in the assignment operator itself). Consider the following program fragment and the operators as they would appear at this point during optimization.

Source Program Fragment
```
a = b * c;
d = b * c + e;
```

Intermediate Language Operators
```
-20    1    REF(a)
-21    1    REF(b)
-22    1    VALUE(-21)
-23    1    REF(c)
-24    1    VALUE(-23)
-25    2    MULTIPLY(-22,-24)
-26    0    ASSIGN(-20,-25)
```

```
-27    1    REF(d)
-32    1    REF(e)
-33    1    VALUE(-32)
-34    1    ADD(-25,-33)
-35    0    ASSIGN(-27,-34)
```

During the forward scan of the operators, the first assignment encountered is ASSIGN –26. The value for this assignment is MULTIPLY –25, which has a reference count of two and is therefore ineligible for result incorporation. Continuing the scan, the Optimizer next encounters ASSIGN –35. This time the value being assigned has a reference count of one; it is eligible for result incorporation because the result of the ADD is used only to provide a value for the target of this ASSIGN. Result incorporation involves adding the identifier of the target reference operator as a third operand to the ADD operator and eliminating the assignment operator altogether. The reference count of the ADD operator is set to zero because the operator no longer produces a value. The final operator would be the following:

```
-34    0    ADD(-25,-33,-27)
```

As might be expected, not all value-producing operators can participate in result incorporation. We have limited the set to those that have analogous hardware operations and whose lengths or sizes are conducive to incorporation in other operators. These include:

1. ADD, SUBTRACT, MULTIPLY, and DIVIDE operators of data type integer, decimal (only if size and scale match), and floating point

2. Conversions to and from integer and floating point

3. Character-string copy operations in which the destination is a varying-length character string larger than the copied value or is a fixed-length character string equal in size to the copied value

4. The ABS operator with a result data type of integer, fixed decimal (only if scale and size match), and floating point

5. The ADDR built-in function

6. Character-string concatenation with the same rules as 3 above

7. Mathematical built-in functions whose result cannot be returned in two hardware registers (that is, for results whose precision is greater than 53).

Conclusions

In this chapter we have described the implementation of global optimization in the VAX-11 Code Generator. Throughout the evolution of the Optimizer our philosophy was to concentrate on those improvements that resulted in the highest payoff for the least cost. Thus, we strove to select optimizations that significantly reduced the running time of the object program without so much compile-time cost that their implementation became impractical. (The record shows that we met this goal: the PL/I compiler produces code that is as highly optimized as any other Digital compiler for VAX-11 machines, and it has a compilation rate of between 2,000 and 4,000 lines per minute, which is significantly better than that of other competing compilers. Our VAX-11 C compiler, which uses the VAX-11 Code Generator, produces code of equivalent quality and its compilation rate is between 4,000 and 7,000 lines per minute.)

Our experience shows that more and more optimization can be added without significantly affecting the amount of time it takes to compile a program. In fact, because many parts of the PL/I compiler are written in PL/I, more optimization reduces the overall compilation time. We have tried not only to implement optimizations that have the highest payoff but also to select those implementation algorithms that run the fastest; in some cases, this meant that we opted for those that were fast but imperfect.

Figures 44 through 49 illustrate the effect of various optimizations on the run time for each of a series of benchmarks. Each column shows the effect on the total run time of the program when the indicated optimization is not performed (and all other optimizations are performed) using the totally unoptimized program as the point of comparison. For example in Benchmark 1 when all optimizations are performed, the running time is about 20 percent of what it would be if no optimizations were performed; if the assignment of local variables to registers is suppressed (and all other optimizations are performed), the running time is 80 percent of what it would be if no optimizations were performed. We have selected a variety of benchmarks; some show that certain optimizations have a significant effect on the running time, and others show a more equitable distribution. Thus, in Benchmark 3, the running time is more significantly affected by the assignment of variables to registers and the removal of invariant expressions from loops than it is by the elimination of common subexpression and peephole optimization. However, in Benchmark 4, the suppression of the assignment of local variables to registers barely affects run time at all. (We include the effects of peephole optimization in these figures as a matter of interest; the Peephole Optimizer executes as a distinct phase following register allocation and is described in Chapter 10.)

The optimization phase can never be totally finished. We are constantly trying to discover new ways to improve code generation. Listed below are several optimizations that we would like to perform in future generations of the VAX-11 Code Generator.

- Better use of the graph during common subexpression elimination would allow us to perform this optimization along longer and irregularly structured flow paths. We could do this by using the dominance information computed during the removal of invariant computation from loops.

- The calculation of discrete lifetimes over actual flow paths rather than lexically over regions would provide better information about the importance of variables and would tell us more specifically the parts of the graph where the value is live.

- Interprocedural analysis of external as well as internal procedures would allow us to compute exactly (or more exactly) the variables that are actually assigned through aliases and those that are uplevel addressed by specific internal procedures.

Even without these, we have extended and invented a considerable number of optimizations. In fact, we spent a lot of development time implementing optimizations in other phases of the compiler—in Write Tree, in the Register Allocator, and in the Peephole Optimizer. The empirical result has been that once we have made an optimization in one part of the compiler—say, the code generation logic—we have opened up the possibility of more optimization in another part of the compiler—say, in peephole optimization.

We next look at these later phases of compilation, including the transformation of operators into instructions and the subsequent optimizations on the program.

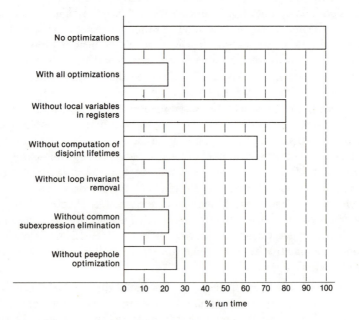

Figure 44.   Effect of optimization on Benchmark 1.

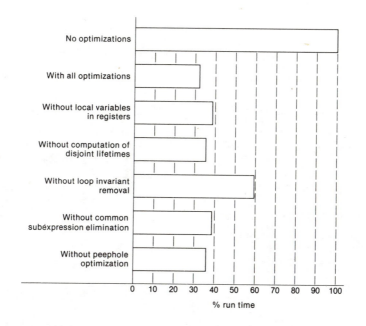

Figure 45. Effect of optimization on Benchmark 2.

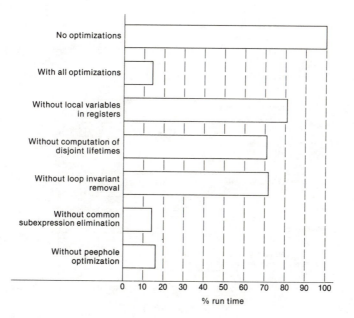

Figure 46. Effect of optimization on Benchmark 3.

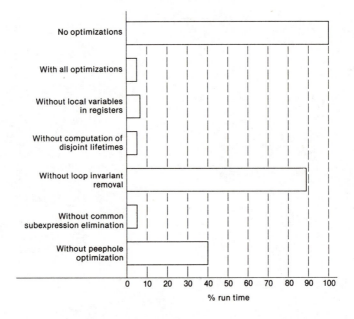

Figure 47. Effect of optimization on Benchmark 4.

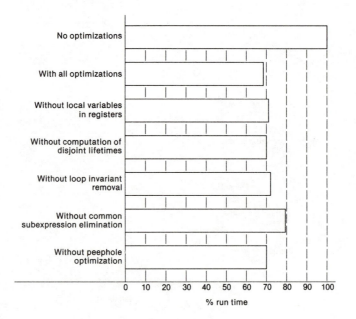

Figure 48. Effect of optimization on Benchmark 5.

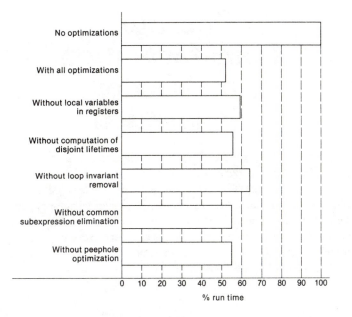

Figure 49. Effect of optimization on Benchmark 6.

8

Operator Transformation and Code Generation

After execution of the front end's storage allocation routine, the VAX-11 Code Generator enters its pure code generation phases in which the operators are transformed into VAX-11 instructions and operand specifiers. The first of these phases is the Local Code Generator, so named because it processes a single operator at a time and generates instructions without regard to the structure of the program as a whole. In this chapter we discuss our philosophy of local code generation and present some detailed information on how this phase of the VAX-11 Code Generator creates instructions for the VAX-11 machine.

Background

When we started bootstrapping the compiler, we had neither a code generator nor access to sources for any of the code generators Freiburghouse had written, although we knew they were written in TBL. We did not at that time have any real inclination to use TBL to write our code generator. However, in the interests of getting the compiler up and running, we decided to use TBL to write the code generator, assuming that we would later rewrite it using some more efficient technique. In fact we never did rewrite it, and that hasty decision proved to be one of our best.

When we wrote our own TBL compiler for the VAX-11, we changed it to suit our needs and our own style of programming and code generation. We added the notion of explicit variables, a *case* action, an *if_not* action, and we made it possible for any action to have a variable number of arguments. A more subtle and (in conceptual terms) more important change was to make the output of all actions explicit in the TBL. In designing our TBL for the Local Code Generator, we provided known variables and let actions modify them explicitly. For example, we defined a variable, *result,* that always holds the address of the current operator, and we defined a number of temporary variables that may be used to hold pointers to operators or operands as we process them.

To give you an idea of the simplicity and elegance of a TBL scheme, we have chosen a fragment from the routine in the Local Code Generator that processes ADD operators:

```
add_op:
        get_data_type(result,temp1);
        case (temp1,

                .
                .
                .

                add_fixed,
                add_flt,
                add_decimal,

                .
                .
                .

                add_long);

        .
        .
        .

add_long:
```

Here, the first actions performed for the interpretation of an ADD operator are obtaining the data type of the value produced by the current operator (as represented by *result*) and storing the numerical value in the variable *temp1*. Subsequently, the *case* action uses the value of *temp1* to determine which TBL routine to branch to. Separate routines exist for add operations involving operands of various data types.

The benefits of the TBL style of code generation soon became obvious. First, it provided much greater flexibility than did the traditional pattern-matching code generation techniques, especially in generation of code for complex coding sequences. Second, it allowed us to elaborate on our code generation scheme as we went along; had we used a pattern-matching scheme, we would have felt compelled to define all possible patterns before we began. (At the very least, we would have had to describe patterns for all possible operand sequences.) For our purposes (and given our prior experience), the latter approach would not have been at all feasible, especially since pattern-matching cannot begin to handle such semantic problems as precision and alignment.

Another advantage of our design approach is that it lets us generate code for special cases in a very straightforward fashion. No cross-coupling is necessary between the Optimizer and the Local Code Generator: the Optimizer does not need to know what the Local Code Generator will generate, and the Local Code Generator does not need to know anything about optimization.

Overview

The Local Code Generator reads an operator, transforms the information in it into a data structure called an *operator node*, determines the opcode of the operator, locates the appropriate TBL interpretative routine to process the

Notes: 13-Nov-78

When generator is entered:

argument specifies base register for locals. This value is placed in a cg-variable. Codepass call specifies fp.

argument specifies the address of a quadword data structure. The first longword of which is to receive the register save mask of the block. The second of which is to be used to allocate storage. A longword in the cg-frame is dedicated to pointing to this quadword value.

A prologue intermediate code list entry is generated by entry to all blocks that require a register save mask and temporaries. It is also generated for entry statements. A prologue entry contains a pointer to the quadword save mask/temporary descriptor.

operator, and passes control to that routine. The TBL routine processes the operands and writes (emits) *code blocks* to the intermediate code list. Code blocks are skeletal machine-language instructions; they contain machine opcodes and operand information, but do not necessarily contain bound addressing information nor (in most cases) any specific register numbers for operands that are to be addressed using registers.

The intermediate code list itself is always built in a strictly linear fashion, with code blocks always added at the end. Thus, it represents the source program from start to finish. However, the Local Code Generator must also represent the structure of the program—which may not be strictly linear—and create and maintain a distinct environment for each nested block or procedure. On the outer processing level, it simply initializes the code list listhead, gets a pointer to the operator file, processes each operator until it reaches the end of the file, and calls the Register Allocator when it has finished. This level of control, shown in Figure 50, is what results in the linear code list.

On the inner level of execution, there is a distinction between two routines: operator processing and block processing. On initial entry to the Local Code Generator, the block processing routine initializes a set of local variables and a data structure called a *prologue descriptor*. Throughout code generation and register allocation, the prologue descriptor will accumulate information about the use of temporaries in the block. The block processing routine then calls the operator processing routine.

The operator processing routine continues reading operators and emitting code blocks until it encounters a PROCEDURE, BEGIN, or BLOCK_END. Then, the following things can happen:

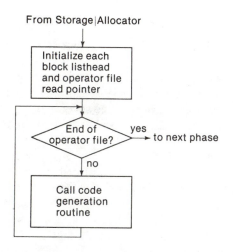

Figure 50. Processing the operator file.

- A **PROCEDURE** or **BEGIN** operator causes the operator processing routine to invoke the block processing routine recursively to create a new block environment.
- A **BLOCK_END** causes the operator processing routine to return either to the block processing routine or to its own earlier incarnation.

The alternate possibilities in the **BLOCK_END** case enable us to distinguish external procedures from internal (contained) blocks and procedures and to generate code for them properly. Consider a source file that contains:

```
a: PROC;
        b: PROC;
        END b;
    .

    .

    .
END a;
c: PROC;
END c;
```

At the end of *b*, the operator processing routine must return to processing operators in procedure *a*. That is, it returns to its previous incarnation. At the end of *a*, however, it must return to the outer control routine so that *c* is properly recognized as a level-one external procedure and not as a procedure internal to *a*. Figure 51 illustrates the levels of recursion for this control flow. The recursion has no effect on the order of the code list, which remains in strictly linear order with respect to the source program.

Temporaries

The prologue descriptor created for each block activation by the block processing routine accumulates information about temporary usage within the block. When we refer to *temporaries*, we are not altering the conventional notion of a compiler temporary as a variable allocated to hold an intermediate result during code generation. We have, however, expanded the notion to include the assignment of the values of local variables to temporaries.

Compiler Temporaries as T-Regs

One of our goals in the design of the Local Code Generator (made possible by the register allocation technique we developed) was to make the Local Code Generator freely assign temporary results to register temporaries, or T-regs. The fact that not all values will necessarily be assigned to registers in the generated code is of no concern to the Local Code Generator. It merely assumes that anything that can possibly be assigned to a register should be

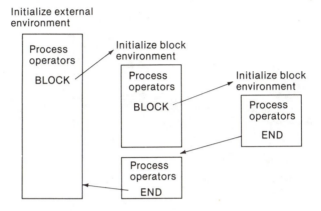

Figure 51. Recursion levels in code generation.

treated as if it will be, and so it assigns results to register temporaries without regard to register numbers, usage spans, the number of registers already allocated to hold results, and so on.

To represent a result assigned to a register temporary, the Local Code Generator allocates an operator node and indicates that it is a register temporary node using the *opcode* field. It then fills in an allocation descriptor in the T-reg node and copies the descriptor to the operator node for the value the T-reg represents. Figure 52 shows the operator node for an ADD operator whose result the Local Code Generator has assigned to a T-reg and illustrates the T-reg node and the allocation descriptors in each.

Each T-reg node has a unique identifier consisting of 12 bits that locate a pointer in an array of pointers. The array is accessed through the prologue descriptor for the block in which the T-reg node is allocated, as illustrated in Figure 53. The prologue descriptor contains a maximum of 64 pointers to these pointer arrays, each of which can hold a maximum of 64 pointers to T-regs. Thus the maximum number of T-reg nodes that can be allocated for a single block during compilation is 4,096. (This has not proved to be a real limit; we have never had a program—or received one from a user—that ran out of space for temporary allocation.)

In the T-reg node, the 12-bit identifier consists of two 6-bit parts. The high-order, base field provides an index to the list of pointers in the prologue descriptor. The low-order, index field gives an index into the array of T-reg node pointers.

The first 16 T-reg nodes in each block are nodes allocated for the 16 hardware registers. Since these nodes are always allocated first, the base portion of the identifications for these registers is 0 and the index portion contains the

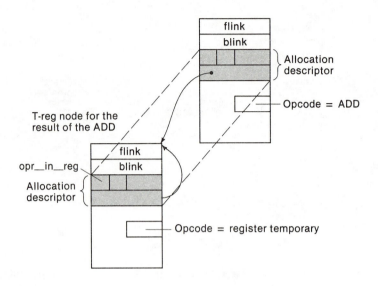

Figure 52. T-reg node allocation.

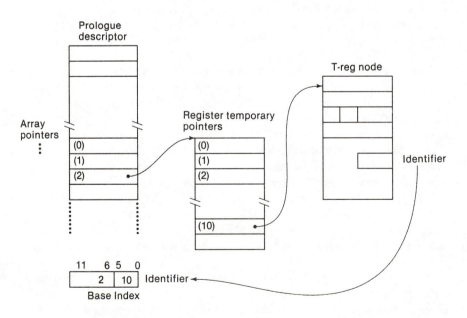

Figure 53. T-reg identification.

values 0 through 15; thus, these nodes can be accessed through their hardware register numbers.

Local Variables as Compiler Temporaries

In our discussion of the Optimizer in Chapter 7, we mention the ASSIGN_REGTEMP (Assign Value to Register Temporary) operator. We describe only the criteria used by the Optimizer to select variables that are eligible for assignment to registers and the modifications the Optimizer makes to the operator file to reflect the selection of a variable. For each of these variables, the Optimizer introduces into the operator file an ASSIGN_REGTEMP operator, whose first operand is the Symbol Table node identifier of the variable's symbol node. The next two operands represent the operator identifiers of the first and last operators that define a given instance of the variable, that is, a determined span of the program over which a particular value that it holds remains valid.

When the Local Code Generator processes these ASSIGN_REGTEMP operators, it allocates T-reg nodes and copies the allocation descriptor from the T-reg node into the ASSIGN_REGTEMP operator node, as it does for other operators when it assigns temporary results to T-regs. Moreover, the Local Code Generator detects when a VALUE operator is referring to an ASSIGN_REGTEMP operator, and in these cases it also copies the allocation descriptor from the T-reg node into the VALUE operator. Consider the following:

```
-2     ASSIGN_REGTEMP(x,34,49,0)
-3     ASSIGN_REGTEMP(z,34,49,0)

-43    VALUE (-2)
-45    VALUE (-3)
-46    ADD(-43,-45)
```

Figure 54 shows the operator and T-reg nodes for these operators.

Building Code Blocks

Each of the code blocks emitted by the Local Code Generator to the intermediate code list consists of a fixed header portion followed by operand specifiers, if any. The fixed portion contains fields describing the type of code block, the opcode of the instruction represented by the code block, the number of operands, and so on. The operand specifiers contain specific information about the size and context of the operands and the manner in which they are addressed. In this section, we describe the types of code block created by the Local Code Generator and provide examples of how the Local Code Generator determines the addressing modes of operands.

The code blocks output by the Local Code Generator describe the instructions and control information needed to write the object file for the program

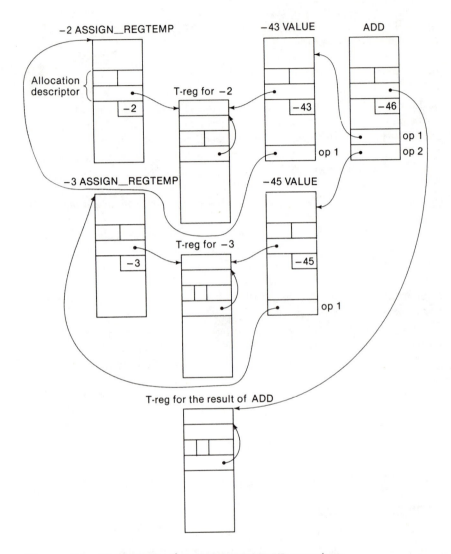

Figure 54. T-reg nodes for ASSIGN_REGTEMP operators.

being compiled. Table 1 summarizes the types of code block and how each is used. Figure 55 illustrates the operators for a simple program and shows which operators result in code block generation and the type of code block generated for each.

Operand Specifiers

Code block operand specifiers are analogous to operand specifiers in VAX-11 instructions. They describe both how the operand is to be addressed (the addressing mode) and the operand's location—which may be in a register, in memory, or in the operand specifier itself. However, a code block operand specifier has a single format for expressing all possible addressing modes, whereas there is a distinct operand specifier format for each VAX-11 addressing mode.

The VAX-11 addressing modes and operand specifier formats are defined in detail in Digital Equipment Corporation's *VAX-11 Architecture Handbook* (Maynard, Mass., 1981). Table 2 summarizes the basic addressing modes and the numeric encoding for each. These codes are also used in the code block operand specifiers and the examples in the rest of this chapter.

Code Block Operand Specifier Format

Figure 56 illustrates a code block operand specifier. The *context* field contains information related to the use of index registers; the *flags* field indicates the type of operand and how other fields are used. For example, if the flag *base_use* is set, it indicates that the *addr1* field contains a T-reg identifier. Similarly, the flag *external*, when set, indicates that the operand is represented by a reference to an external symbol; in this case, the *psect* field must contain the program section number.

Table 1. Code block types.

Type	Usage
Instruction	Represent machine-language instructions, such as ADD, MOV, CLR, and PUSH
Branch	Represent branch instructions
Prologue	Represent the beginnings of blocks
Label	Represent program labels
Statement	Represent source program statements
Block end	Represent the ends of blocks
Literal	Represent immediate data, for example, constants
Conditional move	Represent move instructions introduced by the Local Code Generator for operand specifiers that must be in registers
Load base	Represent instructions required to load the base addresses of program sections into registers

```
                                    Operators              Code blocks

 1              add10: procedure;                      ┌──────────────────┐
                                                       │    Statement 1   │
-33    0000    0    statement (1)                      ├──────────────────┤
 -1    0001    0    procedure                          │                  │
 -2    0002    3    assign_regtemp (X)                 │   Label ADD10    │
 -3    0003    3    assign_regtemp (Z)                 ├──────────────────┤
-34    0004    0    entry (ADD10)                      │                  │
-35    0005    0    end_of_prologue                    │     Prologue     │
                                                       ├──────────────────┤
 2     1                                               │    Load base     │
 3     1       declare (x, z) fixed bin;               ├──────────────────┤
 4     1                                               │                  │
 5     1                 z = 10;                        │    Statement 5   │
                                                       ├──────────────────┤
-36    0006    0    statement (5)                      │  Instruction MOVL│
-38    0007    1    integer (10,0)                     ├──────────────────┤
-39    0008    0    assign (-3, -38)                   │                  │
                                                       │    Statement 6   │
 6     1                 x = x + z;                     ├──────────────────┤
                                                       │ Instruction ADDL3│
-40    0009    0    statement (6)                      ├──────────────────┤
-43    000A    1    value (-2)                         │                  │
-45    000B    1    value (-3)                         │    Statement 7   │
-46    000C    1    add (-43, -45, -2)                 ├──────────────────┤
                                                       │  Instruction RET │
 7     1                 return;                        ├──────────────────┤
                                                       │                  │
-48    000E    0    statement (7)                      │    Statement 8   │
-49    000F    0    return                             ├──────────────────┤
                                                       │  Instruction RET │
 8     1       end;                                    ├──────────────────┤
                                                       │                  │
-50    0010    0    statement (8)                      │     Block end    │
 51    0011    0    block_end (169)                    └──────────────────┘
```

Figure 55. Code blocks emitted for a simple program.

The *addr1* field contains addressing information. The high-order four bits
of this field contain the addressing mode code; low-order bits contain a register number, a T-reg identifier, or other information depending on the addressing mode.

The *addr2* field is used only when the indexed addressing mode is used; the
high-order four bits always contain the value 4, indicating that indexing is
used. It specifies the register (or T-reg) that is the index register for the
operand.

The displacement field contains a variety of information, depending on
other data. For example, it may contain the displacement of an operand from
its base, which may be a register or the base address of a program section.
Or, it may contain a pointer to a label node, an external symbol descriptor, or

Table 2. VAX-11 addressing modes.

Mode	Code	Usage
Literal	0–3	The operand's value is specified in the operand specifier itself.
Indexed	4	(Used in conjunction with other addressing modes.) The index register specifies an offset from the beginning of a data structure whose base address is also in the operand specifier.
Register	5	A register contains the value of the operand.
Register deferred	6	A register contains the address of the operand.
Autodecrement	7	The address of the operand is determined by subtracting the size of the operand from the contents of a register.
Autoincrement	8	The register contains the address of the operand and is incremented by the size of the operand following evaluation of the operand specifier.
Autoincrement deferred	9	The register contains the address of a location containing the address of the operand and is incremented by four (the size of an address) following evaluation of the operand specifier.
Displacement	A,C,E	A byte, word, or longword value is added to the contents of a base register to determine the address of the operand.
Displacement deferred	B,D,F	A byte, word, or longword value is added to the contents of a base register to determine a location containing the address of the operand.

an immediate (as distinct from a literal) value. The VAX-11 Code Generator optimizes the displacement of an operand specifier whenever possible, using byte, word, or longword displacements.

Examples of Operand Specifiers and Addressing Modes

In the remainder of this chapter, we present examples of operand specifiers for different types of instructions and addressing modes. Information in these operand specifiers does not, at this phase of code generation, represent the

Operand specifier fields

Context: Undefined(0), byte(1), word(2), longword(3),
quadword(4), or octaword(5).

Flags: External(1), relocatable(2), label(4), temporary(8),
unbound(10), index__use(20), and base__use(40).

Psect: Program section number if relocatable and
external are specified in flags field.

`m` `r` Addr1: Address mode and register number if
base__use is not specified in flags.
Mode and register number form literal
value if mode is 0, 1, 2, or 3.

`m` `ident` Addr1: Address mode and T-reg identifier if
base__use is specified in flags.

`0` Addr2: Indexing not specified.

`4` `r` Addr2: Indexing specified with a specific
register number if index__use not
set in flags.

`4` `ident` Addr2: Indexing specified with T-reg identifier
if index__use is set in flags.

`data value` Displ: Displacement or actual data
value if label and external
not specified in flags.

`pointer` Displ: Descriptor pointer if label
or external specified in flag.

Figure 56. Code block operand specifier format.

final form of the program. Most of the registers in these examples are specified using T-reg identifiers. (The Register Allocator, described in the next
chapter, updates the operand specifiers with actual register numbers.)
Moreover, the Local Code Generator does not make any attempt to bind

branch instructions to their target labels. The Code Binder performs this task in a later phase.

Figure 57 shows the operand specifiers for a two-operand ADD instruction in which both operands are in registers:

```
ADDL2   Rn,R0
```

The context field in each operand specifier indicates that the operand context is longword (3). The *flags* field in the first operand specifies the *base_use* flag (40); thus, the *addr1* field contains a T-reg identifier (011). The *flags* field of the second operand specifier does not specify the *base_use* flag; thus, the actual register number (0) is specified in the *addr1* field along with the addressing mode code (5).

The next example, shown in Figure 58, is an instruction that uses the indexed addressing mode. The instruction is

```
MOVL    Ry,-displ(FP)[Rx]
```

where the value in the T-reg Ry is to be moved to a location whose base address is specified as a negative displacement from the FP and whose index is specified by the T-reg Rx. The *flags* field in the first operand specifier has *base_use* set (40); thus, *addr1* contains a T-reg identifier. In the second operand specifier, the *flags* field has *index_use* set (20); thus, *addr2* contains a T-reg identifier. The *addr1* field contains the addressing mode code indicating a byte displacement (A) from register D (the FP). The *addr2* field speci-

Figure 57. Operand specifiers for a two-operand ADD instruction.

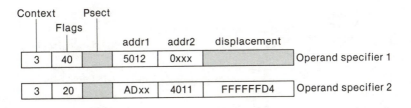

Figure 58. Operand specifiers for an instruction using the indexed addressing mode.

fies indexed mode (addressing mode 4) and the T-reg identifier of the index register (011). The *displacement* field indicates a negative displacement from the FP.

The next example shows how a static variable is addressed by generating a load base code block. Figure 59 illustrates the instruction in the load base code block.

```
MOVAB  psect,Rx
```

Operand 1 represents an external variable, assigned to the program section numbered 2 by the Storage Allocator. The displacement value of 0 indicates that the variable is located at the beginning of that program section. Operand 2's flags indicate a T-reg destination; thus, the *addr1* field contains a T-reg identifier.

The BBC (branch on bit clear) instruction tests a bit in a bit-string variable and branches if the bit is clear. Figure 60 shows one possible configuration.

```
BBC pos,(Rx),label
```

Here, a test is being made to a one-bit, external variable. Thus, the operand specifier for the bit position to be tested consists of a literal operand whose value is 0. The result is an addressing mode code of 0 and an operand value of 0. Operand specifier 2 contains the program section number of the external variable; the context is byte (1); the flag (41) indicates that a T-reg is used for an external reference. The *addr1* field indicates register deferred addressing (mode 6); the T-reg node whose identifier is 012 contains the base address of the program section. Operand 3 specifies the target branch label. Its flag (14) indicates that it is an unbound label; that is, it is not yet bound to a permanent location. The displacement field contains the address of a label descriptor record.

An instruction using autoincrement addressing mode might look like the one shown in Figure 61.

```
MOVL Rn,(Rm)+
```

Here, operand 1 specifies the register containing a source value, which is in a T-reg. In operand specifier 2, the *addr1* field specifies autoincrement mode

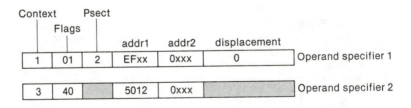
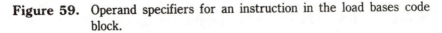

Figure 59. Operand specifiers for an instruction in the load bases code block.

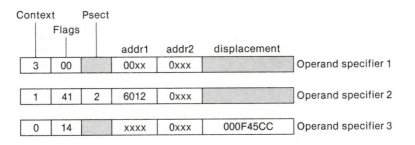

Figure 60. Operand specifiers for a BBC instruction.

(mode 8) and the T-reg identifier (012) of the register whose value is to be incremented following evaluation of the operand specifier. Since the context of this operand specifier is longword (as specified in the context byte), the value is incremented by 4 each time the operand specifier is evaluated.

Our last example, which shows a complex reference, comes from the source code:

```
example: PROCEDURE (y);
DECLARE y POINTER,
        x FLOAT BASED;
        y->x = 5;
```

In this example, the location of x is derived from the value of a pointer y, whose value is passed as a parameter (we assign this floating-point variable a constant value to simplify the example). When the Local Code Generator reads the operator file, there is a single ASSIGN operator to express this assignment. However, the Local Code Generator determines that the reference to x requires an additional instruction to load its effective address into a register. It allocates a T-reg node and emits a MOVL instruction to load the address into the T-reg. The instructions are as follows:

```
MOVL    @04(AP),Rn
MOVF    #1A,(Rn)
```

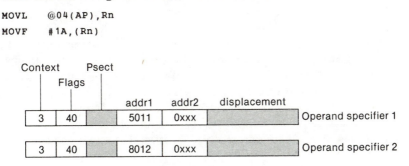

Figure 61. Operand specifiers for an instruction using the autoincrement addressing mode.

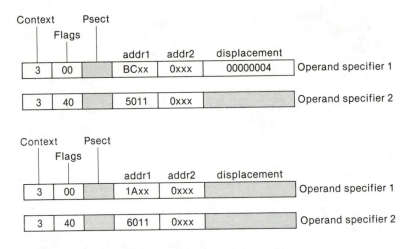

Figure 62. Operand specifiers for a complex reference.

Figure 62 shows the code block operand specifiers. Operand specifier 1 for the MOVL instruction specifies the contents of the parameter *y*. It specifies the position of the argument as a displacement from the AP register C.

The second instruction generated by this sequence is MOVF, which moves the literal floating-point datum 5 (expressed as a short floating-point literal in operand specifier 1) to the address contained in the T-reg node that was allocated to hold the address of the variable in the MOVL instruction.

In this chapter, we presented an overview of how the Local Code Generator transforms the optimized operator file into a sequence of code blocks that will ultimately be VAX-11 instructions. We also gave some detailed examples that illustrate the mechanics of generating code for specific machine instructions.

We have designed a strict, canonical format for operand specifiers that is easy to reduce and—more important—easy to modify as code generation proceeds. The "incompleteness" of the operand specifiers at this point in code generation has its advantages. The T-reg node identifiers are not bound to specific registers. The explicit allocation is performed by the Register Allocator after it decides which uses of T-regs are more important. The Register Allocator is in a much better position than the Local Code Generator to know which instances of temporaries should go into registers. Similarly, branch displacements are not bound, nor is the final addressing of external variables. These bonds are also reserved for later phases of code generation.

9

The Register
Allocator

Most compiler implementations must deal with a fundamental, two-part, hardware-specific problem: register allocation (selecting temporaries and local variables that can be held in general-purpose registers) and register assignment (specifying which register to use for each selected variable or temporary). Instructions that use registers are generally shorter and faster than those that do not; therefore, register allocation/assignment seeks to place as many temporary values and local variables as possible into registers.

Background

The bootstrap compiler used a localized register allocation scheme within the code generator phase. Whenever the code generator generated a computed value, it would assign it to a register. Each value had a usage count, which always reflected the number of references to the value. When the usage count was zero, the value was dropped.

Usage counts provided a good basis for deciding which values to retain when there were insufficient registers and a register was required (say, for a base pointer). In these cases, the code generator simply copied the value with the lower usage count to memory and allocated the freed register (R. A. Freiburghouse, "Register Allocation Via Usage Counts," *Comm. ACM* 17, no. 11, [1974] pp. 638–642).

Although this technique provided a reasonable way to perform register allocation, our assembly-language bias prompted us to modify it. We wanted a register allocator that would use registers as efficiently as any good assembly-language programmer could when coding by hand. Our solid understanding of the VAX-11 architecture and instruction set made us confident that we could design such an allocator.

Register usage on the VAX-11 machines is summarized below.

1. There are 12 general-purpose registers, R0 through R11.

2. There are 4 special-purpose registers, R12 through R15:

   - An Argument Pointer register, AP (R12), used to pass the address of the parameter list to a procedure on invocation. If a procedure has no parameters, AP may be used as a general register.

- A Frame Pointer, FP (R13), containing the address of the beginning of the stack frame for the current block activation.
- A Stack Pointer, SP (R14), containing the address of the current stack location (the "top" of the stack).
- A Program Counter, PC (R15), containing the current program (instruction) counter.

3. Some instructions have as a side effect the destruction of the contents of specific registers. For example, procedure invocations are always assumed to destroy registers R0 and R1 because they may be used to pass return values; string instructions always destroy certain registers; and so on.

4. Some compiler-generated instructions have operands that should, if possible, be addressed with base registers and/or index registers.

Initially, we decided to confine all register allocation, including assignment of temporaries to specific register numbers, to the local code generation phase. Thus, the Local Code Generator, mimicking an assembly-language programmer, would assign registers on an ad hoc basis: each time it encountered a value that could be put in a register, it allocated a register (or registers, as required), beginning with R2.

The two principal problems of this approach are: when a specific register that is required or destroyed by an instruction is active, that register's current contents must be saved, the instruction generated, and then the register contents restored; and when all 12 registers are allocated and a register is required to hold a base or index value in an operand address, a register must be freed to hold the value.

These were the problems we encountered with our first register allocator. Within the Local Code Generator's TBL, we frequently had to generate code sequences that copied the list of active registers, pushed those registers onto the stack, emitted an instruction that destroyed one or more registers, and then restored the registers that had been pushed onto the stack. For example, a MOVC (move character) instruction uses registers R0 through R5. If all these registers were already allocated when the the move character instruction was needed, the assembly-language programmer would write something like

```
PUSHR  #^<R0,R1,R2,R3,R4,R5>   | Push R0 to R5
MOVC3  ...,...,...              | Do the Move Instruction
POPR   #^<R0,R1,R2,R3,R4,R5>   | Get the registers back
```

where the respective instructions PUSHR and POPR push onto the stack and restore the contents of the specified registers. When confronted with this same situation, the Local Code Generator in our first register allocation scheme would execute a set of TBL actions such as

```
get_inuse_mask (temp1);
emit_instr (PUSHR,temp1);
emit_instr (MOVC3,...,...,...);
emit_instr (POPR,temp1);
```

where *temp1* is the variable in which the Local Code Generator stores the mask of all registers currently allocated for instructions.

Clearly, this design resulted in inefficient code sequences and did not closely reproduce the assembly-language code that a good programmer would write. We needed a register allocator smart enough to look at variable and temporary use throughout a single block or section of code, decide which temporaries were referenced more frequently, and assign them to registers. We concluded that we had to separate the distinct actions of register allocation and register assignment and to perform the assignment after code generation rather than before or during it.

Compilers that allocate and assign temporaries and local variables to registers prior to code generation do so based on the frequency of estimated use of the variable or temporary. This approach may require that once a variable or temporary is assigned to a register it remains bound to that register even though the values held by the variable or temporary may have distinct, or disjoint, usages. This is, in fact, true in most implementations.

Although our initial method assigned only compiler-generated temporaries to registers, the change to postcode-generation assignment enabled us to include local variables in register assignment. Moreover, it was clear that the generated code could provide a more realistic picture of a temporary's or a variable's actual usage; the generated code shows exactly how many times the variable is referenced in instructions, not just in the source program. We also knew that from flow analysis within the Optimizer phase we could determine when a variable's or temporary's value ceased to be live, or valid. Thus, we could assign that variable to a register only for that distinct usage and assign it to a different register or to memory for a different usage.

Lastly, we knew that, given the architecture of the VAX-11 instruction set, we could generate instructions using temporary addressing modes and modify them to specify register or memory addressing after we had made final register assignments. We were also confident that, even though we would have to execute another distinct pass over the generated code, we could write a Register Allocator that not only would be efficient in terms of register assignments but also would require a minimum of execution time.

The decision to rewrite the register allocation scheme as a separate phase required a major revision of the Local Code Generator to make it keep track of all instructions that allocated specific registers or destroyed specific registers and to make it compute the usage span of temporaries targeted for assignment to registers. Later, we introduced the necessary logic into the

Optimizer to enable us to include local variables in register assignment and to treat them exactly as we treat temporaries introduced by the Local Code Generator.

Overview

After processing the operator file, the Local Code Generator transfers control to the Register Allocator. At this point the Local Code Generator has built not only data structures to describe the program's block structure and to track usage of all temporaries allocated within those blocks, but also a series of code blocks representing statements, instructions, labels, and so on.

The temporaries for each block are represented by data structures, or nodes (which we call T-reg nodes), allocated by the Local Code Generator. The Local Code Generator allocates a T-reg node for:

- Local variables selected by the Optimizer as candidates for assignment to registers

- Temporaries selected by the Local Code Generator to hold intermediate results

- Temporaries associated with specific hardware registers by the Local Code Generator for specific code sequences.

Each code block contains a header and operand specifiers. Within the operand specifiers, the addressing information remains skeletal. Temporaries representing instruction operands are specified by identifiers of the T-reg nodes allocated by the Local Code Generator.

The Register Allocator uses a heuristic approach to assign a value to each temporary. Then, taking each temporary in order of its value, it assigns the temporary to a register if an eligible one exists. If no register is available, the Register Allocator must allocate the temporary to memory. After determining, for each temporary, the availability of a register, the Register Allocator must fill in the operand specifiers in the code blocks with either the register number (if a register is assigned) or a memory address (if no register is available). This scheme requires keeping track of all register usage in the program on a block-by-block basis. To do this, it manages a number of data structures, each representing a discrete type of information—including program structure, temporary allocation, and register usage. We describe these structures in detail in the following subsections.

Prologue Descriptors

During local code generation, the Local Code Generator allocates a prologue descriptor each time it processes a new block, providing backward and forward links with the previous block. Thus, this prologue descriptor list allows the back end to recreate the program's block structure, which was reduced to a linear form in the operator file. The prologue descriptors contain cumulative information about T-reg use gathered during local code generation, including:

- A count of all T-reg nodes allocated for the block
- Pointers to tables containing pointers to the T-reg nodes (these pointers locate and uniquely identify all T-reg nodes)
- A pointer to a list of T-reg nodes specifying registers specifically allocated for particular operations (the explicit allocation list)
- A pointer to a list of T-reg nodes specifying registers whose contents were destroyed at various points in the program as the side effect of an instruction or a procedure call (the register kill list).

Throughout its operation, the Local Code Generator updates an operand counter in the prologue descriptor each time it emits an instruction to the intermediate code list. Figure 63 summarizes the register control information available through the prologue descriptors.

Register Temporary (T-Reg) Nodes

Each T-reg node, whether it represents a compiler temporary or a local variable, contains allocation and control information as well as specific information, accumulated and set by the Local Code Generator, about the T-reg node's usage priority and its usage span. The usage priority is represented by an integral that is a summation of the individual usages of the temporary. Each time the temporary is referenced in an instruction, the Local Code Generator updates the usage integral (maintained in the T-reg node), using the formula:

$$\text{usage\_integral} = \sum_{i=1}^{n} \text{priority}_i * \left(10^{\min(6,\ \text{loopdepth}_i)}\right) + \text{loopdepth}_i$$

where *priority* is 1 or 4, each *i* is a use of the operand represented by the T-reg node, and *loopdepth* is the current loop nesting level. A priority of 1 indicates that the value can be held either in a register or in memory; a priority of 4 indicates that the value must be in a register. For example, when a temporary is used in the context-index field of an operand specifier, its priority is 4 because if it is not in a register, the Register Allocator will have to generate an additional instruction to load the value into a register when it is needed in the instruction.

The other critical piece of information accumulated by the Local Code Generator is the usage span. The usage span of a temporary represents the time (in terms of first and final use, or reference) over which the value represented by the temporary is valid. The Local Code Generator sets these values by using the current value of the operand counter from the prologue descriptor when it detects the first and final references to a temporary. Thus, the usage span indicates how long the temporary must remain lexically valid. Information from the explicit allocation and kill lists also helps the Register

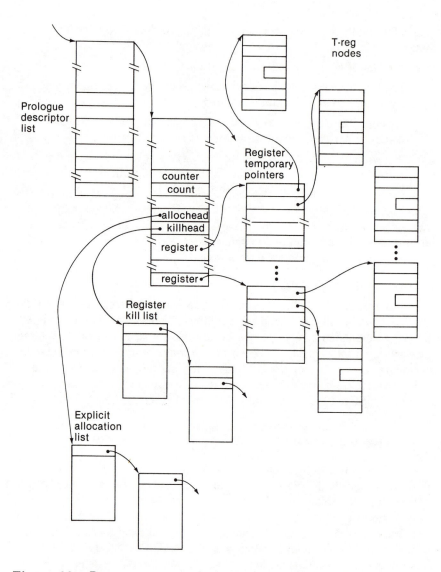

Figure 63. Data structures at the start of register allocation.

Allocator in almost all cases to select a hardware register that will be available for the required span and thus eliminates the need to push and pop register contents.

The Explicit Allocation List

The Local Code Generator makes an entry in the explicit allocation list each time instruction generation requires specific hardware registers. For example, run-time routines generally require that arguments be passed in certain registers. When the Local Code Generator emits an instruction for a call to any of these routines, it makes an entry in the explicit allocation list specifying the register numbers required and the usage span of the program for which they are required. Thus, each entry in this list represents a set of registers that cannot be assigned to variables or temporaries during a specific span of the program.

The Register Kill List

Like the explicit allocation list, the register kill list contains information about specific register usage. The Local Code Generator makes an entry in the register kill list each time it emits instructions or actions that destroy the contents of specific hardware registers. For example, a character-string instruction such as MOVC or CMPC (compare characters) uses specific registers; after the instruction, the previous contents of these registers are no longer valid. Each entry in the register kill list specifies the register(s) whose contents are destroyed and the value of the operand counter at the time the registers are killed.

The Intermediate Code List

In Chapter 8, we described the data structures that constitute the intermediate code list and the information they contain. Holding instructions in the the intermediate code list lets us exploit a fundamental aspect of the VAX-11 architecture, namely, the flexibility of operand addressing. Instruction operands may be held in registers or in memory. The choice of addressing mode does not affect the instruction opcode itself or the number of operands in the instruction. Thus, by generating skeletal machine-language instructions in the Local Code Generator, we can delay the actual binding of operands to specific registers or memory locations until we have looked at the entire program.

The intermediate code list also contains conditional move code blocks. These code blocks represent instructions that load base addresses (either for display pointers or for program sections containing external variables) into registers. The Local Code Generator freely adds these code blocks to the list without regard to the frequency of reference; it lets the Register Allocator make the ultimate decision about whether these addresses need to be held in registers.

Register Assignment

The Register Allocator applies all of the information in these structures—the prologue descriptors, T-reg nodes, explicit allocation list, register kill list, and intermediate code list—during register assignment. Beginning

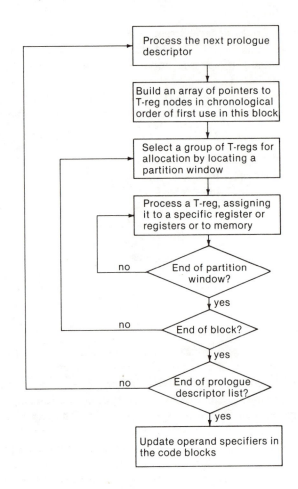

Figure 64. Control flow in the Register Allocator.

with the prologue descriptors built by the Local Code Generator, it performs register assignment a block at a time. Figure 64 summarizes the control flow through the Register Allocator. Each step and each action described in the remainder of this section are performed for each program block.

Register Characterization

Using the pointers in the prologue descriptor, the Register Allocator scans each T-reg node allocated for the current block and captures all the information it has about the temporary's use. As it looks at T-reg nodes, it builds an array of pointers to them. In this array, the pointers are arranged in chronological order according to each T-reg's first (that is, lexically first) use in the program. Concurrently, it calculates a weight factor for each T-reg node and determines which registers are available and which are unavailable for assignment during the temporary's span.

Figure 65 illustrates the chronological array and T-reg nodes. The quadrangles representing T-reg usage spans indicate typical instances of lexical execution, during which the values assigned to T-regs remain valid (as determined by the Optimizer or the Local Code Generator). The T-reg nodes in this figure are numbered according to their identifiers (obtained using the pointers in the prologue descriptors and the pointers in the T-reg node lists) and their order in the chronological array.

Register characterization also entails calculating the T-reg's weight and determining which registers are available for assignment to that T-reg.

Calculating the Weight: Because a T-reg's weight factor indicates the frequency of use of the T-reg, it is very important in the allocation procedure: temporaries with higher weights are given higher priority during the allocation process. The weight is calculated

$$\text{weight} = \frac{\text{usage\_integral}}{(\text{final\_use} - \text{first\_use}) \times \text{number\_of\_registers}}$$

where *usage-integral* is calculated as described earlier (in the subsection on T-reg nodes), the *final_use* and *first_use* are the saved values of the operand counter at the final and first references to the T-reg's value, and *number_of_registers* is the number of hardware registers required to hold the temporary value.

Determining Register Availability: Each T-reg node contains a field specifying which hardware registers can be assigned to the T-reg. In this field, each bit corresponds to a hardware register number: if the bit is set, it indicates that the corresponding register is available; if clear, that the register is not available.

During final register assignment, the Register Allocator continually modifies this field to reflect availability. To initialize this field, the Register Allocator first sets all bits to ones, indicating that all registers are available. (It also sets AP if that register is not needed for parameter access.) Then it scans the explicit allocation and register kill lists to find any registers whose usage spans overlap that of the temporary.

Figure 66 illustrates the register available mask in a T-reg node and in a node in the register kill list. (The Register Allocator takes similar action for each entry in the explicit allocation list.) The mask in the register kill list node (point 1 in the figure) indicates that registers R0 and R1 are killed at a specific program location, as would be the case if a function or procedure call occurred at this point in the program. In the T-reg node (point 2 in the figure), the first and final uses of the temporary specify the span over which the value

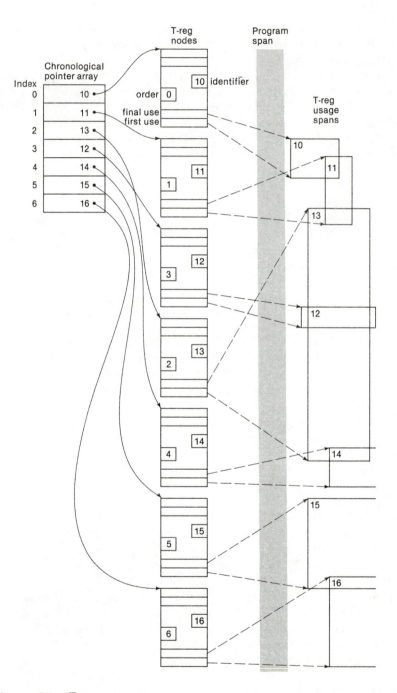

Figure 65. T-reg usage spans.

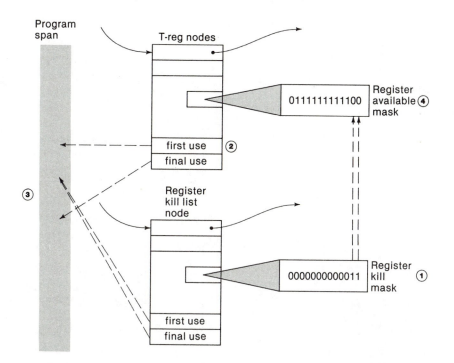

Figure 66. Marking registers from the register kill list unavailable.

the temporary represents must be maintained. Because the program location specified by the kill list node occurs within this span (shown at point 3 in the figure), the Register Allocator clears the bits corresponding to R0 and R1 in the available mask for the T-reg node (point 4), marking these registers unavailable.

Selecting Groups of Register Temporaries for Allocation

After initializing the chronological array and all T-reg nodes, the Register Allocator finds *allocation partitions* within the chronological array to locate points in the program at which no register temporaries are active. An allocation partition is a span of program execution during which some values must be maintained in register temporaries. A point between two partitions indicates a program location at which there are no active temporaries. The Register Allocator uses these partitions as logical breakpoints so that each time it locates a partition point it processes the T-regs in the previous partition.

For each allocation partition, the Register Allocator allocates an array to hold pointers to the T-reg nodes in that partition. In this array, the pointers are arranged according to the weight value assigned to each T-reg: the first

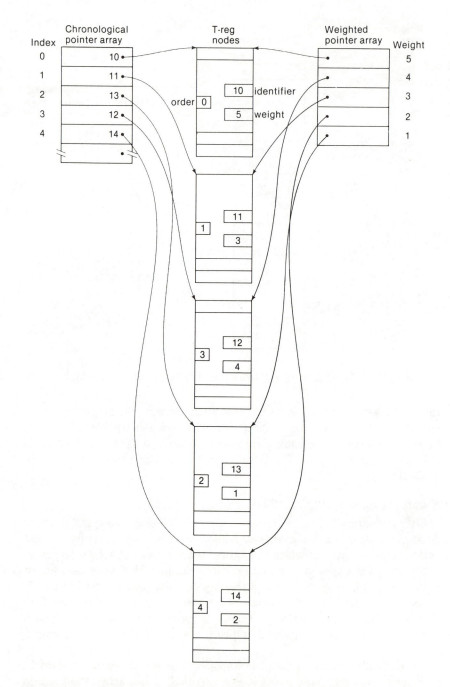

Figure 67. Register temporaries within allocation partitions.

pointer points to the T-reg with the highest weight value, and hence with the highest priority in allocation, and so on. Figure 67 illustrates the relationships between the T-reg nodes, the chronological array, and the sorted pointer array at this point in register allocation.

Selecting a Register and Marking It Used

After reaching an allocation partition point and sorting the T-reg nodes in that partition by weight, the Register Allocator attempts to choose a specific hardware register for each T-reg in the sorted pointer array for that partition. When it selects registers, the Register Allocator uses two masks, one representing register usage and the other register availability. The register use mask in the prologue descriptor for the block indicates which registers have previously been used; this includes all registers previously assigned to a T-reg, explicitly allocated, or destroyed within the current block. The register available mask in the T-reg node indicates which registers are available for that temporary. Figure 68 shows a register use mask indicating that R0 and R1 are the only registers that have been previously used within the current block. Since these registers are not available to the T-reg, the Register Allocator must use another register for the block and accordingly assigns R2 to the T-reg. The number of this register is then added to the register use mask. The Register Allocator sets the available register, number R2, in the T-reg.

Figure 69 summarizes the algorithm for assigning registers to T-regs.

The following list of notes, which are keyed to the diagram in Figure 69, provides some additional explanation.

1. The number of registers needed must always be one, two, or four. (Four is the maximum needed for the largest floating-point value that can be represented on the VAX-11.)

2. If a temporary is used as the base register for an external variable, and if the usage of the temporary is less than three, the Register Allocator sets the base register to PC instead of allocating a base register. (Three or fewer usages of the temporary indicate that it is not worth generating another instruction to load the base address into a register. More usages indicate that it warrants the extra instruction so that in references to external variables we can use the shortest possible displacements.)

3. Certain T-regs (such as those representing values that are passed by reference as arguments to procedures) are marked by the Local Code Generator as requiring memory. When the Register Allocator processes these, it immediately assigns them to memory.

4. When allocating a T-reg, the Local Code Generator may specify a preference for a particular register. When it does, the Register Allocator

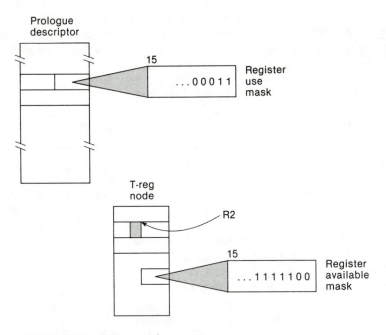

Figure 68. Register use masks.

tries to allocate that register if possible. (For example, when a function return value is assigned to a T-reg, the Local Code Generator will specify a preference for R0 because all function returns must be made using that register.)

5. To find an assignable register, the Register Allocator tries to find one that has already been used within the respective block. To do this, it computes the intersection of the set of registers that are available for allocation (from the T-reg node's register available mask) and the set of registers that have already been used (from the prologue descriptor's register use mask). The Register Allocator then attempts to allocate the required registers from the resulting set. If this set is empty or insufficient, the Register Allocator next computes the intersection of the total set of registers that could possibly be allocated and the available set—that is, it looks beyond those that have been used previously within the current block.

6. After selecting a register, the Register Allocator adds it to the register use mask in the prologue descriptor and places its number in the T-reg node. Thus, the prologue descriptor always reflects the usage of all allocated registers.

7. When a specific hardware register or set of registers has been allocated to a T-reg, the Register Allocator locates the T-reg's pointer in the

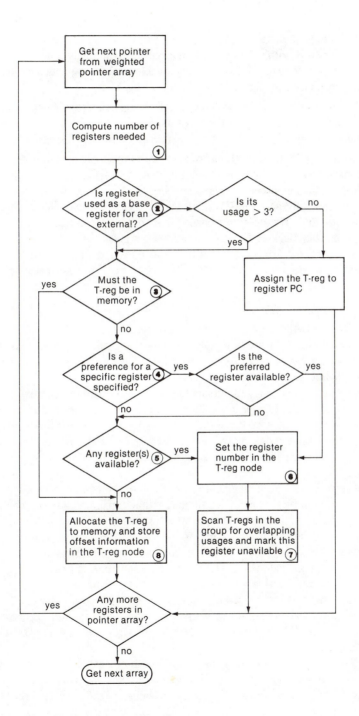

Figure 69. Register selection.

chronological pointer array. From that pointer, it scans both backward and forward within the allocation partition containing this T-reg and marks the allocated register as unavailable in all T-reg nodes whose usage spans overlap that of the current T-reg.

8. When no registers are available, the Register Allocator allocates memory for the temporary in the stack frame for the current block, determines the location, and stores this information in the T-reg node.

At the end of register allocation for a block, the prologue descriptor's register use mask contains a cumulative total (that is, the union) of all registers allocated within that procedure or begin block, as well as all registers that have been explicitly allocated or killed within the block. The Object Module and Listing File Writer—the phase that outputs the final object records—uses this mask as the procedure's entry mask. An entry mask is the set of registers that are used within the procedure and whose contents must therefore be preserved. (R0 and R1 are never part of this set because they are never saved.)

Memory Temporary Allocation

If the Register Allocator finds that no registers are available for allocation, it must allocate memory space to hold the temporary value. Then, it must also modify the operand specifier information in the intermediate code list to reflect the change in the addressing mode.

On the VAX-11 machine, all information associated with the current procedure invocation is contained in a unique data structure, the call frame, which is allocated on the stack by the VAX-11 hardware. For a given procedure invocation, the register designated as the FP points to the beginning of the frame. Thus, FP can be used to address temporaries allocated within the frame.

When register allocation begins, the front end of the compiler must already have calculated, for each block, the amount of stack space required to hold the automatic variables (including arrays, structures, and scalar variables not selected as candidates for allocation to registers) and string and decimal temporaries whose sizes were known at compile time. The Register Allocator uses this computed value as a starting point each time it begins allocating memory for T-regs within an allocation partition and maintains an adjusted value indicating the maximum additional allocation. Thus, it overlays the stack requirements of each partition with the allocation requirements for previous partitions. Figure 70 illustrates the stack layout with overlapping allocations for temporaries.

When it has allocated memory for an operand that was assigned to a T-reg, the Register Allocator updates the T-reg node to indicate that the value is in memory. Then, it records two displacement values in the T-reg node:

• The displacement of the allocated memory from FP

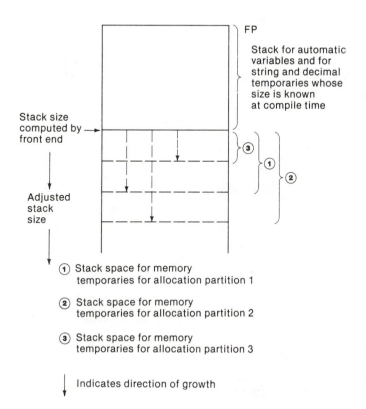

Figure 70. Stack allocation for register temporaries.

- The difference between the computed stack size and the adjusted stack size.

Normally, the Register Allocator will fill in the address of the temporary using its displacement from FP. However, because displacements from the adjusted stack size (which becomes SP—the Stack Pointer) are generally smaller numeric values than displacements from FP, it attempts a final optimization that, if successful, will shorten the size of the operand specifier: the Register Allocator determines whether it can use the SP displacement instead of the FP displacement to address the temporary. It can use SP only if the block does not perform any activity that would change SP in such a way that the Register Allocator cannot calculate its displacement from FP. For example, if the block contained any automatic string or array variables whose sizes were specified dynamically, the Register Allocator would have no way to calculate the stack offset; it then would be forced to use FP addressing. Such information about the block's dynamic use of memory is readily obtained from its block node in the Symbol Table.

When it determines that it can address temporaries using SP, the Register Allocator "reverses" the allocations so that displacements for temporaries of higher usage weights are smaller numbers. Figure 71 shows a T-reg node for a temporary allocated to memory, which is then addressed using SP rather than FP.

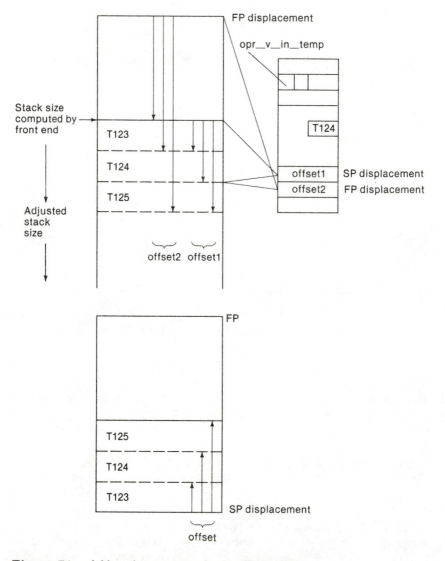

Figure 71. Addressing temporaries by FP and SP.

Updating Operand Specifiers in Code Blocks

After it has processed all the prologue descriptors and T-reg nodes and assigned either hardware register numbers or stack memory locations for each, the Register Allocator begins reading the intermediate code list. Depending on the type of code block, the Register Allocator updates addressing mode codes, register numbers, and displacements in operand specifiers, using the allocation information it has stored in the T-reg nodes. Figure 72 shows a simple example of how the Register Allocator fills in the code block for an instruction with two operands that were assigned to hardware registers.

Processing the Intermediate Code List

As it reads and processes the intermediate code list, the Register Allocator tracks all register usage and maintains the following information for each prologue descriptor:

- The operand counter. Each time the Register Allocator reads a code block header or a code block operand, it increments the operand counter.

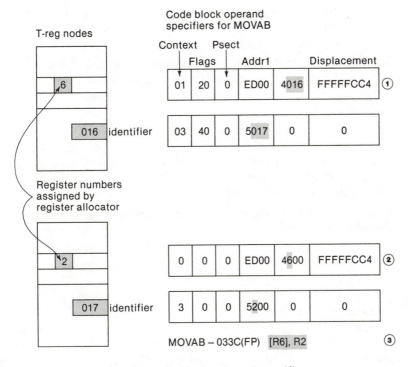

Figure 72. Updating the code block operand specifiers.

- The register state mask. Each time a specific hardware register is allocated or freed, the Register Allocator updates the register state mask to indicate the new register state. This mask always indicates which registers are available for allocation and which are in use.
- The *held register list*. The Register Allocator uses this list to record allocations of hardware registers to temporaries previously allocated to memory.

The held register list works as follows. When the Register Allocator determines that a temporary representing an index register for a machine instruction has been allocated to memory, it must allocate a hardware register and generate an instruction to load the index value into the register. When it does so, it allocates a free register (determined by the register state mask) and places the address of the T-reg node whose value is to be loaded in the position corresponding to the hardware register number in the held register list. A node remains in this list until the corresponding hardware register is required for some other purpose or until the Register Allocator flushes the list. By "holding" registers in this way, the Register Allocator avoids the overhead of releasing the register after each allocation, when in fact the register may immediately be needed again.

During its final pass through the intermediate code list, the Register Allocator performs the following five steps on each code block that represents an executable machine instruction.

1. It processes the first-use list of T-reg nodes (constructed during code generation), updating the register state mask in the prologue descriptor to indicate new registers that now contain valid values and are therefore not available for allocation.

2. It processes the register kill list. If the kill list contains an entry corresponding to the current value of the operand counter, the Register Allocator updates the register state mask to indicate that those registers are now available and removes the addresses of any related T-reg nodes from the held register list.

3. It processes the explicit allocation list. It updates the register state mask to indicate which T-regs are no longer allocated and which are to be allocated for the current instruction. When it allocates registers for the current instruction, it removes the addresses of previous entries for any related T-reg nodes in the held register list.

4. It processes instruction operands, in reverse order, modifying the addressing information to reflect the allocation of a hardware register or memory for each operand requiring either a base register or an index register. By processing them in reverse order, the Register Allocator ensures that if it is forced to compute the addresses of any operands

using the stack, the operand addresses will be pushed onto the stack in the correct order.

5. It processes the final-use list of T-regs and updates the register state mask to reflect all T-regs that no longer have values and thus have become available.

As it reads code blocks from the intermediate code list, the Register Allocator is concerned mainly with processing the operands of instruction code blocks and branch code blocks. It also, however, makes the final determination as to whether the instructions represented by conditional move code blocks are needed. If they are, it processes them; otherwise, it removes them entirely from the code list.

The Acquisition of Base and Index Registers

When it processes code block operands, a primary concern of the Register Allocator is to ensure that temporaries representing base registers or context-index registers have been allocated to registers and not to memory. If it determines that a temporary required to hold a base address or a context-index value has been assigned to memory, the Register Allocator has two remaining courses of action.

First, it looks at the register state mask in the prologue descriptor to see if a register is now free. During register allocation, it had to mark all registers unavailable that were allocated to T-regs whose usage spans overlapped that of the current temporary. However, when the Register Allocator processes the code list, it can try to use registers that may be available for only a single instruction (such as a register allocated to two T-regs whose spans do not overlap); it keeps track of these usages in the held register list.

If it finds a register in this way, the Register Allocator generates an instruction to load the contents of the memory location allocated for the T-reg into the free register and inserts the code block and operands for this instruction into the code list just before the current instruction. For example, an ADD instruction using a T-reg base register that was assigned to a hardware register (say, Rn) might look like this:

```
ADDL2   x(Rn)[R4],destination
```

However, if the temporary was allocated to memory and if the Register Allocator determines that a register, say R3, is available at this point, it generates two instructions instead of one for this ADDL2, as follows:

```
MOVL    offset(SP),R3
ADDL2   x(R3)[R4],destination
```

If no registers are available, the Register Allocator next checks the held register list to see if there are any registers whose values are not already being held for this code block. If there are any registers in the list whose final use is beyond that of the current temporary, it allocates one of these registers on the assumption that it is better to free registers that would otherwise hold values too long. When it locates a register, it stores its number in the operand specifier and generates the MOVL instruction required to load the operand's value into the register.

If it cannot allocate a register using the held register list, it inserts instructions to compute the operand address on the stack and updates the operand specifier with a stack-deferred addressing mode. Figure 73 illustrates this situation. Assume that if T-reg 123 had been allocated to a register, say Rn. Then, this SUBL2 instruction might be as follows:

```
SUBL2   x(Rn)[R4],destination
```

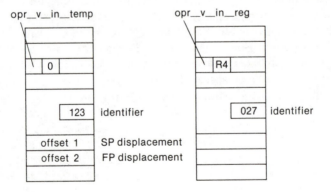

T-reg nodes before code block processing:

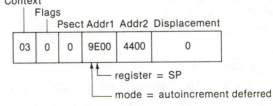

Figure 73. Emulating base register usage on the stack.

After failing to allocate a register for T-reg 123, the Register Allocator generates the following instruction to push the address of the operand onto the stack:

```
ADDL3   #x,offset(SP),-(SP)
```

The notation –(SP) indicates that it is pushing the resultant value onto the stack and decrementing SP. The Register Allocator then modifies the operand specifier in the code block, as illustrated in Figure 73, to use the computed value. The resulting instruction is

```
SUBL2   @(SP)+[R4],destination
```

where the notation @(SP)+ indicates that the operand's base address is taken from the stack and the stack pointer incremented.

Effects of Register Allocation on a Sample Program

The sample program shown in Figure 74 illustrates the effectiveness of our Register Allocator.

Figure 74. Disjoint register allocation example.

```
1    reg_example: PROCEDURE(a);

     REG_EXAMPLE:
             .entry REG_EXAMPLE,<r2,r3,r4,r5,r6,r7,r8>
             movab  -164(sp),sp

2
3    DECLARE (a,b) FIXED BINARY(31),
4            (i,j(32)) FIXED BINARY(31),
5            char1 CHARACTER(32),
6            extern_func ENTRY(FIXED BINARY(31),FIXED BINARY(31))
7                        RETURNS(FIXED BINARY(31));
8
9        DO i = a TO 32;


             movl   @04(ap),r3
```

NOTE 1 (Refer to text.)

```
             movl   r3,r4
             cmpl   r4,#32
             bgtr   vcg.2
             moval  -164(fp)[r3],r2
     vcg.1:
```

Figure 74 *(continued)*

10	SUBSTR(char1,i,1) = 'A';

```
movb    $CODE+12,-33(fp)[r4]
```

11	j(i) = 0;

```
clrl    (r2)+
```

12	END;

```
        aobleq #32,r4,vcg.1
vcg.2:
```

13	
14	IF char1 = 'test_string'
15	THEN DO;

```
cmpc5   #32,-32(fp),#32,#11,$CODE+1
bneq    vcg.3
```

16	b = j(i);

```
movl    -164(fp)[r4],r8
```

17	END;
18	ELSE DO;

```
        brb     vcg.4
vcg.3:
```

19	i = 1;

NOTE 2 (Refer to text.)

```
movl    #1,-164(fp)
```

20	b = extern_func(j(i),i);

Figure 74 *(concluded)*

```
pushal  -164(fp)
movl    -164(fp),r2
pushal  -164(fp)[r2]
calls   #2,EXTERN__FUNC
```

NOTE 3 (Refer to text.)

```
movl    r0,r8
```

21   END;

    vcg.4:

22
23 label1:
24   DO i = b TO 32;

NOTE 4 (Refer to text.)

```
movl    r8,r7
cmpl    r7,#32
bgtr    vcg.6
moval   -164(fp)[r8],r6
```
    vcg.5:

25   SUBSTR(char1,i,j(i)) = 'b';

```
cvtlw   (r6)+,r2
movc5   #1,$CODE,#32,r2,-33(fp)[r7]
```

26   END;

```
aobleq  #32,r7,vcg.5
```
    vcg.6:

27 END;

```
ret
```

In this program, the variable i has three distinct usages. Because the Optimizer phase of the compiler can detect these distinctions (or lives), the Register Allocator can, and does, assign i to different registers or to memory depending on its use.

In the sample program, we show both the PL/I source lines and the generated assembly-language code. The i, whose value is derived from the parameter a, is assigned to a register (R4 at note 1) for its first use. It is assigned to memory (note 2) for its second use because it is used as a parameter to be passed by reference in the call to *extern_func*. Last, it is assigned to a different register (R7 at note 4) for its third use.

This program also demonstrates the effects of gathering information about register use and destruction. Because we always try to assign registers using lower-numbered registers first, the register assignments in the first DO-loop (line 9) are registers R2, R3, and R4. In the last DO-loop (line 25), however, we are using registers R6, R7, and R8. We do not use R2 and R5 in this instance because the MOVC5 instruction is known to destroy the contents of registers R0 through R5. Thus, the Register Allocator does not use those registers for T-regs whose usages overlap this instruction.

In both cases, we have avoided using R0 and R1 because they are either used by the string instructions or are destroyed by the procedure calls. Moreover, because R0 is used to pass return values, it does contain the value of b on return from the call to *extern_func* (note 3); but its value is immediately loaded into another register, R8, because there is another definition of b in the THEN clause and both values must be in the same register.

Conclusions

An early article by Edward S. Lowry and C.W. Medlock on object code optimization in the OS/360 FORTRAN compiler concluded that register allocation provided one of the most important techniques for optimization (in "Object Code Optimization," *Comm. ACM,* 12 no. 1 [1969] pp. 13–22). In our case, the payoff has been very high: the Register Allocator makes a significant contribution to optimization, yet it represents less than 2 percent of the total execution time of the compiler.

We believe that the single most important aspect of our Register Allocator is that it executes after code generation. Because there is some debate as to whether register allocation may be more efficient if performed during code generation, we state here some of the benefits of our approach, many of which became apparent only after we had begun implementing and using the technique we have just described.

We can assign temporaries to registers based on total register usage. Our technique not only assigns temporaries by giving weights to those more heavily used, but also ensures that there will be no interfering register usage because of an intervening instruction or sequence of instructions.

We could have used more than 16 registers. Once we had generalized the assignment of temporaries to registers without regard to which phase allocated the temporary or for what purpose, we discovered that we could put as many objects into temporaries during code generation as we wanted to, without having to worry about conflicts in assigning them to registers. For example, the conditional loading of base pointers into registers is possible for just this reason. We allocate the temporaries during code generation and, if during register assignment we determine that there are insufficient registers or that a pointer is not referenced, we eliminate the instruction required to load the pointer into a register.

Knowledge of register use and destruction is confined to a single phase of the compiler. Only the Local Code Generator knows about specific register use. This knowledge is confined to small portions of the TBL that interprets the operator file. The Optimizer never needs to know about register use, and it can freely assign local variables to registers without regard to (possibly) generating code sequences that would destroy specific registers.

The Optimizer, Local Code Generator, and Register Allocator remain totally independent phases. When we modify the Optimizer, we do not affect any part of the Register Allocator. Although there was interplay between these phases during our development work—for example, when improvements in the Register Allocator encouraged us to modify the Optimizer to generate more temporaries—they are and have always been fully distinct phases.

Our design is suitable for a language-independent common code generator. By removing all knowledge of the machine and its registers beyond the generation of local code sequences, we ensure that the majority of optimizations remain language independent. In fact, the article by Lowry and Medlock mentioned above presaged the development of machine-dependent optimizers for multiple source languages. In it, the authors suggested that "the area of analysis and transformation of programs is extremely fruitful for programming research." Our experience shows that these techniques were indeed fruitful in the implementation of a successful, highly optimized compiler and code generator.

10

Peephole Optimization

After the Register Allocator completes its processing of the intermediate code list, and just before final code binding, the VAX-11 Code Generator executes a phase that attempts final optimizations on the instructions in the intermediate code list. The Peephole Optimizer scans generated object code for certain patterns within small ranges of instructions (the so-called peepholes). When it detects a pattern, it replaces the instruction sequence with a more efficient instruction sequence.

The classic candidates for peephole optimization are redundant move instructions and branches over branches. For example, code generators commonly produce the pattern:

```
        branch-if-operand-equal    label1
        unconditional-branch       label2
label1:
```

A peephole optimizer can readily detect this pattern and replace it with the obviously more efficient:

```
        branch-if-operand-not-equal    label2
label1:
```

Moreover, a peephole optimizer will then check whether *label1* is referenced; if not, it removes the label from the generated code.

Another common property of peephole optimizers is that they continually backtrack over instructions that were previously optimized to see if any optimizations have produced new patterns that are eligible.

This chapter describes how we implemented the Peephole Optimizer phase of the VAX-11 Code Generator, some of the peepholes we chose to detect, and our success in meeting our objectives.

Objectives

The original peephole phase in our bootstrap compiler had a very different structure from the one we now use. It defined classes of peephole; when it detected a pattern of code belonging to a given class, it executed a chain of routines. If a given routine could not apply a peephole, it passed control to the next routine, and so on until it reached the end of the chain. A particular peephole routine could not be used for several different patterns because the routines were ordered in a fixed way.

Our goals in redesigning the peephole optimizer were threefold: to detect and optimize as many patterns as possible, to make its execution time negligible, and to make it very simple to add new patterns. We also hoped to develop more comprehensive peepholes, ones that would do more than merely look at and reduce operand specifiers.

Design

The Peephole Optimizer executes after the Register Allocator. (Although, like other optimizations, its execution can be suppressed by a command option.) Its primary inputs are a series of tables—describing instructions, peephole classes, and pattern-matching routines—and the intermediate code list.

To achieve our goal of detecting and matching as many patterns as possible, we classified instructions according to peephole classes and put this information in a table indexed by machine instruction opcode values. Each peephole class comprises a set of related instructions, any of which might begin a pattern we are looking for. For example, the peephole class for fixed-point binary test instructions includes the instructions TSTB, TSTW, and TSTL. (These instructions compare a byte, word, or longword datum with zero.) This classification of instructions by the Peephole Optimizer reflects yet another exploitation of the VAX-11's orthogonal instruction set. Given three instructions differentiated only by the size of their operands, a peephole pattern can match all three. Another, more complex example is the peephole class of three-operand instructions on fixed-point binary (integer) data. This class comprises the following instructions:

```
ADDB3, SUBB3, MULB3, DIVB3, BISB3, BICB3, XORB3
ADDW3, SUBW3, MULW3, DIVW3, BISW3, BICW3, XORW3
ADDL3, SUBL3, MULL3, DIVL3, BISL3, BICL3, XORL3
```

Thus, a sequence beginning with any of these instructions will match a single pattern defined in the Peephole Optimizer.

We have defined approximately 25 peephole classes. For each class, we define a table that lists which peephole pattern-matching routines might find a match on a peephole in that class. A given peephole pattern-matching routine is not restricted to a single peephole class, but in fact many pattern-matching routines are applied to more than one peephole class. This scheme greatly enhances the number of possibilities for finding matches: the Peephole Optimizer can potentially detect and optimize approximately 1,000 different patterns.

Figure 75 illustrates the organization of the peephole tables and routines. In the drawing, the lists of pattern-matching routines for the classes described

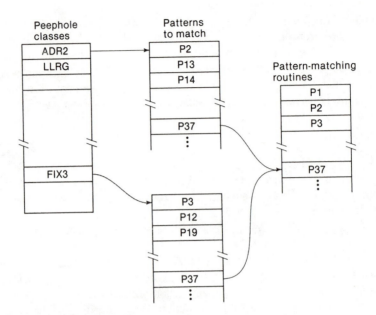

Figure 75. Peephole tables and pattern-maching routines.

above overlap at peephole routine P37. Optimization of this peephole consists of detecting and removing redundant tests that follow instructions that set a condition code. That is, given the pattern

```
instruction op1,op2,op3
conditional-branch label-n
       .
       .
       .
conditional-branch label-m
test-instruction op3
```

it detects that the *test-instruction* is redundant (because *op3* has already been tested) and removes it.

Scanning the Intermediate Code List

The second major input to the Peephole Optimizer is the intermediate code list, which at this point has been processed by the Register Allocator but not by the Code Binder. The Peephole Optimizer can modify the target addresses of branch instructions, change addressing modes in operand specifiers, remove dead code, and so on. When it processes the code list, the Peephole Optimizer performs the following tasks:

1. It reads the next code block and checks the type code. If the code block is a branch or instruction code block, the Peephole Optimizer begins its search for a peephole pattern (step 3).

2. If the code block is a label code block, it checks the Symbol Table to see if the label is referenced. If not, it removes it and returns to read the next code block. For any code block type other than branch, instruction, or label, it merely reads the next block.

3. When it reads an instruction or branch code block, it reads the instruction table to get the peephole class and locates the list of pattern-matching routines for that class.

4. It dispatches control to the first, or next, pattern-matching routine. The pattern-matching routine executes and, if it detects its given pattern, performs its optimization.

5. If the optimization is successful, the pattern-matching routine sets a flag called *reduced* and returns; otherwise, it returns without setting this flag.

6. When a pattern-matching routine returns with a *reduced* status, the Peephole Optimizer backs up over the code list, usually about five code blocks (not counting statement code blocks) and continues. The number of code blocks it backs up represents the maximum number of instructions in any peephole sequence.

7. If the pattern-matching routine returns without a *reduced* status, the Peephole Optimizer tries the next pattern-matching routine in the table (step 3). It continues through the table until a routine returns a *reduced* status, or until all routines have been tried and none returned *reduced*.

Figure 76 summarizes this control flow.

Some Peepholes

This section presents some examples to illustrate some of our considerations in selecting and optimizing peepholes.

Peepholes Involving Temporaries

A number of peephole patterns involve the use of temporaries that are subsequently reused, as in:

```
ADDL3    x,y,temp
MOVL     temp,z
```

Here, the values of x and y are added and the result is stored in a temporary. The temporary is subsequently the source operand of the MOVL in-

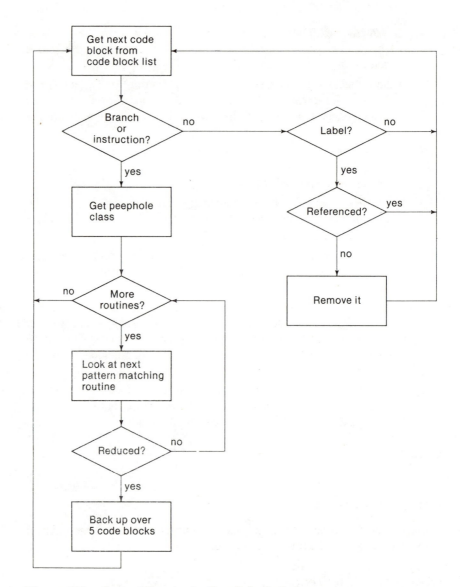

Figure 76. Control flow in the Peephole Optimizer.

struction, which stores it in *z*. This pattern occurs frequently and clearly is eligible for transformation to:

```
ADDL3    x,y,z
```

The primary consideration in performing peephole optimizations on this and similar sequences is the need to verify that the temporary is no longer needed following the MOVL instruction. Because information in the operand specifier indicates whether that use of the operand is the last use of a temporary, the Peephole Optimizer can easily test whether this is the last use and, if so, perform the optimization. Most peephole optimizers would have to look ahead to see whether the operand is used again; ours has the information readily encoded. This is a major factor in the success of our second goal—a fast Peephole Optimizer.

Generating Stack Addressing

In a similar optimization, the result of an operation is pushed onto the stack. For example, the Peephole Optimizer transforms instruction sequences such as

```
ADDL3    x,y,temp
   .
   .
   .
PUSHL    temp
```

to the single instruction

```
ADDL3    x,y,-(SP)
```

where the destination operand of the generated ADD instruction indicates that the result is to be pushed onto the stack and the SP register decremented accordingly. In this peephole, the limiting criteria are that no intervening instruction may modify the stack and that the PUSHL must represent the last use of the temporary.

Operand Reduction

As the preceding example shows, the Peephole Optimizer can in some cases eliminate instructions because it knows more about the program than does the Local Code Generator. The Local Code Generator produces only one instruction at a time, without regard to whether operands will eventually be in registers or in memory. The Peephole Optimizer, however, does have such information, which lets it detect and optimize patterns such as

```
ADDL3    x,y,temp
MULL3    z,temp,w
```

in which a three-operand instruction storing its result in a temporary is followed by a three-operand instruction that consumes that temporary. For a pattern like this (which it detects for both integer and floating-point operations), the Peephole Optimizer can change the second three-operand instruction to a two-operand one, as follows:

```
ADDL3    x,y,w
MULL2    z,w
```

Here, it stores the result of the ADD instruction directly in the destination for the MULL2 instruction because in a two-operand multiply instruction the destination operand contains one of the multipliers. This optimization decreases the execution speed of the resulting program in only two cases:

- If the temporary, *temp,* is in memory. In this case, the Peephole Optimizer eliminates the addressing base and displacement that would be required to specify the temporary as an operand in two places.

- If both the temporary, *temp,* and the final destination, *w,* are registers.

Thus, the Peephole Optimizer performs this peephole only if the execution speed will improve, which is not the case if we end up with additional memory accesses in the interests of shortening the instruction stream.

Conclusions

Our approach to peephole optimization has proved very efficient. Not only is it simple to add peephole pattern-matching and optimization routines, but the cost of adding them—in terms of both development time and compiler execution time—is so small that we can add them whenever we see a pattern in generated code that can be reduced.

For comparison purposes, we compiled the source code of the Optimizer (written in PL/I) without running the peephole optimization phase, built a version of the PL/I compiler using this Optimizer, and then used this version of the compiler to compile the Optimizer's sources. The following figures show the differences in object module size and execution time in the resulting compilers.

	Optimizer Compiled with Peephole	Optimizer Compiled without Peephole
Size	25,630 bytes	27,618 bytes
Time	57.65 seconds	61.04 seconds

Thus the effect of performing peephole optimizations on the Optimizer is a 7 percent space reduction and a 5.5 percent reduction in run time. (Additional statistics on the effect of peephole optimization are illustrated in Figures 44 through 49 at the end of Chapter 7.)

We successfully met our original goals. Our Peephole Optimizer recognizes 10 to 20 times as many patterns as do other peephole optimizers. Moreover, in an average compilation, the peephole optimization phase consistently represents less than 2 percent of the total time required for compilation. Third, other programmers who subsequently worked on the compiler found it quite simple to contribute and incorporate peepholes (and not only simple, but fun). This is one of the few areas of compiler design and development in which there is a nearly instant improvement in generated code. Discovering a peephole, adding it to the Peephole Optimizer, and incorporating the augmented Peephole Optimizer in the compiler could take as little as 20 minutes. Finally, we have documented in this chapter not only peepholes that reduce the size of operands in the code list, but also some that remove entire instructions; thus we met our underlying goal of developing comprehensive peepholes.

11

Beauty and the Beast

The traditional topics of books about compiler design are parsing, symbol table construction, and simple semantic analysis. Other topics of interest in this specialized field—such as code generation—have been slighted. Computer science courses in compiler construction reinforce the tradition by ending the semester before reaching the topic of code generation. It was our intention to break with this tradition. Most of our discussion is devoted to the lesser known part of a compiler, the back end. We found working on the code generation phases very interesting and gratifying.

We include this chapter for readers who may feel that our book would not be complete without more information on parsing and semantic analysis and for readers who are curious about how we approached design considerations in building the front ends of compilers for two different programming languages. Here, we discuss from an engineering standpoint how we addressed parsing and semantic analysis for the two languages, and we compare not only the two front ends but the techniques we used in their implementation.

Background

Before we finished the PL/I compiler, we wanted to prove that we could use our back end in constructing another compiler. To do this, we had to implement another front end. Because Digital already had corporate compiler products for most of the interesting modern languages (and because we had to find a project for which we could be funded), we were limited in our choice. We chose C (or C chose us: given the growing interest in the language, the historical relationship between PDP-11s and UNIX, and the growing relationship between VAX/VMS and VAX/UNIX, a union seemed inevitable).

Although C is also a procedure-based language that provides for declarations of data in structures, it has little else in common with PL/I. Yet, to prove our point about common code generation, we needed to construct a C compiler front end that was "plug-compatible" with our PL/I front end. That is, it had to produce a Symbol Table and a set of trees for C statements that could then be processed by the back end with no language-specific changes to the latter.

Our first task was to organize the major functions of the compiler so that it consisted of an execution envelope containing all processing that was not specific to PL/I. It was in the middle of this envelope that we would put the language-specific front end. In addition to the code generation routines in the back end, the envelope had to contain common procedures and routines that:

- Initialized common data structures
- Processed compiler command lines into a common data structure
- Allocated and manipulated the Symbol Table
- Allocated and manipulated trees
- Provided I/O functions for source, preprocessor, object, and listing files
- Issued error messages in the standard format required by the VAX/VMS operating system.

The compiler's common routines perform initialization and command interpretation and then invoke the language-specific front end for each source file. When the front end—working with Write Tree—is complete, the envelope enters the optimization phase, which is the beginning of the back end's work. At the end of code generation for a given source file, the compiler can reinitialize itself and perform another compilation without having to be reloaded.

If the back end were indeed language independent, the details of the input language syntax and semantics should be unimportant. Our approach to implementing a C front end was indeed diametrically opposite to the original PL/I approach. Our title for this chapter is an appropriate metaphor for our expectations about the distinctions between the two projects (if not about the distinctions between the languages themselves). We already had a solid, well-engineered PL/I compiler, and we were proud of its performance. Given our experience with it and the relative simplicity of the C language compared with PL/I, we thought that a C compiler would be significantly smaller and faster than our PL/I compiler. The PL/I compiler, previously beautiful, would begin (we thought) to look like a beast in comparison.

The Beast

One of our important initial goals (and a self-imposed constraint) in building the PL/I compiler was to minimize the changes to the compiler's front end. We knew that it was a well-tested, solid design. We also wanted to avoid designing any new language features until we had acquired sufficient expertise in both the compiler internals and the PL/I language. (One lesson we learned the hard way was that it was imprudent to add new features to the language simply because we knew how to implement the change in the compiler. Adding new language features requires careful consideration. We have seen compiler designers fall into the trap of trying to solve everyone's problems and ending up with poor language design.)

The PL/I parser and semantic analysis phases were based on mature designs for processing the PL/I language and not on current state-of-the-art theories and techniques. Each method used, though simple and elegant, was specific to the processing of PL/I. We think this approach has real merit and should be considered by serious compiler designers and implementors who want to build production-quality compilers. In fact, our experience showed that once the parser was designed and stabilized, it not only worked very well, it was easy to modify and understand.

PL/I Syntax

Before describing the PL/I front end, we present a short introduction to the language syntax. This should help those who are not familiar with PL/I as well as those who want to understand just how we see it in order to parse it.

PL/I is syntactically a well-defined language. Most PL/I source code consists of sequences of identifiers that may be followed by comma-delimited lists of items enclosed in parentheses. Related sequences are separated from other sequences by semicolons. Assignment statements and arithmetic expressions require a special treatment; assignments because they involve a punctuation separator (an equal sign), arithmetic expressions because they represent either constant or computed values.

From this perspective on the language, it appears that a very general, straightforward parser can be built and combined with a more complex semantic analyzer to form the basis for a PL/I front end. Although this general approach is not necessarily the most efficient way of parsing and semantically analyzing a PL/I program, it demonstrates that the task is intuitively uncomplicated. Take a simple example, a stream output statement.

```
PUT SKIP(2) FILE(outfile)
        LIST('Values are:',array(1,2,3),b,c);
```

Here, the identifiers are PUT, SKIP, FILE, and LIST. Some are followed by parenthesized expressions or lists of items. A language defined in this way can be parsed with a generalized syntax scanner that recognizes these simple repeated sequences and records their presence in a table. The semantic processor must then assign meaning to the combination of sequences, write a symbol table, and emit a set of trees.

Experienced PL/I programmers will no doubt think of some exceptions to this simplified set of syntax rules. Exceptions do exist, and in fact our PL/I front end handles much more complicated cases than the one described above. However, many commonly encountered parsing problems are really no more complicated than this one.

The Structure of the Beast

The PL/I compiler front end consists of four separate parts that communicate via the Symbol Table and the operator trees. The multiphase structure of the PL/I front end is dictated by PL/I semantics, which allow free ordering of declarations and usage. Because names are not necessarily declared before their use, the compiler must process the entire source file before the Symbol Table is complete.

Though necessitated by the PL/I declaration semantics, the division of the front end into several phases also provides programming modularity and functional separation of tasks. Given a well-defined input, each phase had a well-defined result. We built diagnostic aids to dump the contents of the Symbol Table and operator trees at the divisions between the phases. Thus, we could divide the work on the compiler front end among ourselves. This arrangement worked quite well, and we can recall few instances in which debugging involved more than one phase of the compiler. In the PL/I compiler, the distinct phases are:

- PASS1, the syntactic parser and token recognizer
- The lexical analyzer, which includes the source file I/O and preprocessor routines (this phase is essentially a slave of PASS1)
- DECLARE, the declaration processor
- PASS2, the semantic analyzer that merges parse and declaration information.

With the exception of the lexical analyzer, all of these front end procedures are written in PL/I or TBL programs whose interpreters are written in PL/I.

PASS1: PASS1 embodies the parser and syntactic recognizer for the PL/I language. The result of PASS1 is the Symbol Table and a linear representation of the program trees. The trees are functionally correct after PASS1, but references to the Symbol Table remain unresolved. References to identifiers and constants in the program are passed to the next phases as textual information in a special form of REF operator called an SREF. Symbol Table lookups are not allowed in PASS1 because the total Symbol Table is not formed until the entire source program has been processed. Thus, trees created by PASS1 have neither data type nor size information.

The structure and methodology of PASS1 is simple and elegant. The actual logic for the parser is encoded and written in TBL. The TBL for PASS1 implements a high-level language specifically designed to parse PL/I source text. Actions in PASS1's TBL include actions that match the token type, save and restore information on a parse stack, and write trees from the contents of the stack. The PASS1 TBL logic is interpreted at compile time by an interpreter written in PL/I. Though using TBL results in a table-driven parse, it is important to remember that in TBL a table is expressed in algorithmic form rather than a numerical form consisting of arrays of small, constant integers. Moreover, the logic of the parse is easy to discern from reading the TBL program. This logic is simply a top-down, left-to-right, predictive scheme that uses a recursive descent logic with operator precedence for parsing arithmetic expressions. Recursive descent parsers are considered inefficient, usually because they require extensive look-ahead (to find a particular token) or backtracking (when a prediction proves wrong). If carefully planned and implemented, however, these problems can be avoided in a recursive descent parser. For example, the PL/I parser never backtracks and it needs a look-ahead only in one case, and that is to recognize an assignment statement. Since it is only a single case, we put the logic to recognize an assignment statement in the lexical scanner, which records the occurrence of assignment statements as a side effect of its scan.

Statements are parsed as follows: at the start of a statement, the lexical analyzer is called to return a vector of recognized tokens. The token vector spans the start of the statement to a semicolon or the keyword THEN. The token vector contains values corresponding to the type of token recognized. The values themselves are tightly encoded to optimize run-time efficiency. All white space and noise in the source (including comments and line marks) are removed in the process of building the recognized token vector. When it has a complete vector of tokens, PASS1 predicts the statement type by examining the first token after the last label (indicated by a colon). Because PL/I statements generally start with standard keywords, only a simple table lookup is required. Assignment statements, the noted exception, are recognized as statements that end in semicolons and have equal signs that are not embedded in parentheses.

IF statements can also have equal signs at this level, but they terminate with the keyword THEN. THEN keywords require even more special processing. Because PL/I has no reserved words, the parser must be able to distinguish uses of names as keywords and uses of the same names as user-defined identifiers. Given

```
IF then THEN then = ^then;
     ELSE then = then & else;
```

the lexical scanner must differentiate the keywords (shown here in uppercase) from their other uses (shown here in lowercase). To do so, it asks two questions: is the THEN beyond two tokens of the previous label or start of a statement? Is the THEN preceded by a right parenthesis, an identifier, or a constant? If both of these are true, then this occurrence is the keyword THEN.

Having found the statement keyword and knowing the statement type, PASS1 begins executing the TBL source that has the logic to parse that statement's syntax. The output of a set of trees for this statement is then well defined.

When it encounters a PROCEDURE statement, PASS1's TBL performs a recursive transition. It parses and recognizes the new procedure before returning to the containing (outer) procedure. For example, the syntax of the PL/I RETURN statement is as follows:

```
optional_label: RETURN;
```

Or, if the procedure is a function, it is the following:

```
optional_label: RETURN(expression);
```

For a program source statement like

```
end_of_program: RETURN(arg1+1);
```

the lexical analyzer would produce a token vector something like:

```
identifier 'end_of_program'
colon
identifier 'return'
left paren
identifier 'arg1'
plus sign
fixed point decimal constant 1
right paren
semicolon
```

The TBL routine that processes RETURN statements in PASS1, shown below, is entered after the label and the keyword RETURN have been processed.

```
return_stmnt:
if current_token(semi_colon)
    THEN [
        emit_operator(return_op);
        ]
    ELSE [
        /* The procedure is a function and the
        /* RETURN must be followed by a left paren
        match_current_token(left_paren);
        call(process_expression);
        save_on_stack;    /* Save the value of the
                          /* expression on the stack
        match_current_token(right_paren);
        match_current_token(semi_colon);
        /* Emit valued return operator
        /* using the value on stack
        emit_operator(return_op,top_element);
        ]
    RETURN;
```

This routine emits one of two trees depending on whether the optional expression is present and whether the presence of the expression is detected by the placement of the semicolon. The action *match_current_token* issues an error message if it does not find what it is looking for.

Advocates of state-of-the-art parsing techniques might dismiss this direct method of parsing as uninteresting. Most will think it inadequate for producing meaningful error messages. They may also think that this form of parser is hard to modify. From our standpoint, all these assessments are simply wrong. Meaningful, pinpoint-location error messages result from a careful design. Ease of modification comes from careful implementation.

In fact, the PL/I compiler can produce explicit error messages for syntax problems. The logic for the parse scan is controlled by the actions in the TBL program like those shown in the fragment above. At any point, a general error or mismatched token can result in an error as specific as:

`'+' found where ';' was expected`

This is a very fine level of detail.

The Lexical Analyzer: The job of a lexical scanner is to differentiate sequences of input characters into recognizable units. Each programming language may have different names for the units, but generally they include:

- Identifiers
- Numbers
- Punctuation characters.

In our compiler, the lexical analysis routines also perform all source input and preprocessor functions. Because source file I/O routines perform similar functions in all compilers, we packaged these routines in our common envelope.

Preprocessor functions are modifications of the source text at compile time by lexically recognizable directives in the source file. PL/I has several common preprocessor functions. The ones supported in our compiler are

`%REPLACE token1 BY token2;`

which replaces all occurrences of *token1* with *token2*, and

`%INCLUDE file-name;`

which copies text from the given file into the current source. These statements are processed entirely by the lexical analyzer and are never seen as tokens by PASS1. Many compilers implement preprocessor functions as a separate pass over the source. We think that this is wasteful and that most users have no need for the intermediate, preprocessed source representation.

The best lexical analyzers keep per-character processing time to the absolute minimum. One of our goals for the PL/I compiler was to make the compilation as fast as possible. Since the lexical scanner is the only part of the compiler that processes each character of the source, we wanted very much to reduce that per-character processing time in order to decrease the overall compilation time.

Like many traditional lexical analyzers, the bootstrap compiler's was a finite-state automaton. It was written in PL/I with a table of state transitions that were driven by individual input characters. On the VAX-11, we had a unique opportunity to use the machine's extensive set of character-string instructions; we therefore rewrote the lexical analyzer in assembly language, without changing its basic algorithms. For example, we designed the new lexical scanner to use the string instructions called SPANC and SCANC. These are single instructions that skip over long sequences of related characters and interpret a table of values much like a translation instruction. They stop on certain values encoded in the tables. For instance, a SCANC instruction can be set up to scan for legal characters in identifiers, numbers, and constants. Using these instructions in conjunction with the other VAX-11 string instructions meant that we rarely had to process single characters in the source file. By rewriting and restructuring the lexical scanner in VAX-11 assembly language to use these string instructions, we reduced the compilation time required by PASS1 by half and increased the overall performance of the compiler by one-tenth. This was our first major compile-time improvement.

We made further improvements by tightly encoding the token vector given to PASS1. Since the PASS1 source refers to token types by using named constants, there was no reason to give the token type constants reasonable values. In fact, to minimize the lexical processing time, we gave the punctuation tokens their corresponding ASCII values in decimal. For example, the plus sign (+) was assigned the value 43. This meant that the other token types, such as identifiers, had to be given values that overlapped the ASCII set but that were invalid characters in a PL/I source file. For example, the token type for identifiers was given the value 25, the ASCII code for the CTRL-key/letter-Y sequence.

A third improvement we made to this pass was to make the tokens for all identifiers and constants canonical, so that all identifiers were made uppercase and all numbers were made well formed. Syntactic errors such as invalid numerical characters are covered up by passing on a correct constant to PASS1—usually a 1—thus eliminating the need to check whether this error caused additional errors that should not be reported.

DECLARE: We call the second phase of the PL/I front end DECLARE. It gives order to lexically unrelated declaration information and forms a well-structured Symbol Table. The result is that declarations appear to occur in a lexically correct order even though they were not specified that way in the source file. To do this, DECLARE scans the rough Symbol Table constructed by PASS1 and analyzes the data. It performs consistency checks on all attribute information and applies the PL/I language defaults (for example, if a variable is declared only FIXED, DECLARE will add the attribute BINARY and a precision attribute of 31). This is the phase that detects and reports user declaration errors and inconsistencies.

DECLARE also processes expressions specifying extent and size information and reduces them to their simplest forms. In most cases these are constants, but PL/I also allows run-time evaluation of such expressions.

When DECLARE has finished, the Symbol Table is in a state that will allow later phases to perform lookup functions on specific identifier strings.

PASS2: The workhorse of the PL/I front end is PASS2. It combines the syntactically correct trees produced by PASS1 and the validated Symbol Table produced by DECLARE into fully expanded and semantically correct trees. These trees are then given to Write Tree for simplification and eventual output to the Optimizer.

PASS2 sequentially processes individual trees created by PASS1. Each tree is rooted in a node that does not yield a value. For example, the ADD operator yields a value, but the ASSIGN operator does not. Therefore, when it encounters an ASSIGN operator, PASS2 stops building the tree and begins processing it.

The logic for PASS2's tree processing is encoded in another TBL program. Like those written for PASS1 and the Local Code Generator, the TBL for PASS2 is unique: it is written for the specific purpose of semantically analyzing trees. These TBL actions are operations that verify the data type and insert a new operator if a conversion is needed.

During expansion of the PASS1 trees into fully expanded trees, PASS2 performs all of the following functions:

- Expands references from textual form into Symbol Table references with addressing information and data type.

- Expands array references or dynamic extents into offset calculations.

- Checks each operator for semantic correctness. If necessary, it inserts operator trees for data type conversions. If it cannot determine any semantic meaning, it issues an error message.

- Adds operators to the procedure prologue to cause proper initialization and dynamic storage allocation.

When a tree is fully processed, it is passed on to Write Tree to be reduced for processing by the Optimizer.

Domesticating the Beast

Our PL/I compiler front end is not the pinnacle of compiler technology. We took a well-proven design and implementation and tailored it to fit the VAX-11 architecture and VAX/VMS methodology. We took full advantage of the VAX-11 instruction set and our experience with it. The resulting high-quality compiler is a successful tool for producing quality software.

We were comfortable with the structure of the PL/I front end, mainly because it fit well with our earlier operating system software methodology. In its modularity, functional separation of components, and approachability, it resembles an operating system. We borrowed many internal concepts of VAX/VMS in our construction of the Local Code Generator and in our memory allocation and data structure design.

Implementing our second compiler front end was less gratifying. We started the C compiler project with less expertise in the language than we had with PL/I at the same point. Moreover, we lacked a language expert. We also soon discovered that the C language was a moving target: gone were the advantages of ANSI standards and competitors' reference manuals documenting a relatively stable language. For answers to troublesome questions, we used several C compilers to which we had gained access for experimentation.

Each C compiler that we tried had different levels of sophistication and support. Some checked for a particular error, some did not. Some laid out memory for structures on VAX-11 one way and some another. Compatibility with UNIX was also an important goal. Eventually, we gravitated to a "standard," but one that might be uniquely ours! We wanted to implement the compiler front end using C as the implementation language and to bootstrap our compiler from another C compiler in much the same way that we had bootstrapped PL/I. We did this bootstrapping backward, as we had with PL/I. We had the additional advantage of knowing that the back end was thoroughly debugged, so we could concentrate on debugging the front end. This did require work.

A first major decision in the actual design of the C front end was to ignore the lessons that we had learned in doing the PL/I front end. This time we would do a textbook implementation. The C language is simply structured, regular, and modern, and as such seemed a perfect candidate for building a state-of-the-art front end. We have come to refer to it as the Beauty.

The Beauty

The Beauty—our C compiler—is constructed around an LALR(1) grammar and a parser that traverses the LALR(1) description tables using the source token sequence to drive the traversal. The result is a single-pass front end that generates trees directly, source statement by source statement. Unlike PL/I, the C language adapts well to this scheme because all declarations must precede use. As a reference is processed, all of the Symbol Table information needed for that reference must already have been processed or an error results.

In the implementation of C, we encountered several technical issues we had not foreseen and for which we had to supply solutions. We had expected the LALR(1) parser to be easy and fast to implement. Many tools exist to build

such parsers, and we in fact borrowed both an internal Digital parse table generator and a parser that had been successfully used to build other parsers.
However, we soon found we had to spend considerable development time in
generating the LALR(1) grammar. Many common programming languages
are not strictly context free. LALR(1) parse schemes work best for context-
free grammars, less well for context-sensitive cases. And C did not form a
natural LALR(1) grammar. Although the language definition in the *C Programming Language* (Brian W. Kernighan and Dennis M. Ritchie, Prentice-
Hall, 1978) closely resembles an LALR(1) grammar description, it is not a
formal LALR(1) definition, and we in fact had several problems trying to
adapt C into the framework of the grammar. For example, our parse table
generator did not allow operator precedence to be incorporated in the grammar description. This meant that our LALR(1) description for C had 13 levels
of reduction just to parse expressions (in addition to the parsing of the statements surrounding the expression). Languages like PASCAL have only three
or four precedence levels and as a result have far less complex grammars.
The level of complexity in the C grammar was also not without cost in terms
of execution time.

The development of the C parser was also frustrated by our desire to incorporate the LALR(1) grammer in a single-pass semantic phase. One of the subtle problems we encountered in C was the syntactic distinction between a
function declaration and a function definition. The distinction is not necessarily in the syntax of the function declarator itself, but rather in the presence of
a trailing "}" character. Potentially, a LALR(1) parser cannot detect the presence of the "}" if it is more than a token away; thus, the parser must process
function declarations and function definitions the same way and then perform
the specific semantic checks later. For example:

```
struct tnode *f() {    /* a definition of a function */
       .               /* returning a pointer */
       .               /* to tnodes */

       .
       }
struct tnode *f();     /* a declaration of the same */
```

This syntax is not ambiguous to a human reader; our parse problem was a
result of the structure of the compiler—in this case, because the semantic
analysis phase needed to know whether a definition or a declaration is in
progress when it is processing the "f" token. If the compiler checked syntax
independently from semantics, this would have been easier. As it was, we had
to put special cases in the grammar to process this correctly.

Depending on the sophistication of the LALR(1) tools available, the development of a grammar description can be a frustrating process of primarily
blind iteration. Each change to our grammar caused a potentially substantial

loss of time, in contrast to the comparative ease with which we had changed the TBL for the PL/I front end. Once the grammar was complete—and its development took four months—we could begin building a compiler. Remarkably, the grammar remained relatively stable during the compiler development.

One potential benefit of LALR(1) parsing is that error messages can be very explicit; in addition, it can incorporate simple local error correction. Since we had borrowed our parser from another compiler group, we had a chance to experiment with automated local error correction. Although we were impressed by the success of the error correction technique for other languages, we soon removed much of it because C proved to have many constructions that cause problems for recovery schemes. For example, consider the difference between

+ +

and

++

The first of these is an error, the second is not! We also found that nonsyntactic errors were handled no better than in our PL/I compiler, although we had been led to believe that with LALR(1) they would be.

While constructing the lexical analyzer for the C compiler, we had to contend with the fact that the C language has rich and powerful preprocessor functions. We constructed the C lexical analyzer to behave like the PL/I lexical scanner and to process all preprocessor and I/O functions. This prevented the parser from knowing the actual nuances of the input source. We considered making the lexical scanner a part of the common compiler envelope; but we felt that, because the lexical scanner for C was more complex than its PL/I counterpart, it would be unreasonable to make a common routine. It should be possible to construct a common lexical scanner, but we chose not to do so.

The parser was implemented to traverse the LALR(1) tables based on lexically recognized token sequences and to call a semantic action routine when it reached a reduction point. The semantic action routine would perform its processing on the basis of context information maintained on a semantic stack. The semantic action routines themselves are usually small, but because C requires more than 100 different actions, the technique was cumbersome. The parser would call one large routine that processed all actions, specifying which action it was to perform. This meant that the action processing routine became a monolithic module starting with a C SWITCH statement (a case construction). This lack of modularity in our semantic actions became a major problem. Moreover, because each semantic action routine was intimately involved with actions in other routines, it was not easy to break up the module. Although we were never able to separate all the actions, we moved as much code as possible from this module into external subroutines, some of which were used only in one place.

Typically, a semantic action processes the current token and either places a tree address on the semantic stack or combines a stacked tree with the current token and leaves a new tree on the top of the stack. Even in simple cases, this scheme is conceptually difficult because the predecessor and successor states of a semantic action are hidden in the order of the LALR(1) table traversal. Of course, this might not be true of a simpler grammar specification. It helped to remember that the processing usually proceeded left to right.

Another cumbersome problem of the "do it all at once" method was that even though error detection and diagnostic output were easy to implement, semantic error recovery was difficult. An example of a semantic error is a data type mismatch in an assignment. At first, instead of recovering from the error, the compiler terminated after the first such error. Our final implementation took a nondetection and nonpropagation approach: the semantic action routine issued an error, set a static variable that recorded the occurrence of the error, and then left the stack in a state as if the error had not occurred. During the final reduction for a statement, the statement trees could be discarded without further error, based on the value of the static error flag. This scheme minimized the severity of semantic errors because in most cases we found routes to clean recovery. As a result, our C compiler has many "warning" diagnostics and few severe semantic error diagnostics. (Though beneficial to future users of the compiler, this scheme was frustrating to us as the initial implementors and would be to future modifiers of the compiler. This is probably an axiom of software engineering.)

Near the end of the first stage of our implementation, we discovered several more flaws in the single-pass design. One problem was that trees need to be written in lexical order. Sometimes not all of the necessary semantic information is available when the tree should be completed. This is the case when processing the SWITCH construction. It is necessary at the point of the SWITCH invocation statement to generate trees to verify that the index value is within the range of the specified options. Until the SWITCH construction is fully processed, however, these limits are not known. We considered several solutions to this chicken-and-egg problem.

1. Create trees referencing memory temporaries that are initialized to the constant extents of the SWITCH options. We dismissed this solution because we invariably received comments on how terrible the generated code looked.

2. Put a branch around the SWITCH construction and delay the SWITCH trees until after the entire construction has been passed to Write Tree. Our inspection of other compilers dealing with this problem shows that this is a popular approach. Unfortunately, it causes real havoc during optimization. We rejected it for basically the same reasons we had rejected solution 1.

3. Implement solution 2, but have the Optimizer rearrange the construction. Since our Optimizer was to be a common part of all compilers, we did not want to clutter it up with language-specific items. Thus we rejected this approach.

4. Backpatch the operators when the values are known. We unanimously rejected this because it violated our sense of software engineering esthetics.

5. Rescan the operators after reading the entire source file and fill in the proper construction.

We chose the last option. The front end recognizes the occurrence of SWITCH statements and forces a second pass over the program. This second pass constructs and inserts the optimal SWITCH trees for the limit value tests. The code generated using this approach looks better than that for any of the other solutions; the total cost for rescanning the trees is less than 5 percent of the total compilation time. Later, we found several other language constructs that could make use of the second pass. If a program contains none of these constructs, the compiler does not perform the second pass.

We expected the single-phase C front end to outperform the three-phase PL/I front end in every respect. We were disappointed. Each front end requires about the same time on an equivalent program. The bottleneck in the C compiler is the parse table traverse loop. In searching the LALR(1) tables, the parser consumes up to 25 percent of the front end processing time in an eight-instruction loop. However, because the compiler met our initial goal of compiling source code at a rate of more than 2,000 lines per minute, and because we were not positive that we could obtain any substantial improvement without significant redesign, we did not go back to fix the problem.

What Is the Moral?

Our experience with using the same code generator for two different language compilers has proved to be a success. Although we encountered problems in implementing the C compiler, they were front end problems that we would have faced had we been implementing a compiler from scratch. The fact that we had a code generator made the time to commercial production very short for the second compiler. And, given the proven worth of the back end's optimization and code generation techniques, we feel that this is another production-quality compiler.

The development effort for the VAX-11 C compiler required only 2 man years, compared with 11 for the PL/I compiler and its large run-time library (not including the years of development spent by Freiburghouse on his earlier versions of both a full PL/I and the subset). Comparing the relative merits of the internal designs requires more thought, and such thought yields an apt analogy to most areas of applied engineering. The PL/I front end had the benefit of several generations of design and implementation, spanning the time from the origination of Freiburghouse's compilers through almost two product releases of VAX-11 PL/I. The C compiler's front end had the benefit of modern theory in computer science. What distinguishes the two is simply the level of real engineering experience that they embody. Although the dragon sometimes wins, it is engineering, not science, that is the best weapon.

12

Concluding
Remarks

The three years we devoted to the design and development of compilers resulted in two products—the VAX-11 PL/I and VAX-11 C compilers. The PL/I compiler has been available on VAX-11 systems since November of 1980. The C compiler was made available in the spring of 1982. Our back end also contributed to work on two other compiler projects: a PEARL compiler completed in Digital's European Software Engineering group in Reading, England, concurrently with the PL/I project, and a fourth compiler still under development at Digital Equipment Corporation in the United States.

In preceding chapters, we have summarized our opinions about different phases of the compiler and explained, whenever possible, why we made certain design decisions and what their ultimate effect has been. Here, we discuss compiler design as an engineering experience and conclude with some statistics illustrating the comparative weights of the language-specific and the common phases in each of our compilers.

We feel strongly that a fundamental element of our success is that we approached the problems as engineers and not as theoreticians. Although we benefited from current literature on the subject of compiler design and from an existing design and its documentation, we approached our task—writing and debugging code—empirically. It was not until we had written essentially the entire compiler that we thoroughly understood it. Once we understood all the pieces and how they interacted, we began the process of reengineering.

More than half this book is devoted to some aspect of optimization—the Optimizer itself, Write Tree's reductions, the Register Allocator, and the Peephole Optimizer—because these are the phases of the compiler that were most frequently revised and rewritten. We have concluded that, when it comes to optimization, engineering is far more important than theory. Our basic technique could actually be called repeated engineering. By continually looking at the code we were generating, we continually saw areas for potential improvement. The solutions always lay in better software engineering, especially in the cases of the Optimizer and the Register Allocator. For example, because significant portions of the compiler itself are written in PL/I —including the Optimizer—each optimization we added further increased the compile-time performance of the compiler.

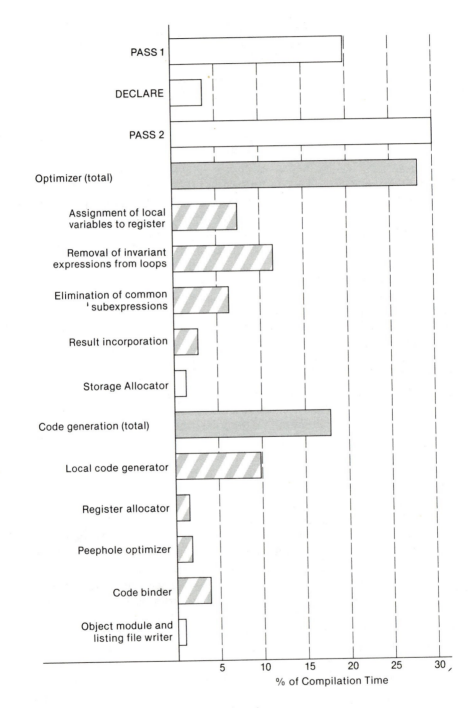

Figure 77. PL/I compiler execution-time summary.

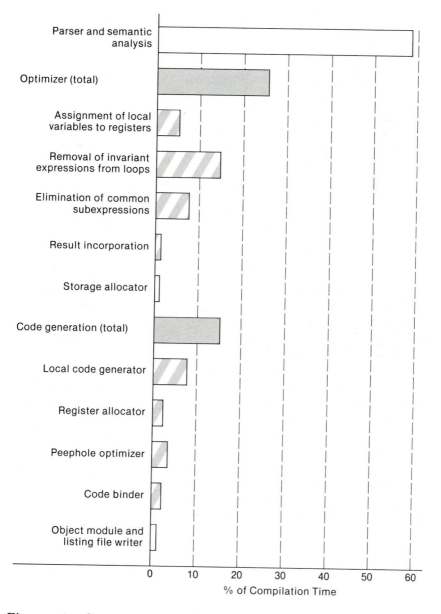

Figure 78. C compiler execution-time summary.

In modifying existing phases to increase optimization, we did adhere to the basic payoff rule: the change had to improve the generated code without degrading compile-time performance. For example, the development of a comprehensive algorithm for the removal of invariant expressions from loops required us to restructure the way the front end built the loop control operators. This change did not affect the performance of the compiler but made a large improvement on the generated code. One rule we never followed: "If it works, don't touch it."

An obvious corollary to repeated engineering is never to be afraid to try something even though there is no guarantee that it is exactly the right thing to do. In some cases, this attitude leads to felicitous results. Our decision to use TBL, for example, was made hastily with the assumption that it was probably not the best way to do code generation. Since we wanted to get the compiler running, we used TBL for expedience. And we never abandoned it. On the other hand, our original register allocation scheme was far from optimal; but by going ahead and doing it, we at least created a compiler that gave us something to look at—real code—and something to fix—a working compiler.

Several engineering tools enabled us to revise and rewrite substantial portions of the compiler without jeopardizing other portions. Most important is the overall compiler design and its division into unique phases. Because the inputs and outputs of each phase were well defined, changes in one phase did not necessarily affect any other. This modularity also allowed us to work in parallel on the various parts of the compiler, without affecting one another's work. Second, the diagnostic tools that dumped the intermediate program representations following each phase and the debugger we adapted to the specific purpose of debugging the compiler were invaluable. And finally, it was well worth the effort to write a comprehensive test system against which we could measure each new version of the compiler.

And measure we did. The compiler itself, when requested, outputs statistics indicating how much time it spends in each of its phases. Throughout our development work on the compiler, we watched these numbers closely. Their final (current) values are shown in Figures 77 and 78. These figures summarize, in terms of execution time, what percentages of time each of our compilers spends in its major phases. The optimization and code generation phases are broken down into more detailed categories.

Appendix

Optimized
Code Examples

On the following pages, we present some examples of optimized PL/I programs and a C program. Explanatory notes accompany the first few; afterward, the reader is invited to discover independently the optimizations and permutations.

Figure 79. A binary search program, optimized.

```
1        binsearch: procedure;

         BINSEARCH:
             .entry BINSEARCH,<r2,r3,r4,r5,r6,r7>
```

NOTE The base address of static data (in the program section named $DATA) is loaded into a register.

```
             movab   $DATA,r1
```

```
 2 |  1     /*
 3 |  1               binary search
 4 |  1     */
 5    1     declare (i,il,it,iu,k,mid) fixed bin(31);
 6    1     declare vn fixed bin(31);
 7    1     declare (nhits,misses) fixed bin(31);
 8    1     declare ibuf(10000) fixed bin(31) static;
 9    1
10    1         do i = 1 to 10000;
```

NOTE The first value of the variable *i* is loaded into register R3.

```
             movl    #1,r3
```

Figure 79   *(continued)*

NOTE The base address of the array *ibuf* is assigned to a register outside the loop.

```
        moval   (r1),r2
vcg.1:
```

11	2	ibuf(i) = 7 * i;

NOTE References to successive elements of the array *ibuf* are made using autoincrement addressing mode.

```
        mull3   #7,r3,(r2)+
```

12	2	end;

```
        aobleq #10000,r3,vcg.1
```

13	1	nhits = 0;
14	1	misses = 0;

NOTE The variables *nhits* and *misses* are assigned to consecutive registers (R5 and R6) and therefore can both be cleared with a single instruction.

```
        clrq    r5
```

15	1	do i = 1 to 10;

NOTE The second instance of the variable *i* is assigned to register R7.

```
        movl    #1,r7
vcg.2:
```

16	2	do it = 1 to 17500;

NOTE The variables *it, il,* and *iu* are also assigned to registers.

```
        movl    #1,r4
vcg.3:
```

17	3	il = 1;

```
        movl    #1,r3
```

Figure 79 *(continued)*

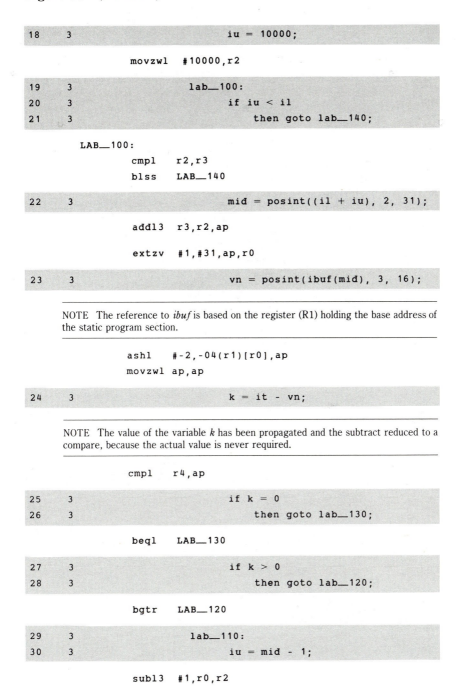

| 18 | 3 | iu = 10000; |

```
movzwl  #10000,r2
```

19	3	lab__100:
20	3	if iu < il
21	3	then goto lab__140;

```
LAB__100:
        cmpl    r2,r3
        blss    LAB__140
```

| 22 | 3 | mid = posint((il + iu), 2, 31); |

```
addl3   r3,r2,ap

extzv   #1,#31,ap,r0
```

| 23 | 3 | vn = posint(ibuf(mid), 3, 16); |

NOTE   The reference to *ibuf* is based on the register (R1) holding the base address of the static program section.

```
ashl    #-2,-04(r1)[r0],ap
movzwl  ap,ap
```

| 24 | 3 | k = it - vn; |

NOTE   The value of the variable *k* has been propagated and the subtract reduced to a compare, because the actual value is never required.

```
cmpl    r4,ap
```

| 25 | 3 | if k = 0 |
| 26 | 3 | then goto lab__130; |

```
beql    LAB__130
```

| 27 | 3 | if k > 0 |
| 28 | 3 | then goto lab__120; |

```
bgtr    LAB__120
```

| 29 | 3 | lab__110: |
| 30 | 3 | iu = mid - 1; |

```
subl3   #1,r0,r2
```

Figure 79 *(concluded)*

| 31 | 3 | goto lab__100; |

```
        brb    LAB__100
```

| 32 | 3 | lab__120: |
| 33 | 3 | il = mid + 1; |

```
    LAB__120:
        addl3   #1,r0,r3
```

| 34 | 3 | goto lab__100; |

```
        brb    LAB__100
```

| 35 | 3 | lab__130: |
| 36 | 3 | nhits = nhits + 1; |

NOTE Addition and assignment are reduced to a single increment instruction.

```
    LAB__130:
        incl    r6
```

| 37 | 3 | goto lab__150; |

```
        brb    LAB__150
```

| 38 | 3 | lab__140: |
| 39 | 3 | misses = misses + 1; |

```
    LAB__140:
        incl    r5
```

| 40 | 3 | lab__150: |
| 41 | 3 | end; |

```
    LAB__150:
        aobleq  #17500,r4,vcg.3
```

| 42 | 2 | end; |

```
        aobleq  #10,r7,vcg.2
```

| 43 | 1 | end; |

```
        ret
```

Figure 80. Strength reduction.

```
1                 example: PROCEDURE;

                  EXAMPLE:
                  .entry EXAMPLE,<r2,r3,r4,r5,r6,r7>
                  movab  -800(sp),sp
```

```
2  |  1     /*
3  |  1              variables addressed within loops
4  |  1     */
5     1     DECLARE (i,k,loop) FIXED BINARY(31);
6     1     DECLARE (iter1,iter2,iter3) FIXED BINARY(31);
7     1     DECLARE (a,b,x) FLOAT BINARY(24);
8     1     DECLARE (y(100),z(100)) FLOAT BINARY(24);
9     1
10    1         iter1 = 10;
11    1         iter2 = 1000;
12    1         iter3 = 100;
13    1         DO i = iter3 TO 1 BY -1;
```

```
                  movzbl #100,r5
                  moval  -400(fp),r3
            vcg.1:
```

```
14    2              y(i) = float(i, 24) * 2.;
```

```
                  cvtlf  r5,r2
```

NOTE This instruction represents a strength reduction; a multiplication by 2 has been reduced to an add operation.

```
                  addf3  r2,r2,-(r3)
```

```
15    2                    END;
```

```
                  sobgtr r5,vcg.1
```

Figure 80   *(continued)*

16	1	DO k = 1 TO iter3 BY 1;

```
        movl    #1,r4
        moval   -400(fp),r3
vcg.2:
```

17	2	z(k) = FLOAT(k, 24) / 2.;

```
        cvtlf   r4,r2
```

NOTE Here, division by 2 has been reduced to a multiplication by 1/2. This is another example of strength reduction.

```
        mulf3   #.5,r2,(r3)+
```

18	2	END;

```
        aobleq  #100,r4,vcg.2
```

19	1	DO loop = 1 TO iter1;

```
        movl    #1,r7
vcg.3:
```

20	2	a = 0;

```
        clrl    r3
```

21	2	DO i = 1 TO iter2;

```
        movl    #1,r6
vcg.4:
```

22	3	DO k = 1 TO iter3;

```
        movl    #1,r4
        moval   -800(fp),r0
        moval   -400(fp),ap
```

Figure 80 *(concluded)*

NOTE The conversion of i to a floating-point value followed by the computation of $((x\text{-}1.)/(x+1.))\times x\times.39$ has been moved outside of the loop because it is an invariant expression. The instructions between the CVTLF and the compiler-generated label *vcg.5* compute the expression.

```
        cvtlf   r6,r5
        subf3   #1.,r5,r2
        addf3   #1.,r5,r1
        divf2   r1,r2
        mulf2   r5,r2
        mulf2   #.39,r2
vcg.5:
```

| 23 | 4 | x=FLOAT(i,24); |
| 24 | 4 | a=((x-1.)/(x+1.))*x*.39+a; |

NOTE The resultant inner loop requires only an update of the variable a and then an addition. Both $y(k)$ and $z(k)$ are addressed using autoincrement addressing modes.

```
        addf2   r2,r3
```

| 25 | 4 | y(k) = z(k) + a; |

```
        addf3   r3,(ap)+,(r0)+
```

| 26 | 4 | END; |

```
        aobleq  #100,r4,vcg.5
```

| 27 | 3 | END; |

```
        aobleq  #1000,r6,vcg.4
```

| 28 | 2 | END; |

```
        aobleq  #10,r7,vcg.3
```

| 29 | 1 | END; |

```
        ret
```

Figure 81. *relax2,* optimized.

```
1                 relax2: PROCEDURE(eps);

        RELAX2:
                .entry RELAX2,<r2,r3,r4,r5,r6>
                movab  X,r3

2     1
3     1         %REPLACE false BY '0'B;
4     1         %REPLACE m BY 40;
5     1         %REPLACE n BY 60;
6     1         %REPLACE true BY '1'B;
7     1
8     1         DECLARE x(0:m,0:n) FLOAT BINARY(24) EXTERNAL,
9     1                 xnew FLOAT BINARY(24),
10    1                 eps FLOAT BINARY(24);
11    1         DECLARE i FIXED BINARY(31),
12    1                 j FIXED BINARY(31);
13    1         DECLARE done BIT(1) ALIGNED;
14    1
15    1     start:
16    1         done = true;

        START:
                movb   #1,r5

17    1
18    1         DO i = 1 TO m - 1;

                movl   #1,r6
        vcg.1:

19    2         DO j = 1 TO n - 1;

                movl   #1,r4
```

NOTE The base address of $x(i,1)$ is computed and moved outside of the loop.

```
                mul13  #61,r6,r0
                moval  04(r3)[r0],r1
        vcg.2:
```

Figure 81 *(concluded)*

20	3	xnew = (x(i-1,j)+
		x(i+1,j)+
		x(i,j-1)+
		x(i,j+1)) / 4;

NOTE Array references to successive elements *x(i,j)* are made by using R1 as a base address. The last reference in the loop to *x(i,j)* uses autoincrement addressing.

```
addf3   -244(r1),244(r1),r2
addf2   -04(r1),r2
addf2   04(r1),r2
mulf2   #.25,r2
```

21	3	IF abs(xnew - x(i,j)) > eps
22	3	THEN done = false;

```
subf3   (r1),r2,r0
bicw2   #8000,r0
cmpf    r0,@04(ap)
bleq    vcg.3
clrb    r5
```

23	3	x(i,j) = xnew;

```
vcg.3:
    movf    r2,(r1)+
```

24	3	END;

```
aobleq  #59,r4,vcg.2
```

25	2	END;
26	1	IF ^done
27	1	THEN GOTO start;

```
blbc    r5,START
```

28	1	END;

```
ret
```

Figure 82. The towers of Hanoi, optimized.

```
1                hanoi: PROCEDURE RETURNS(FIXED BINARY(31));

     HANOI:
               .entry  HANOI,<r2,r3,r4>
               movab   $DATA,r1

2 |  1      /*
3 |  1            towers of hanoi
4 |  1      */
5    1      DECLARE nf(1:20) FIXED BINARY (31) STATIC,
6    1              no(1:20) FIXED BINARY (31) STATIC,
7    1              nt(1:20) FIXED BINARY (31) STATIC;
8    1      DECLARE (i,jp,k,n) FIXED BINARY (31);
9    1
10   1              i=1;

               movl    #1,r4

11   1              k=2;

               movl    #2,r3

12   1              n=20;

               movl    #14,r2

13   1              jp=1;

               movl    #1,r0

14   1      l1:
15   1              IF n=1
16   1                  THEN GOTO 13;

     L1:
               cmpl    r2,#1
               beql    L3

17   1              no(jp) = n;
```

Figure 82 *(continued)*

```
                        movl    r2,76(r1)[r0]
```

| 18 | 1 | nf(jp) = i; |

```
                        movl    r4,156(r1)[r0]
```

| 19 | 1 | nt(jp) = k; |

```
                        movl    r3,-04(r1)[r0]
```

| 20 | 1 | k = 6-k-i; |

```
                        subl3   r3,#6,r3
                        subl2   r4,r3
```

| 21 | 1 | l2: |
| 22 | 1 | n = n-1; |

```
                L2:
                        decl    r2
```

| 23 | 1 | jp = jp+1; |

```
                        incl    r0
```

| 24 | 1 | GOTO l1; |

```
                        brb     L1
```

| 25 | 1 | l3: |
| 26 | 1 | jp = jp-1; |

```
                L3:
                        decl    r0
```

| 27 | 1 | IF jp=0 |
| 28 | 1 | THEN GOTO l5; |

```
                        beql    L5
```

| 29 | 1 | n = no(jp); |

Figure 82   *(concluded)*

```
            movl    76(r1)[r0],r2
```

```
30    1                         IF n<=0
31    1                            THEN GOTO 13;
```

```
            bleq    L3
```

```
32    1              14:
33    1                            i = nf(jp);
```

```
            movl    156(r1)[r0],r4
```

```
34    1                            k = nt(jp);
```

```
            movl    -04(r1)[r0],r3
```

```
35    1                            no(jp) = -n;
```

```
            mnegl   r2,76(r1)[r0]
```

```
36    1                            i = 6-i-k;
```

```
            subl3   r4,#6,r4
            subl2   r3,r4
```

```
37    1                            GOTO 12;
```

```
            brb     L2
```

```
38    1              15:
39    1                            END;
```

```
        L5:
            ret
```

Figure 83. A shell sort, written in PL/I, optimized.

```
1               shell: PROCEDURE(v, n);

        SHELL:
                .entry SHELL,<r2,r3,r4,r5,r6,r7>

2  | 1    /*
3  | 1           shell sort
4  | 1    */
5    1    DECLARE n FIXED BINARY(31) VALUE,
6    1            v(0:100) FIXED BINARY(31);
7    1    DECLARE strcmp ENTRY(FIXED BINARY(31) VALUE,
8    1                         FIXED BINARY(31)
                               VALUE) RETURNS(FIXED BINARY(31));
9    1    DECLARE i FIXED BINARY(31),
10   1            j FIXED BINARY(31),
11   1            gap FIXED BINARY(31),
12   1            temp FIXED BINARY(31);
13   1
14   1            gap = DIVIDE(n, 2, 31, 0);

            moval   @08(ap),r7
            div13   #2,r7,r5

15   1            DO WHILE(gap > 0);

            bleq    vcg.7
            decl    r7
            moval   @04(ap),r4
        vcg.1:

16   2            DO i = gap TO n - 1;

            movl    r5,r6
            cmpl    r6,r7
            bgtr    vcg.6
        vcg.2:

17   3                j = i - gap;

            sub13   r5,r6,r3

18   3                DO WHILE(j >= 0);

            blss    vcg.5
        vcg.3:
```

Figure 83   *(concluded)*

| 19 | 4 | IF strcmp(v(j), v(j+gap)) > 0 |
| 20 | 4 | THEN DO; |

```
addl3   r3,r5,r2
pushl   (r4)[r2]
pushl   (r4)[r3]
calls   #2,STRCMP
tstl    r0
bleq    vcg.4
```

| 21 | 5 | temp = v(j); |

```
movl    (r4)[r3],r0
```

| 22 | 5 | v(j) = v(j + gap); |

```
movl    (r4)[r2],(r4)[r3]
```

| 23 | 5 | v(j + gap) = temp; |

```
movl    r0,(r4)[r2]
```

| 24 | 5 | END; |
| 25 | 4 | j = j - gap; |

```
vcg.4:
        subl2   r5,r3
```

| 26 | 4 | END; |
| 27 | 3 | END; |

```
        bgeq    vcg.3
vcg.5:
        aobleq  r7,r6,vcg.2
vcg.6:
```

| 28 | 2 | gap = DIVIDE(gap, 2, 31, 0); |

```
        divl2   #2,r5
```

| 29 | 2 | END; |

```
        bgtr    vcg.1
vcg.7:
```

| 30 | 1 | END; |

```
        ret
```

Figure 84.   A shell sort, written in C, optimized.

```
1                    shell(v,n)
2                    int v[],n;

      shell:
                     .entry shell,<r2,r3,r4,r5,r6,r7>

3                    {

                     moval  (ap),r7

4    1                   int gap,i,j,temp;
5    1
6    1                   for (gap = n/2; gap > 0; gap /= 2)

                     movl   08(r7),r6
                     divl3  #2,r6,r4
                     bleq   vcg.6
                     movl   04(r7),r3
      vcg.1:

7    1                       for (i = gap; i < n; ++i)

                     movl   r4,r5
                     cmpl   r5,r6
                     bgeq   vcg.5
      vcg.2:

8    1                           for (j = i-gap;
                                     j >= 0 &&
                                     v[j] > v[j+gap];
                                     j -= gap). {

                     subl3  r4,r5,r1
                     blss   vcg.4
                     addl3  r4,r1,r2
                     cmpl   (r3)[r1],(r3)[r2]
                     bleq   vcg.4
      vcg.3:
```

Figure 84   *(concluded)*

9	2	temp = v[j];

```
        movl    (r3)[r1],r2
```

10	2	v[j] = v[j+gap];

```
        addl3   r4,r1,r0
        movl    (r3)[r0],(r3)[r1]
```

11	2	v[j+gap] = temp;

```
        movl    r2,(r3)[r0]
```

12	2	}

```
        subl2   r4,r1
        blss    vcg.3
        addl3   r4,r1,r0
        cmpl    (r3)[r1],(r3)[r0]
        bgtr    vcg.3
vcg.4:
        incl    r5
        cmpl    r5,r6
        blss    vcg.2
vcg.5:
        divl2   #2,r4
        bgtr    vcg.1
vcg.6:
```

13	1	}

```
        ret
```

Glossary

ADD_OFFSET operator Intermediate Language operator used to represent an address within an aggregate or string. Its operands represent the position of the referenced item from a base address.

addressing mode On the VAX-11, a code indicating the manner in which operands in a machine instruction are to be addressed.

alias Denotes variables whose values might be modified under some other name, such as variables that share the same storage.

alias node A node in the flow graph generated by the Optimizer. This node does not represent any sequence of program operators but provides the Optimizer with a way to generate graph edges to represent hidden flow caused by aliased labels.

allocation partition A span of program execution during which some values must be maintained in register temporaries. The Register Allocator uses the division between partitions to determine at what points all registers are available.

AP The Argument Pointer register on the VAX-11. When a procedure is invoked, this register always points to the argument list of the called procedure's parameters. When not in use for procedure calling, AP may be used as a general register.

argument In PL/I, the expression or reference associated with a procedure's parameter in a particular invocation of the procedure. For example, in *CALL* $p(x, 3 \times i)$, the arguments of p are a reference to x and the expression $3 \times i$. In PL/I, the arguments as written are analyzed by the compiler to determine actual arguments.

ARG_VAL operator Intermediate Language operator that denotes storage containing the value of its operand.

array node A data structure in the Symbol Table that describes an array, including its dimensions, bounds, and the data type and size of its elements.

assembly language A language closely related to a computer's machine language. Assembly language allows locations and other values to be referenced symbolically.

assignment statement Statement in a programming language that assigns a value to a variable.

239

ASSIGN_REGTEMP operator   Intermediate Language operator introduced by the Optimizer. This operator specifies a variable that the Optimizer has determined is a candidate for assignment to a register and contains the operator identifiers of the first and last operators that reference the variable.

ASSIGN_REPEAT operator   Intermediate Language operator that assigns a specified value to all elements of a given array.

attribute   Any one of a set of bits in a symbol node that specify various properties such as data type and storage class.

autodecrement addressing mode   VAX-11 addressing mode in which a register contains the address of the operand and is decremented by the size of the operand prior to evaluation of the operand specifier.

AUTO_DECREMENT operator   Intermediate Language operator introduced by the Optimizer so that an autodecrement addressing mode will be generated to address an array whose elements are visited in descending order during execution of a loop.

autoincrement addressing mode   VAX-11 addressing mode in which a register contains the address of the operand and is incremented by the size of the operand following evaluation of the operand specifier.

AUTO_INCREMENT operator   Intermediate Language operator introduced by the Optimizer so that an autoincrement addressing mode will be generated to address an array whose elements are visited in ascending order during execution of a loop.

automatic   A class of PL/I variables for which storage is allocated when the block that declares the variable is activated. The storage is released when the block is deactivated.

back end   Collectively, the phases of the VAX-11 Code Generator that execute after all language-specific work of parsing and semantic analysis has taken place. These phases are Write Tree, the Optimizer, Local Code Generator, Register Allocator, Peephole Optimizer, Code Binder, and Object Module and Listing File Writer.

based   A class of PL/I variables for which unique storage is not allocated, but for which storage is described. A pointer is always used to specify the storage actually accessed.

base pointer   (1) In an array or structure reference, the memory location of the beginning of the aggregate from which successive elements are addressed. (2) In references to variables that do not have explicit storage allocated for them, the address of the variable's storage.

base register   The register containing a memory location to be used in addressing a program variable.

basic block   *See* **basic node**.

basic node   A sequence of operations in a flow graph that can be entered at only one point even though that sequence of operations may have more than one exit. In this book, the term **node** is used to avoid confusion with other types of block.

begin block   A block in PL/I delimited by BEGIN and END statements. A begin block is activated when control reaches the BEGIN statement as a result of normal control flow in the containing block.

bind   To associate one object with another in order to control the interpretation of references to the first object. Examples are binding a procedure parameter to an argument and binding references to labels to unique memory locations.

block   A construction in a programming language that both defines a scope for interpreting names and controls the allocation of variables declared within the block.

block activation   VAX-11 hardware context created each time a block is entered, including information on the allocation of storage for automatic variables declared in the block and hardware information required to connect this block activation to the previous block activation.

block node   A node in the Symbol Table representing a procedure or begin block in the source program.

Boolean minimization   *See* **Boolean optimization.**

Boolean optimization   Optimization in which logical and relational tests followed by branch instructions are short-circuited so that if part of a test fails, for example, the code to compute the second part of the test is not executed.

bootstrap   Technique for implementing a compiler on one hardware machine by using an existing compiler for the same language on a host machine (usually a different machine). The technique requires compiling all parts of the compiler on the host machine with a code generator that generates code for the target machine, and then taking this output to the target machine.

bootstrap compiler   The VAX-11 PL/I compiler as it existed after its bootstrap to the VAX-11 and before extensive modifications for optimization.

BUILD_STRUCTURE operator   Intermediate Language operator that builds a single aggregate value from a list of element values.

call frame   VAX-11 hardware context, created each time a call instruction is executed. It contains saved copies of registers specified by the call target, the saved PC (Program Counter), AP (Argument Pointer), FP (Frame Pointer), the processor status, and a longword that specifies the address of a condition handler.

Code Binder   The phase of the VAX-11 Code Generator that performs final address displacement calculations, binding branch instructions to their target addresses.

code block   Data structure created by the Local Code Generator to hold information about instructions that are being emitted, including the instruction opcode, skeletal addressing information about the operands, and the addressing mode.

code improvement   *See* **optimization.**

common subexpression elimination   The program optimization in which a compiler detects expressions that are computed more than once with absolutely equivalent results and then reorders the program so that the computation is performed only once.

compilation unit   The part of a source program that is processed by a simple invocation of the compiler. In VAX-11 PL/I, this unit can contain one or more external procedures and related declarations.

compiler   A program that translates a program written in a language such as PL/I, C, and FORTRAN into object code.

compile time   Existing or taking place during compilation of a program. Contrast with **run time.**

condition handler   A procedure designated to receive control when an exception condition (either hardware or software generated) occurs.

constant   (1) A value that does not change during program execution. (2) The source language construction denoting such a value.

constant folding   The optimization in which expressions containing constants are detected, the operation performed, and the expression replaced with the result (such as the reduction of $2+7$ to 9).

constant identifier   (1) A named constant. (2) In the TBL compiler, a numeric constant defined by a LET directive.

CONSTANT operator   Intermediate Language operator denoting a constant value. The value is defined by a token node in the Symbol Table.

containing   Denotes the programming construction that contains another. For example, a block b is the containing block of x if b contains x but does not contain a nested block that itself contains x.

CONVERT operator   Intermediate Language operator specifying the conversion of a variable or result to the data type required for an operation or result.

copy propagation   *See* **value propagation.**

copy subsumption   *See* **value propagation.**

cross-compiler   A compiler that runs on one machine producing code that executes on another machine.

current block   The block containing the program element being processed.

DAG   *See* **directed acyclic graph (DAG).**

data type   Classification of variables, constants, and operators that specifies the set of values an object may assume and the internal representation of those values.

declaration   A construction in a programming language that establishes a specific meaning for a name. In most languages a name may be declared more than once, each declaration having a different scope.

DECLARE   (1) The phase specific to the front end of the VAX-11 PL/I compiler that verifies that all data declarations are consistent, fills in default attributes if necessary, and builds permanent trees needed by PASS2. (2) The PL/I language keyword that identifies a data declaration.

defined   A class of PL/I variables in which a variable's storage is specifically associated with the storage of another, as in:

```
DECLARE a(10) FIXED;
        b FIXED DEFINED(a(2));
```

Here, *b* references the second element of *a*.

definition point   A point in the execution of the program at which a variable is potentially assigned a value or modified.

depth-first order   The ordering of nodes in a flow graph so that the first node in the list is the outermost node (leaf) in the graph.

descriptor   Data structure containing the address of a procedure argument and other information describing the argument.

directed acyclic graph (DAG)   A directed graph with no cycles. In compiler theory, a DAG may be used to represent a set of computations that involve no control flow. A vertex that has exiting edges represents an operation; the opposite vertices of the exiting edges are the operands of the operator.

discrete lifetime   *See* **disjoint lifetime.**

disjoint lifetime   The differentiation between different instances of a variable, that is, program spans in which the value that a variable holds is distinct. The Optimizer computes disjoint lifetimes so that the Register Allocator can more efficiently assign registers to local variables.

display pointer   Pointer to the stack frame of a block activation that is an ancestor of another block. Display pointers are used to resolve uplevel references, that is, references to names declared in containing blocks.

dominator   *See* **loop dominator.**

dope vector   *See* **descriptor.**

DO statement   PL/I statement that begins a DO-group. The statement may specify repetitive execution of the group, or it may be used simply for syntactic grouping.

dynamically sized   Denotes items whose sizes, which are not known at compile time, must be computed at run time.

END statement   PL/I statement denoting the end of a procedure, begin block, or DO-group.

entry point   Point in a sequence of executable statements (in a procedure) at which execution of the procedure can be invoked. The beginning of the sequence is the normal entry point. In PL/I, a procedure may have additional entry points.

executable statement   In PL/I, a statement that does something when the program is executed, in contrast to statements such as DECLARE which are processed entirely at compile time.

explicit allocation list   A list of T-reg nodes maintained by the Register Allocator to keep track of all registers that are currently allocated.

expression   A construction in a programming language that denotes the computation of a value, such as $x+2$.

external procedure   In PL/I, a procedure that is not contained in any other procedure.

flow graph   Series of data structures built to gather information about a program in order to perform optimizations. The program flow information in a flow graph (whose principal structures are called either basic blocks or nodes) describes the control flow in the program based on labels, branches, calls to external procedures, and so on.

FP   The Frame Pointer register on the VAX-11. This register points to the call frame for the current block and is linked by a pointer to the previous block.

front end   Collectively, the procedures and phases specific to the compilation of source programs for a single programming language. The primary tasks of a front end are parsing and semantic analysis.

function procedure   A procedure that returns a value.

global optimization   Optimization of a program an entire block at a time, in contrast to optimizations that examine and optimize only a single node of the program at a time.

grammar   The rules governing the syntax of a programming language.

held register list   List of pointers to register temporary nodes for hardware registers, used by the Register Allocator to record registers allocated for use in hardware instructions requiring operands to be in registers.

identifier   (1) Numerical value used to identify a Symbol Table node, an operator, or a register temporary node. *See* **node identifier, operator identifier**, and **T-reg identifier**. (2) In VAX-11 PL/I, a sequence of letters, digits, underscores, and dollar signs specifying a program entity such as a procedure or variable name.

IF statement   PL/I statement specifying conditional execution of a statement or group. It may have the form IF-THEN-ELSE. In the PL/I front end, PASS1 translates IF statements and ELSE clauses by generating LABEL, BR_TRUE, and BR_FALSE operators.

IMMEDIATE operator   Intermediate Language operator denoting a value that is stored immediately in the operator.

indexed addressing mode   VAX-11 addressing mode in which an index register specifies an offset from the beginning of a data structure whose base address is also in the operand specifier. This addressing mode is always used in conjunction with another addressing mode.

index register   On the VAX-11, a register whose contents are used to address a program variable by first multiplying the contents of the index register by the size (in bytes) of the variable being addressed.

intermediate code list   List of data structures, called code blocks, created by the Local Code Generator. It contains a lexical sequence of the generated instructions of the source program.

intermediate language   Within a compiler, a language into which a program is translated before its final transformation into object code. The elements of the language are normally some specific type of data structure (such as trees), not characters as in the original source language. A compiler may use several intermediate languages. In our compiler, the Intermediate Language is the set of operators defined in Chapter 5.

interpreter   A program that faithfully performs the actions specified by elements in another program. For example, when a computer is implemented using microcode, the microcode is an interpreter for the computer's machine language.

keyword   In PL/I, an identifier with a language-defined function, for example, IF.

kill list   A list of T-reg nodes maintained by the Register Allocator to keep track of all points in the program at which the contents of specific registers are destroyed.

label   In the Intermediate Language, a symbol node denoting a point in the program that can be the target of a GOTO operator or any of the various branch operators. A LABEL operator in the operator file relates the symbol node to the actual point in the program. In a source program, the user-specified identifier denoting such a point.

LALR(1)   Acronym for a parsing technique known as "Look ahead 1 moving left to right." LALR(1) is a refinement on the more complex LR parsing technique for the bottom-up parsing of context-free grammars.

level-one   (1) Denotes a variable that is not a member of a structure. (2) Denotes a variable that is itself a structure but not a member.

lexical   Denotes the source program form of the program, that is, as a sequence of characters.

lexical analyzer   In a compiler, the phase or routine that scans the source text. While scanning, it identifies and separates the lexicons (vocabulary) of the language to be parsed. Common terminology refers to these recognized lexicons as "tokens."

limit of an operator   The identifier of the operator that most recently defined or potentially defined a value for any of the current operator's operands, and thus the farthest point backward in the program that the operator can be moved. The limit of an operator is very important in both elimination of common subexpressions and removal of invariant expressions from loops.

linker   A system program that can combine several object modules into a single object program that is ready to load and execute. Its functions include resolving intermodule references, finding modules in libraries, and assigning storage locations.

live variable analysis   Analysis of specific program variables to determine precisely when they are assigned values and the duration of the program for which those values must remain valid. The information gathered during live variable analysis helps the Optimizer determine when the value of a variable may be assigned to a register.

loader   A system program that will load an object program into memory and initiate its execution. On the VAX-11, the functions of the linker and loader are combined; the image activator executes a bound program image.

Local Code Generator   Phase of the VAX-11 Code Generator that reads the linear file of operators and operands and constructs an intermediate form of the program's instructions and operand specifiers.

loop dominator   A node in the flow graph that is always executed if the loop of which it is part is executed.

loop invariant removal   The optimization technique in which computations that are performed within loops but that do not change during execution of the loop are reordered in the program so that the computation occurs only once and not each time through the loop.

machine language   The language actually accepted by the computer.

MACRO   The VAX-11 assembly language.

member   *See* **structure.**

memory temporary   The result of an operation which must be kept for later use and for which the compiler allocates dynamic memory in the stack frame for the block activation. For example, the compiler generates memory temporaries to hold the results of string operations.

MULTICS A timesharing operating system that runs on certain Honeywell computers. The system features virtual memory and is implemented mostly in PL/I.

nesting level The lexical nesting level of blocks in the program. The imaginary outermost block has a nesting level of zero, each external procedure has a nesting level of one.

node A data structure that has a distinct relationship to other, similar structures. In the VAX-11 Code Generator, the term describes the structures in the Symbol Table as well as the basic nodes in a flow graph.

node identifier An unsigned 15-bit value that uniquely identifies a node in the Symbol Table.

n-tuple An *n*-operand operator. *See also* **triple** and **quad.**

object code The representation of a program produced by a compiler, usually machine code or something closely related that will be accepted by a system's linker. Sometimes, however, the compiler may produce an intermediate form of code that will be processed by an interpreter.

object module Output from a compiler consisting of the object code produced by a single invocation of the compiler.

object module analyzer VAX/VMS system program that reads object modules and reports on the syntactic correctness of its records.

Object Module and Listing File Writer Phase of the VAX-11 Code Generator that writes out the object module records created during compilation and a listing file showing the program's source code and, optionally, the generated machine language instructions.

object program A program in a form ready for loading into a computer's memory and execution.

ON-unit The PL/I language construct for the definition of condition handlers for specific purposes.

operand In the Intermediate Language, an argument to an operator that specifies the parameters of the operation.

operand counter A field in the prologue descriptor for a block that is updated by the Local Code Generator each time it emits an instruction to the intermediate code list. The value of this field is particularly important in the recording of the first and last uses of register temporaries.

operand specifier In the encoding of a VAX-11 instruction, the information required to address an instruction operand, including the addressing mode, displacement from a base register (if any), the name of the register, and index register (if any).

operator   In the Intermediate Language, the collector of information about a specific program statement or action. Operators can have from 0 to 255 operands.

operator file   Internal file of operators in a linear format, in which operators are arranged in buffers for easy access by the back end of the VAX-11 Code Generator.

operator identifier   A 15-bit negative value that uniquely identifies an operator, both in its tree form on input to Write Tree and in its linear form on output from Write Tree.

operator node   A structure built by the Local Code Generator to describe an Intermediate Language operator.

optimization   The attempt to decrease the execution time of generated code.

Optimizer   Phase of the VAX-11 Code Generator that performs global optimizations such as loop invariant removal and common subexpression elimination.

parameter   (1) A name declared as a procedure parameter and bound to an argument when the procedure is invoked. (2) A class of PL/I variables in which a variable's storage is associated with the storage of a corresponding procedure argument.

PARAM_PTR operator   Intermediate Language operator that references an item in a parameter list.

parent block   The block containing the current block. *See also* **containing**.

parsing   The process of converting a source program to trees (or one very big tree) in accordance with a grammar.

PASS1   Phase specific to the front end of the VAX-11 PL/I compiler that reads the source file, performs syntactic parsing and lexical analysis, and begins building the Symbol Table.

PASS2   Phase of the front end of the VAX-11 PL/I compiler that combines the syntactically correct trees produced by PASS1 and the validated Symbol Table produced by the DECLARE phase into fully expanded and semantically correct trees.

pattern matching   (1) Code generation technique in which patterns of code to be generated and patterns of operands are predefined in a table and code is generated based on selection of a pattern from the table. (2) Optimization technique in which a specific pattern of operations is replaced with a shorter pattern.

PC   The Program Counter register on the VAX-11, used to point to the instruction currently being executed.

peephole   A pattern of code easily distinguished as a pattern that can be reduced to a shorter, more efficient form.

Peephole Optimizer   Phase of the VAX-11 Code Generator that performs peephole optimization by recognizing and reducing peepholes.

predecessor   In the flow graph constructed by the Optimizer, a node that precedes another node in the graph such that execution can flow from it into a successor.

procedure   A part of a program that can be invoked from one or more points in the program. The invocation is referred to as a procedure call. In general, a procedure has a set of parameters which are bound to specific arguments when the procedure is invoked. If a procedure invocation returns normally, control returns to the point of invocation.

program   Specification of a computation in some language. The term usually means an object that can be manipulated with its entire structure as determined by the rules of the language.

prologue code   Code generated by the compiler to initialize the call frame on block activation. It executes before the first executable statement at any entry point.

prologue descriptor   Data structure built by the Local Code Generator to accumulate information about a program block. It contains pointers to lists of register temporaries allocated in the block, a mask containing a summation of all registers used, and various control information.

quad   An operator with four operands; used in some compilers in the construction of trees.

recursive descent parse   A common parsing technique for programming languages, usually combined with expression analysis using operator precedence. A recursive descent parser analyzes a program's syntax using mutually recursive routines that scan the current input stream.

reduction   (1) In Write Tree, the process of following trees to their roots and performing optimizations on them so they represent a computation more efficiently. (2) In the Peephole Optimizer, the process of replacing instruction sequences with shorter or faster instruction sequences.

reference   In PL/I, a construction which denotes a name declared in the program.

REF operator   Intermediate Language operator representing a reference to data and to all the information required to locate it in memory.

region   (1) A collection of one or more nodes in a flow graph that are connected via a unique flow path. (2) The nodes in the flow graph that represent a discrete, disjoint lifetime of a variable.

Register Allocator   Phase of the VAX-11 Code Generator that determines what registers are available for allocation to temporaries created by the Local Code Generator and assigns specific registers to temporaries.

register temporary   Result of an operation that must be kept for later use and assumed to be assignable to a register during program execution. In the VAX-11 Code Generator, the use of register temporaries is extended to apply to local variables that the Optimizer determines can be assigned to registers.

register temporary node   *See* **T-reg node.**

result incorporation   Optimization in which two instructions are replaced with a single instruction. On the VAX-11, this involves replacement of a two-operand arithmetic instruction that is followed by a move instruction that stores the result of the first instruction with a single three-operand instruction.

run time   Existing or taking place during a program's execution. Contrast with **compile time.**

SAVE_RESULT operator   Intermediate Language operator used to capture the value of a variable and save it for later reference.

scope   The part of the source program in which the interpretation of a declared name supersedes other declarations with the same name.

semantic analysis   The process of transforming parse trees into an explicit form from which code can be generated.

SETS operator   Intermediate Language operator used by the front end to tell the Optimizer about definitions of variables that the Optimizer could not otherwise detect, such as when a variable is modified as a side effect of an input/output operation.

source language   The programming language accepted by a compiler, such as PL/I, C, and PASCAL.

source program   The sequence of characters that is the original written form of the program, as distinct from the various forms into which the compiler transforms it.

SP   The Stack Pointer register on the VAX-11, whose contents always point to the top of the stack.

stack frame   Software context created each time a block activation occurs. The stack frame is created immediately below the call frame created by the hardware and consists of a saved parent pointer, saved AP, pointer to a linked list of ON-unit descriptors, and stack memory allocated for automatic variables and compiler temporaries.

statement   In PL/I, one component of the sequence forming a source program. PL/I statements are frequently referred to by their identifying keywords, such as DO, CALL, END.

static   Class of PL/I variable for which storage is allocated in a fixed memory location and retained throughout the execution of a program.

Storage Allocator   A language-specific phase that reads the Symbol Table and writes object module records describing how storage is to be allocated for static variables.

storage class Classification of variables according to the way in which storage is allocated for them. In PL/I, the storage classes are automatic, based, defined, parameter, and static.

strength reduction An optimization in which a single operation is replaced by a faster operation, such as replacing division by 2 with multiplication by ½. (*See* **result incorporation.**)

structure A variable composed of member variables that may themselves be structures. In PL/I, structures are declared using level numbers, as in:

```
DECLARE 1 s,
        2 x,
          3 (a,b) FIXED,
        2 y CHARACTER(6);
```

Here, *s* is a structure. *x*, *y*, *a*, and *b* are members. *x* is a substructure. *See also* **level-one.**

subgraph A collection of related nodes in the flow graph, usually those representing a discrete lifetime of a variable.

subroutine *See* **procedure.**

successor In the flow graph constructed by the Optimizer, a node that follows another node in the graph such that execution can flow into it from a predecessor.

symbol node A node in the Symbol Table representing a name declared in the program, in contrast to compiler-generated labels or variables.

Symbol Table A collection of data structures, called nodes, that contain information about the program's structure, variable names, and tokens.

TBL (Table Building Language) (1) A high-level language designed to function as a machine tailored to a specific use. (2) A compiler that compiles statements written in a TBL program into a binary form that must then be interpreted by a user-written interpreter.

temporary Variable generated by the compiler to hold the result of an operation. *See also* **register temporary** and **memory temporary.**

token node In the Symbol Table, a data structure representing an identifier or constant and containing its spelling.

Translation Systems, Inc. A private corporation founded by R. A. Freiburghouse to develop and market PL/I compilers to various manufacturers. This ancestor of the VAX-11 Code Generator uses a common PL/I front end, for which code generators produce code for different hardware computers.

tree In the VAX-11 Code Generator and its compilers, a tree-like data structure that represents a statement, expression, or reference in the program.

T-reg *See* **register temporary.**

T-reg identifier   A 12-bit value that uniquely identifies a T-reg node and which the Register Allocator uses to indicate the T-reg allocated for a particular instance of a variable or a temporary.

T-reg node   In the VAX-11 Code Generator, a data structure representing a register temporary introduced by the Local Code Generator to hold a temporary result or the value of a variable designated by the Optimizer as a candidate for assignment to a register.

triple   An operator with three operands; used in some compilers in the construction of trees.

uplevel   (1) Denotes a reference to a variable declared in a containing block. (2) An attribute applied by the code generator to a block in which such references can be made.

use-definition list   In the flow graph of a program developed by the Optimizer, the list of all operators that either assign values to or reference the value of the variable for which the list is constructed. There is one such list for each of up to 32 variables selected as candidates for assignment to registers.

USE operator   Intermediate Language operator that refers to a value produced by a previous operator.

VALUE operator   Intermediate Language operator that produces the current value of a reference.

value propagation   Optimization in which variables that are used only to assign values to other variables are removed from the computation.

variable   (1) An entity to which values may be assigned in the course of a computation. (2) In the VAX-11 Code Generator, a symbol node in which the *variable* attribute is set.

VAX-11   Computer architecture developed by Digital Equipment Corporation. It is a 32-bit machine with memory management capabilities to support multiprogramming.

VAX-11 Code Generator   The common routines that make it possible to write compilers for various programming languages by writing front ends that produce a Symbol Table and well-structured trees that express the source program in terms of the Intermediate Language.

VAX/VMS   Operating system for the VAX-11 hardware.

Write Tree   Phase of the VAX-11 Code Generator that accepts trees from the front end, reduces them, and writes them into a linear form that is then passed to the Optimizer.

Index

Index